SHAKESPEAREAN GOTHIC

Shakespearean Gothic

Edited by
Christy Desmet and Anne Williams

UNIVERSITY OF WALES PRESS
CARDIFF
2009

British Library Cataloguing-in-Publication Data
A catalogue record for this book is available from the British Library.

ISBN   978-0-7083-2093-8 (hardback)
        978-0-7083-2092-1 (paperback)
e-ISBN 978-0-7083-2262-8

Printed by Gutenberg Press, Tarxien, Malta

For our Mothers:
in memory of Rosemary Desmet (1925–2007)
and
in gratitude to Gary Palmer Williams

CONTENTS

Contents

ACKNOWLEDGEMENTS

We would like to thank the contributors to *Shakespearean Gothic* for their intelligence, hard work and patience. We would also like to thank Andy Smith, Ennis Akpinar of the University of Wales Press and the participants in the session on Shakespearean Gothic at the 2005 International Gothic Association meeting in Montreal. David Schiller and John Boyd deserve special mention for their support during this long process. Ily, the Jack Russell, and Oliver, Domingo and Percy (the Bad Brown Tabbies) were always sympathetic listeners whenever editorial problems needed to be addressed. We are dedicating this volume to our mothers, who started us on our separate literary journeys toward the Gothic.

The photographs of Ellen Terry as Ophelia, Lady Macbeth and Mamillius are reproduced by kind permission of the National Portrait Gallery, London. The photograph of the set from the 1984 Royal Shakespeare Company production of *Hamlet* is reproduced by permission of Donald Cooper. The image of Hamlet and the Ghost from the 1992 Royal Shakespeare Company production of *Hamlet* is reproduced with the permission of the Shakespeare Centre Library. Finally, we would like to thank the Goettingen University Library and the German Shakespeare Society for permission to reproduce the images from the *Boydell Shakespeare Gallery* that accompany Frederick Burwick's essay.

ILLUSTRATIONS

Contributors

Frederick Burwick, UCLA
Christy Desmet, University of Georgia
Marliss C. Desens, Texas Tech University
Susan Allen Ford, Delta State University
Diane Long Hoeveler, Marquette University
Jeffrey Kahan, University of LaVerne
Rictor Norton, Independent Scholar
Marjean D. Purinton, Texas Tech University
Yael Shapira, Hebrew University of Jerusalem
Jessica Walker, University of Georgia
Carolyn A. Weber, Seattle University
Anne Williams, University of Georgia

Introduction

ANNE WILLIAMS AND CHRISTY DESMET

Shakespeare and the Gothic were born together in the eighteenth century. By 'Shakespeare' we mean the canonical figure in place by the 1790s, England's national poet and candidate for the greatest writer of the Western tradition, the Shakespeare who, as Harold Bloom would later claim, invented 'the human'. But the concept of 'Gothic story' that sprang fully armed from Horace Walpole's dreaming brow in 1764 has only recently begun to be regarded as a significant phenomenon, though it has also inspired some grandiose claims.

The essays in this volume attest to the importance and complexity of this simultaneous parturition. Yet the phrase 'Shakespearean Gothic' sounds paradoxical or oxymoronic. What could Shakespeare have to do with the Gothic, that repository of cheap thrills? What could be Shakespearean about the mad monks and fainting heroines of early Gothics, the vampires and werewolves of its later incarnations? A casual survey of early Gothic writing (1764–1820) reveals a plenitude of conscious and unconscious Shakespearean elements. If the two were born together, however, their native relationship was quickly suppressed. 'Shakespeare' continued his upward path towards Parnassus throughout the nineteenth century, while the Gothic went underground, subsisting in the realm of shilling shockers and penny dreadfuls, or in pulpy serials such as *Varney the Vampire*. Thus, when professional literary criticism was institutionalized around the beginning of the twentieth century, scholars assumed that 'Shakespeare' had no relation to the Gothic whatsoever.

To uncover the secret relation between this unlikely pair provides something of a Gothic story in itself, a tale of two long-lost relatives reunited at last. But what, exactly, is the nature of their kinship? Though separated virtually at birth, these literary siblings do not re-enact the Shakespearean and Gothic plot convention of separated twins. In attempting to clarify their subtle and complex relationship, one might be reminded of Carl Jung's theory that every personality consists of an ego and its 'shadow', the conscious and unconscious dimensions of a single self. The shadow exists only insofar as the ego, the subject's public face, casts its inevitable shadow. As 'Shakespeare' materialized as the father of English literature in the eighteenth-century imagination, his figure cast a growing shadow, which from Horace Walpole onwards came to be called Gothic. Beginning with Walpole, enthusiasts of the 'barbarous' and the medieval argued that Shakespeare's plays justi-fied their sensational material, 'monstrosities' of all kinds. Thus, a complete portrait of Shakespeare must include his Gothic 'shadow'. And it follows, that in order to read the Gothic clearly, we should contemplate its Shakespearean origins.

Ironically, the construction of Father Shakespeare, his canoniza-tion, was inspired by the English desire to defend him against the strictures of French neoclassical critics. Voltaire and many others complained that Shakespearean drama was barbarous, untutored, violating the 'rules' at every turn. Shakespeare carelessly mixed prose and verse, tragedy and comedy, natural and supernatural. He paid no attention to the notions of decorum that banished murders from the stage and demanded that Cordelia's cruel death be rewritten as something more edifying. Certainly, English critics were enjoined to 'first follow Nature', but Pope and others believed it to be orderly and rational. Yet Shakespeare the barbarian dramatist was simultaneously praised as 'Nature''s premier poet. During the century, Shakespeare's defenders gradu-ally realized that instead of pruning Shakespeare to follow the rules, as the French wished to do, they should reformulate the rules themselves. As Walpole remarked in 1772, 'Shall we fail to soar, Sir, because the French dare not rise above the ground?' After all, even Pope had suggested that truly great poets 'Snatch a grace beyond the reach of art'.

Shakespeare, in short, was established as 'sublime', a new aesthetic that shifted significant reader response from the realm of judgment to the realm of feeling. In his second preface to *Otranto*, Walpole grounded the Gothic in feeling – in terror. He also claimed that his 'Gothic story' was inspired by England's national poet, who authorized his violations of classical decorum. In *Hamlet* and *Macbeth*, in particular, Gothic writers found irregularity, irrationality and a sublime ignorance of 'the rules'. They revelled in a promiscuous mixing of literary modes, of fiction and history, of the real and the supernatural, of the medieval and the barbarous. Readers of Shakespeare and writers of the Gothic began to see that 'Nature' was a more capacious category than hitherto had been recognized. In producing 'the Gothic' in and through 'Shakespeare', critics and novelists alike began to redefine 'nature', and particularly 'human nature'.

The processes that led to the canonization of Shakespeare and the rise of the Gothic are too complicated to summarize here. A number of excellent books have treated various aspects of the process, including Gary Taylor's *Reinventing Shakespeare* (1993), Michael Dobson's *The Making of the National Poet: Shakespeare, Adaptation and Authorship, 1660–1769* (1992) and Don-John Dugas's *Marketing the Bard: Shakespeare in Performance and Print, 1660–1740* (2006). The history of the Gothic has been largely rewritten in the past two decades and includes such indispensable resources as David Punter's *The Literature of Terror* (2nd edition, 1996), Maggie Kilgour's *The Rise of the Gothic Novel* (1995), E. J. Clery's *The Rise of Supernatural Fiction, 1762–1800* (1995), James Watt's *Contesting the Gothic: Fiction, Genre and Cultural Conflict, 1764–1832* (1999) and Robert Mighall's *A Geography of Victorian Gothic Fiction* (1998). Feminist critics have also caused a revolution in our thinking about the Gothic, beginning with Ellen Moers's chapter on 'Female Gothic' in *Literary Women* (1976), Sandra Gilbert and Susan Gubar's *Madwoman in the Attic* (1978), Kate Ellis's *The Contested Castle: Gothic Novels and the Subversion of Domestic Ideology* (1989), Eugenia DeLamotte's *Perils of the Night:*

A Feminist Study of Nineteenth-Century Gothic (1990) and Diane Long Hoeveler's *Gothic Feminism: The Professionalization of Gender from Charlotte Smith to the Brontës* (1998). There are many others, for the Gothic has burgeoned into a virtual industry, although one still not quite matching the Shakespeare trade.

These three apparently separate stories – the creation of 'Shakespeare', the birth of 'the Gothic' and the rise of the novel as an expression of female subjectivity – do, however, share one element. Each attests to eighteenth-century culture's increasing fascination with the notion of subjectivity itself. In *The Making of the Modern Self: Identity and Culture in Eighteenth-Century England* (2004), Dror Wahrman argues that during the eighteenth century a new sense of 'self' emerged. By 'self', he means 'a very particular understanding of personal identity, one that presupposes an essential core of selfhood characterized by psychological depth, or interiority, which is the bedrock of unique, expressive individual identity'.[1] Wahrman's index contains two references to 'Gothic literature' and only nine to Shakespeare. But their mutual development throughout the century also supports his thesis.

Shakespeare increasingly 'materialized' during this period – as a statue in the Poet's Corner in 1741 and in the numerous scholarly editions that appeared during the century. In *Marketing the Bard*, Don-John Dugas explores the ways in which material culture affected this evolution. Between the expiration of the Licensing Act in 1695 and the passing of the Act for the Encouragement of Learning (1709), numerous attempts in Parliament to pass another Licensing Act were foiled by powerful London booksellers, such as Jacob Tonson and his nephew, Jacob Jr. They objected because they wished to avoid the return of 'licensing', which involved censorship, and were eager instead to protect the interests of those – such as themselves – who owned copyrights. In 1709, the Tonsons published their edition, which, as Dugas argues, essentially 'repackaged' the bard. To publish an 'edition' of Shakespeare was implicitly to elevate his standing, although it is unclear whether the Tonsons regarded Shakespeare as extraordinarily worthy. But, at any rate, Tonson's edition of Shakespeare contained many of the features we now associate with scholarly editions. They hired Nicholas Rowe as editor, and *The Works of*

Mr William Shakespeare contained biographical information as well as criticism. In publishing 'scholarly' editions, critics were according Shakespeare the same respect that hitherto had been reserved for classical authors.[2]

Shortly thereafter, in 1711, John Dennis published the first work of literary criticism devoted exclusively to Shakespeare, and the Tonson editions were supplanted by those of Pope (1725), Theobald (1733), Warburton (1747), Johnson (1765), Capell (1768) and Malone (1790). The editing of Shakespeare was familiar enough and controversial enough for his editors to serve Pope well as objects of satire in *The Dunciad* (1728). The editors, however, felt increasingly hampered by the lack of historical fact as interest in Shakespeare the man and Shakespeare the artist was growing. They created his biography out of sparse materials and increasingly read his writing as an expression of a unique sensibility. As Margreta de Grazia argues in *Shakespeare Verbatim: The Reproduction of Authenticity and the 1790 Apparatus*, 'new interests emerged' in Edmond Malone's edition that became and remain fundamental to Shakespeare studies. The Malone edition was

> the first to emphasize the principle of authenticity in treating Shakespeare's works and the material relating to them; the first to contain a dissertation on the linguistic and poetic particulars of Shakespeare's period; the first to depend on facts in constructing Shakespeare's biography; the first to include a full chronology for the plays; and the first to publish, annotate and canonize the 1609 sonnets.[3]

A fascination with Shakespeare's lyrics is both consistent with the growing prestige of the lyric mode (itself also a marker of the birth of modern selfhood) and with the scholar's assumption that the key to Shakespeare's greatness resided in his unique genius. The reader needed to see how Shakespeare's mind illuminated human experience. The Shakespeare admired for the mirror he held up to nature thus had become a lamp that shed its unique radiance on mankind.

However, if public discourse on Shakespeare implicitly had posited a 'modern' self, the shadow cast by Shakespeare – the

Gothic – implied more occult dimensions of this new phenomenon, the human self. Horace Walpole's 'Gothic Story' in 1764 emerges out of a curiously literal manifestation of the Gothic castle as individual self. For nearly two decades, Walpole built his country villa Strawberry Hill in his own image, constructed, as he would write in his *Description of the Villa* (1784), 'to please my own taste, and to some degree to realize my own visions'.[4] It was a public declaration of eccentricity, in fact, a 'queer space' as defined by architectural historian Aaron Betsky (1997). Since the publication of Timothy Mowl's *Horace Walpole: The Great Outsider* (1996), critics have examined the hitherto unacknowledged relationship between Walpole's sexuality and his creative works. But, while flamboyantly manifesting Walpole's own sense of himself as different, Strawberry Hill is also designed to imply the presence of secrets. In seeking to create 'gloomth' (a word that he coined), Walpole wanted to create an edifice that cast a shadow. Most tellingly, he constructed at ground level a series of pointed arches, perhaps eighteen inches high at their peaks. They were filled with vertical iron bars, suggesting that a dungeon lay beneath Strawberry Hill.

In producing *Otranto* though an implicitly psychoanalytic process, Walpole in effect explored that dungeon. Walpole's fictional interpretation shows that the public self is not as it appears: the most cheerful surface may hide terrible secrets; the most powerful ruler is subject to inevitable ruin. Walpole's narrative experiment, which he rationalized by appealing to Shakespeare, brought to consciousness the shadows cast by his house, the secrets lurking in the immaterial dungeons of what would be called the unconscious. Strawberry Hill's shadow was the Castle of Otranto. Walpole's projection of himself as a Gothic structure of mysteries and terrible secrets prefigures the Freudian self that would emerge in rational discourse more than a century later. If humanity resides within the individual self, as the evolving discourse on Shakespeare implied, that self, Horace Walpole suggested, was a man-made structure of considerable antiquity, strongly defended against external threats but concealing within itself dark unknown forces enclosed in the dungeon of an unconscious mind.

After Walpole, the Gothic rather systematically explored the contrasting fates of male and female selves. Nor is it anachronistic to find in Shakespearean Gothic adumbrations of psychoanalysis. In *Shakespeare in Psychoanalysis* (2001), Philip Armstrong argues that

> Shakespeare precedes psychoanalysis epistemologically, just as he does historically: that is, the modes of narrative, rhetoric, imagery and characterization that Freud, Rank and Jones encounter in Shakespearean drama all help to shape the development of psycho-analytic notions about dreamwork, the operations of the unconscious and the nature of the self.[5]

Armstrong also writes that Freudian theory did not colonize Shakespeare; instead, 'the Shakespearean text slips in ahead of psychoanalytic theory, so that at the critical moment of "discovery" Freud finds Shakespeare there before him'.[6] Freud does not simply notice that Hamlet suffers from an Oedipal conflict; Hamlet's struggles teach Freud about its nature and dimensions.

In authorizing the 'barbarous' and the irrational, in affirming the burden of the past, Shakespeare invited us to contemplate the human elements that escape the bounds of reason and do not obey its laws. The Gothic tradition enthusiastically explored the dark shadows of post-Enlightenment culture. Its periodic lapses into conventionality enact a reality of psychoanalysis: the uninterpreted nightmare evokes terror; the familiar monster elicits a yawn or a giggle. The old nightmares lose their power, but new ones appear to take their place. Mina Harker replaces Emily St Aubert, Schedoni becomes Dr Jekyll.

However, enthroned in high culture, 'Shakespeare' also has cast a significant shadow, one that confirms his Gothic affinities and ironically echoes the birth of 'Shakespeare' in confrontations with French theory. As Richard Wilson writes in *Shakespeare in French Theory: King of Shadows* (2007), the Bard has provided the shadowy, monstrous Other necessary to French theorists in constructing their own political and aesthetic theories. In the revolutionary chaos that fostered the Gothic in England, French readers of Shakespeare figured him as the dangerous, 'uncanny prefiguration of the unpoliced revolutionary mob'. To such readers the graveyard scene in *Hamlet* 'came to symbolize the popular justice that the savants of the salons thought had been repressed in France'. In his first chapter, tellingly called 'Gothic Shakespeare', Wilson explores the origins of this French idea that Shakespeare was 'a savage and moral monster, a barbaric negation of the Enlightenment'.[7]

The essays in this collection explore Shakespeare and the Gothic from various critical perspectives. Part I, 'Gothic appropriations of "Shakespeare"', focuses on how Gothic writers employed the Bard for their own ends. In 'Reading Walpole reading Shakespeare', Anne Williams examines Horace Walpole's most overtly Shakespearean works: his paradigmatic Gothic novel *Otranto*, his history vindicating Richard III and his blank-verse tragedy about an apparently virtuous mother who confesses to the terrible sin of having seduced her own son. Williams argues that Shakespeare gives Walpole, who was tormented by his own family romance, a means of working through his fears of illegitimacy and its consequences for his 'father' and beloved mother. Rictor Norton explores the popular notion that Ann Radcliffe, as a Gothic novelist, was herself the 'Shakespeare of romance writers'. Radcliffe's Shakespearean epigraphs and other quotations are not, as Norton argues, mere embellishments, or tokens to legitimize her writing. Instead, Radcliffe's characteristic affects are derived from her reading of Shakespeare. In 'The curse of Shakespeare', Jeffrey Kahan discusses William Henry Ireland's Shakespeare forgeries as a context for his later Gothic novels, arguing that they not only function collectively as an apology for Ireland's early forgeries but also seek to rehabilitate his literary reputation and to dramatize his position as a literary martyr.

However, Gothic novelists also rewrote Shakespeare's persons and plays in their own idiom. Part II, 'Rewriting Shakespeare's plays and characters', examines some of these appropriations. In 'Shakespearean shadows' parodic haunting of Thomas Love Peacock's *Nightmare Abbey* and Jane Austen's *Northanger Abbey*', Marjean D. Purinton and Marliss C. Desens examine the 'performative Gothic' in two novels that use Shakespeare to parody

Gothic conventions. For Peacock and Austen, Shakespeare thus becomes a stage for dramatizing late eighteenth-century social anxieties. Carolyn A. Weber, in 'Fatherly and daughterly pursuits: Mary Shelley's *Matilda* and Shakespeare's *King Lear*', discusses how, in *Lear*, Shelley found a complex portrayal of father–daughter relations that spoke to her anxieties about her own role as daughter and author. 'Into the madman's dream: the Gothic abduction of *Romeo and Juliet*', by Yael Shapira, takes a look at the dark side of Gothic appropriation through M. G. Lewis's evocation of *Romeo and Juliet* in *The Monk*. In the hands of Ambrosio, a villainous Romeo, Shakespeare's romantic plot becomes a tool for coercion and cruelty as the Bard's lovers are refigured as rapist and victim. In 'Gothic Cordelias: the afterlife of *King Lear* and the construction of femininity', Diane Long Hoeveler discusses Amelia Opie's *Father and Daughter* as a rewriting of *King Lear* and considers that novella's own literary progeny. The ascendance of the father and daughter as a paradigmatic family relation based on pathos and obedience brings Shakespeare to bear on the evolving notion of English national character. Opie's Gothic *Lear* recast Shakespeare's tale of unaccommodated man, naked and alone on the heath, as a family drama based on unfailing and unconditional love.

Was Shakespeare the Gothic's father or its creature? All literary genealogies eventually turn back on themselves, and Shakespeare's is no exception. Part III of *Shakespearean Gothic* therefore considers 'Shakespeare as [a] Gothic writer'. In '"We are not safe": history, fear and the Gothic in *Richard III*', Jessica Walker uncovers a latent Gothicism in *Richard III*, Shakespeare's play about a much maligned king in whose defence Walpole himself took up rhetorical arms. Walker argues that Shakespeare, like Walpole, turns for inspiration to England's medieval origins, troubling the boundary between (barbaric) past and (civilized) present in a way that would become characteristic of the Gothic as a genre. Christy Desmet's 'Remembering Ophelia: Ellen Terry and the Shakespearizing of *Dracula*' focuses on the symbolic presence of the Shakespearean actress in Stoker's late Gothic, where Terry functions as a liminal figure whose combination of theatricality and artifice redeems the Shakespearean plots that link the vampire and his foes, but also shows how delicate and permeable the distinction between being and seeming, living and undead, can be. Kenneth Branagh, it has been noted, filmed Ophelia's funeral in what seems to be Highgate Cemetery, which significantly is also the location of Lucy Westenra's family tomb. In a wide-ranging examination of Branagh's artistic past, Susan Allen Ford's '"Rites of Memory": the heart of Kenneth Branagh's *Hamlet'* traces the Gothic ancestry of Branagh's film as he seeks to create a *Hamlet* to supersede all *Hamlets*. The Afterword to *Shakespearean Gothic*, by Frederick Burwick, concludes the volume with a tour of Boydell's Shakespeare Gallery to show that, while Gothic novelists were busy appropriating Shakespeare's plots and characters, the Shakespeare that spectators encountered in the theatre simultaneously was being shaped to satisfy the public's taste for Gothic horror. Gothic novels are famous for their tangled genealogies, and the story of *Shakespearean Gothic* is no different. Athena sprang fully armed from the head of Zeus; Milton's Sin was born spontaneously from Lucifer's pride in exactly the same manner. But for a genre like the Gothic, obsessed as it is with family romances, the line between Shakespeare and his Gothic heirs is indeed a tangled one. The essays in this volume seek at least to begin the process of sketching out a genealogy for this Shakespearean Gothic.

Notes

[1] Dror Wahrman, *The Making of the Modern Self: Identity and Culture in Eighteenth-Century England* (New Haven and London: Yale University Press, 2004), p. xii.

[2] Don-John Dugas, *Marketing the Bard: Shakespeare in Performance and Print, 1660–1740* (Columbia and London: University of Missouri Press, 2006), p. xi.

[3] Margreta de Grazia, *Shakespeare Verbatim: The Reproduction of Authenticity and the 1790 Apparatus* (Oxford: Clarendon Press, 1991), p. 2.

[4] Horace Walpole, *A Description of the Villa of Mr Horace Walpole* (1784; London: The Gregg Press Limited, 1964), p. iv.

[5] Philip Armstrong, *Shakespeare in Psychoanalysis* (London and New York: Routledge, 2001), pp. 41–2.

[6] Ibid., p. 42.

[7] Richard Wilson, *Shakespeare in French Theory: King of Shadows* (London and New York: Routledge, 2007), p. 5.

PART I

Gothic Appropriations of 'Shakespeare'

1

Reading Walpole Reading Shakespeare

ANNE WILLIAMS

Walpole's Gothic, both literary and architectural, is a thing of shreds and patches. *The Castle of Otranto* was inspired by the fragment of a nightmare concerning a 'gigantic hand in armour', and chapter 1 begins with the fall of an enormous helmet into the castle's courtyard. Walpole pieced together his story from patches of history, folk tale, kidnapped romance, medieval superstition and Shakespearean allusions. Strawberry Hill, the villa that Walpole constructed over nearly forty years, is a pastiche of Gothic designs, imitated (in wood or papier mâché) as adornments for fireplaces, ceilings and library shelves – to say nothing of battlements and turrets made of lathe and plaster. Walpole's prolific writings appear in an equally heterogeneous range of genres. His body of work, in short, seems as disjointed as the armour of Alphonso the Good.

Yet the works of the 1760s reveal an unexpected kinship. Walpole published *The Castle of Otranto* in 1764, and in February 1768 *Historic Doubts on the Life and Reign of King Richard the Third*. Six months later, he printed at Strawberry Hill fifty copies of *The Mysterious Mother*, a tragedy in blank verse. These works mark the climax of Walpole's creative activity. With the exception of the Beauclerc Tower (1776), built to house illustrations of the play, Walpole's original work was essentially finished by the end of the 1760s. Despite their seeming diversity, however, these works share one important characteristic: they are all 'Shakespearean'. Walpole appropriated, rewrote and impersonated his precursor. I propose that under the aegis of Shakespeare, Walpole finally lived up to the Horatian motto he had chosen for his library ceiling – *'fari quae sentiat*: he says what he feels'.[1]

Walpole plays Shakespeare

[Horace Walpole's] features were covered by masks within masks … He played innumerable parts and over-acted them all.

Thomas Babington Macaulay

The Castle of Otranto and *The Mysterious Mother* are overtly fictional, though Walpole repeatedly teases us about their relation to reality. *Historic Doubts* is also a kind of romance, a wish-fulfilment fantasy disguised as history. All belong to other times and places – medieval Italy, fifteenth-century England and sixteenth-century Narbonne. All involve sexual transgressions and the abuse of power and family secrets. *Otranto* describes a failed Oedipal struggle in which a grandson learns that his grandfather had usurped the throne, knowledge that destroys 'The House of Manfred'. *Historic Doubts* seeks to exonerate the sins of a 'father' – a king – who was *not*, Walpole insists, history's murderous monster. *The Mysterious Mother* enacts the opposite process. In this tragedy, an apparently virtuous woman confesses to a sexual liaison with her son, and, learning that he has married the resulting sister/daughter, kills herself.

Shakespeare's influence in these works appears both in the old-fashioned sense of verbal echoes, formal imitation, repeated characters and themes, and in Harold Bloom's concept of influence as an unconscious struggle between literary fathers and sons. Each work appropriates Shakespearean 'authority' in different ways.[2] As Kristina Bedford has shown, *Otranto* has a 'Shakespearean sub-text' produced by Walpole's 'constant allusion and imitation', and E. L. Burney shows that he imitated the rhythms of Shakespearean blank verse in his prose, particularly when the aristocratic characters are speaking.[3] In the second preface to *Otranto*,

Walpole invokes Shakespeare in order to defend his own aesthetic choices and defends him against Voltaire. It seems that having removed several layers of his protective anonymity in the first edition, Walpole assumes the armour of Shakespearean authority and then takes up arms against his 'father''s foreign enemies.

Walpole's relation to Shakespeare in *Historic Doubts* is, however, oddly covert. Readers might well assume from the title that Shakespeare, largely responsible for the image of Richard as monster, is his chief antagonist. Yet Shakespeare's name appears only four times in the text. Early in his treatise Walpole writes: 'I did not take Shakespeare's tragedy for a genuine representation, but I did take the story of that reign as a tragedy of the imagination. Many of the crimes imputed to Richard seemed improbable, and what seemed stronger, contrary to his interests.'[4] Whereas in *Otranto*, Walpole had justified his violations of novelistic realism by claiming Shakespearean precedent, writing as a historian he reproaches Shakespeare for being insufficiently realistic. Shakespeare's Richard, however, cannot be escaped entirely. He haunts the text much as the ghost of Hamlet's father haunts him. *Historic Doubts* does, however, involve a sort of Bloomian Oedipal struggle. But, instead of meeting the father on his own ground (as Wordsworth confronts Milton in epic blank verse), here the aspiring son chooses to challenge him in another genre, and one that Shakespeare never essayed: the scholarly history in prose. Walpole's deep emotional investment in this project is evident from the energy he exerted in answering his critics, eventually publishing a supplement almost as long as the original document.

This shadowy conflict apparently whetted Walpole's purpose in Shakespearean endeavours. In writing *The Mysterious Mother*, he dons a suit of Shakespearean armour, adapting 'Shakespearean' language to create a 'Shakespearean' tragedy set in Shakespearean times. Despite his scandalous plot, however, Walpole's Shakespearean imitation is flat, at least to my ears. Here, too, he blurs the line between history and fiction, justifying his theme of double incest by citing historical precedent. He avoids the Shakespearean ghosts that had enlivened the 'barbarity' of *Otranto*. *The Mysterious Mother* is downright decorous. Walpole obeys the unities of time, place and action – though declaring this choice unintentional. And the crucial bed-trick is buried sixteen years in the past.

This 'Shakespearean' device strikes readers nowadays as psychologically unconvincing. How could Edmund, her son, have confused his mother's aging body with that of Beatrice, the young maid? Marliss Desens points out that, in the works of Shakespeare and his contemporaries, the bed-trick device almost invariably serves to restore dynastic or legal rights, as when, in *All's Well that Ends Well*, Helena tricks her husband into consummating their marriage. Such questions of verisimilitude are thus beside the point. But when the purpose of the trick is primarily sexual, to make possible the birth of a mythic hero, actual shape-shifting usually takes place. Merlin, for instance, transforms Uther Pendragon into a copy of Igraine's husband so that Arthur may be conceived. Walpole's adoption of the convention, however, does suggest something about his motives in writing the play. His plot demanded that the countess become pregnant by her son but in the least blameworthy way imaginable, in a moment of erotic insanity. This relatively sanitary solution, however, still dismayed Walpole's friend William Mason. He insisted that the mother's motive must be jealousy, not lust, and sent Walpole his suggested revisions. Walpole kindly thanked him for his comments and ignored them.

E. J. Clery has argued that *The Mysterious Mother* registers Walpole's ambivalence in the face of changing cultural conceptions of female sexuality.[5] I believe, however, that Walpole's anxiety is far more immediate. Thus, before continuing to trace his debts to Shakespeare, we need to ask another question. Why did Walpole's Shakespearean experiments embody such seemingly adolescent anxieties about fathers, mothers and sons? Walpole turned forty-seven a month after completing *Otranto*. Lady Walpole had died in 1737, Sir Robert in 1745. Nevertheless, in his fifth decade, their son was impelled to write of impotent sons, guilty/innocent fathers and innocent/guilty mothers. What could account for this belated preoccupation?

An unconscious confession

Freud acknowledged that the poets had discovered the unconscious before him. But Horace Walpole's contribution to this collective enterprise was surprisingly concrete. In writing *Otranto*, Walpole inadvertently stumbled upon the process of Freudian psychoanalysis. As he confessed to William Cole on 9 March 1765, he had awakened from the disturbing dream of 'a gigantic hand in armour' resting on 'the uppermost bannister of a great staircase'. He felt driven to explain its presence, and to do so, spontaneously adopted the proto-Freudian technique of 'free association': 'I sat down and began to write, without knowing in the least what I intended to say or relate.'[6] In trying to make sense of his nightmare, Walpole also engaged inadvertently in an over-determined exercise in self-analysis. His nightmare involved a house, which Walpole hinted was his own Strawberry Hill: 'The scene is undoubtedly laid in some real castle.'[7] Walpole had been remodelling and adding to his villa since around 1749, creating a miniature castle designed 'to please my own taste, and in some degree to realize my own visions'.[8] Thus this 'house dream' about his 'dream house' inevitably concerned himself. *The Castle of Otranto* constitutes a 'psychoanalysis' of both Strawberry Hill and its author Horace Walpole.

The terror and horror emerging from Walpole's exercise in free association seem incongruent with his dwelling's whimsical character, whose name sounds more pastoral than Gothic.[9] But in telling its story, Walpole unconsciously 'realizes' (in several senses) that Strawberry Hill has its ancient, dark, labyrinthine aspects. It *literally* embodies (in words) its master's fatal secret.[10] In the second preface, Walpole declared his desire that *Otranto* would free his readers from the present world, where 'the resources of fancy have been dammed up' (p. 9). But *Otranto* portrays a world that is anything but free; it tragically embodies 'the Law of the Father', patriarchal culture's symbolic order. This law inextricably entangles the destiny of fathers and sons. Furthermore, just as *Otranto* seems an unlikely 'reading' of Strawberry Hill, the hero/villain Manfred's fate is oddly incongruent with Walpole's secure position near the top of the social hierarchy. Yet if Manfred is Walpole's Jungian 'Shadow' – the dark double repressed in any man's unconscious – this 'psychoanalysis' of his house compels us to ask whether Horace Walpole may also have feared himself 'illegitimate' in some way.

Horace was known as the youngest son of Sir Robert Walpole, the first British politician to be called 'prime minister', and, next to the king, the most powerful man in England. His corrupt political career ended with his resignation from office in 1741, shortly after Horace returned from his Grand Tour. Sir Robert (now Earl of Orford) died in 1745, leaving Horace several lucrative political sinecures, a seat in Parliament and the lease of a house in London's Arlington Street. Nearly fifty years later (1791), he would inherit Sir Robert's title, becoming the fourth (and last) earl. Horace behaved as Sir Robert's loyal son, devoting himself to cataloguing the former prime minister's art collection and, later, to defending his memory and reputation. But Horace may have felt anxious about playing his designated role as the great man's youngest son, for two reasons.

First, Horace Walpole was what we would now call gay, though the concept of homosexuality would not be articulated until the twentieth century.[11] Sneers at his 'effeminacy' were published both before and after his death. In 1764, Walpole was engaged with William Guthrie in a pamphlet war concerning the expulsion of Henry Seymour Conway, Horace's favourite cousin, from his political office and military command. Guthrie attacked Walpole as being 'by nature muleish, by disposition female, so halting between the two that it would very much puzzle a common observer to assign him to his true sex'.[12] Similar aspersions appeared in the nineteenth century. In *Table Talk* (1835), Samuel Taylor Coleridge remarked of *The Mysterious Mother* that 'No one with a spark of true manliness, of which Horace Walpole had none, could have written it.'[13] Thomas B. Macaulay, reviewing a new edition of Walpole's letters (1833), wrote that his mind and imagination were 'unhealthy', a Victorian euphemism for same-sex attraction: 'Nothing but an unhealthy and disorganized mind could have produced such literary luxuries as the works of Walpole.'[14]

W. S. Lewis, Walpole's twentieth-century editor and champion, vigorously denied these insinuations. Lewis apparently cautioned

R. J. Ketton-Cremer, Walpole's authoritative biographer, to avoid the speculations that might arise from some of Horace's letters to his Eton friend, Lord Lincoln. In his preface to the first edition (1940), Ketton-Cremer thanks Lewis for helping him to avoid any 'misinterpretations' of Walpole. Though Lewis apparently wanted to protect Walpole from an identity that he considered embarrassing, he was a scrupulous scholar and published the Lincoln letters twenty years afterwards in the Yale *Correspondence* (vol. 30). These look very much like love letters, and though Lewis did not censor or suppress them, he did attempt to control their interpretation. In his head-note to the most passionate, Lewis asserted that here, '[Walpole] appears in the character of one of [Lincoln's] mistresses'.[15] Lewis succeeded in diverting attention from the question of Walpole's sexuality for most of the century. Not until Timothy Mowl's revisionist biography, *Horace Walpole: The Great Outsider* (1996), did anyone confront this aspect of the father of 'Gothic'.

Mowl's biography goes overboard in the opposite direction. He supposes that Walpole's 'homosexuality' explains everything about him, and the figure who emerges in this analysis is a rather unpleasant stereotype. Walpole was, writes Mowl, 'a notably effeminate bachelor with a strong vein of malice in his writings; but if he had homosexual tendencies, he appears to have been too fastidious ever to have given way to them'.[16] Mowl's unexamined assumptions about homosexuality are troublesome, as his reading of Walpole is uninformed by the extensive scholarship on gender and sexuality published since the 1980s. This body of work demonstrates, among other things, the dangers of imposing our own assumptions about sexual behaviour on historical periods so different from our own.[17] To read Walpole as simply 'homosexual' is to misread him, though not for the reasons Lewis feared. Walpole was undoubtedly 'queer', but he was not in the closet, for the closet did not yet exist.

I see no evidence that Walpole's sexual orientation rendered him so irrevocably an 'other' that he lived a life of internal exile, as Mowl argues. Though sodomy was illegal in eighteenth-century England, Walpole belonged to the fortunate class who could behave as they pleased without fear of legal reprisal or social ostracism. Walpole's eccentric allegiance to 'deviant' aesthetic norms, widely recognized as an explicit personal statement, caused him to be celebrated, not condemned. I also doubt that anxieties about sexual identity alone could have generated the energy driving Walpole's sixty-year-long project of self-expression – in his letters, his house, his collections, his books, his private printing press. In fact, in decrying Walpole's 'effeminacy', Guthrie, like Coleridge and Macaulay after him, were *themselves* writing as outsiders, as middle-class observers of a closed, if not closeted, aristocratic coterie. Nevertheless, if we read carefully the meta-phorical dimensions of Walpole's various creations – *Otranto* above all – it seems clear that he was haunted by a fear far more threatening to a man living at the top of the patriarchal hierarchy. It is more than likely that Horace was not a Walpole.

Public secrets

In 1833, Lady Louisa Stuart wrote: 'In a word, Horace Walpole himself was generally supposed to be the son of Carr Lord Hervey, and Sir Robert not to be ignorant of it.'[18] Lady Louisa's source was her grandmother, Lady Mary Wortley Montagu, whose journals and letters she had read before supervising their destruction. W. S. Lewis emphatically rejects Lady Louisa's claim, for various reasons even more threatening than the rumours about Walpole's sexuality. It had been obvious to contemporaries of this youngest 'son' that Horace did not resemble the Walpoles, either physically or intellectually. Furthermore, Sir Robert and Lady Walpole had not been living as husband and wife for several years before Horace's birth. This event was not announced in the press, though babies born to Sir Robert's sister Dolly (Viscountess Townshend) and to his cousin and friend Sir William Wyndham appeared about the same time.[19] Again, according to Lady Louisa, Sir Robert had ignored Horace until he began to show signs of intellectual precocity at Eton. Lewis had four reasons for rejecting these rumours. First, since Lady Mary was the primary source of the gossip, he assumed that it must be not only false but also mali-cious. He states that there was no such gossip while Horace was alive and that none of Sir Robert's many political enemies had ever attacked him for this scandalous situation. Finally, he asserts that if Horace had known anything about his mother's amours, he would never have adorned her memorial in Westminster Abbey with an epitaph praising her many virtues and a statue representing 'Modesty'.

However, none of these arguments holds up to careful scrutiny. Horace was indeed extraordinarily hostile toward Lady Mary. Lewis appears to assume that the feelings must have been mutual. But one sees little malice evident in either Lady Mary or Lady Louisa. And, as Robert Halsband observes in his essay 'Walpole versus Lady Mary', 'in their attitudes towards each other they present very different aspects – benign on hers, bitter on his'.[20] There is a simple explanation for Horace's revulsion toward this woman old enough to be his mother, a revulsion that extended to hinting that she suffered from syphilis.[21] Lady Mary was an unimpeachable source of information about Sir Robert and Lady Walpole's marriage. She had been an intimate friend of Sir Robert's wayward sister Dolly and of the second Lady Walpole, Sir Robert's long-time mistress Maria Skerrett, whom he married, much to Horace's dismay, a few months after his mother's death. Horace also appears to have believed – wrongly – that Lady Mary and Maria were kin.[22] Lady Mary, in other words, was an all too reliable source of information about his parents' marriage and his claim to the name of Walpole.[23] Furthermore, despite Lewis's denial, there was plenty of contemporary gossip regarding Sir Robert's and Lady Walpole's quite public infidelities and Horace's paternity.

The marriage of the prime minister and his lady evoked some gossipy interest in the public at large, and was an item of amused satire among his political enemies.[24] Lady Louisa points out that Gulliver's elaborate defence of the virtue of the Lilliputian Treasurer's wife was clearly understood as a satire on Walpole's complaisance about his wife's 'gallantry':

> Those ironical lines also, where Pope says that Sir Robert Walpole
>> Had never made a friend in private life,
>> And was, besides, *a tyrant to his wife*,[25]

are equally well understood as conveying a sly allusion to his good-humoured unconcern about some things that more strait-laced husbands do not take so coolly. Openly laughing at their nicety, he professed it his method 'to go his own way and let madam go hers'.[26]

Lord Holland, whose reminiscences were composed around 1826, recounted the following: 'The scandalous chronicle reported [Horace] to be the son of a Lord Hervey. In affected humour, laborious application to trifles, occasional and unprovoked malignity, and whimsical ingenuity of understanding, he certainly bore some resemblance to that family.'[27] (Incidentally, the Lord Hervey in question was the elder half-brother of John, Lord Hervey, Pope's 'Sporus'.) After Lady Walpole died in 1737, Lord Egmont noted in his journal that 'Sir Robert, it is likely, is not very sorry. She was as gallant, if report be true, with the men as he was with the women; nevertheless they contrived to live together and to take their pleasures their own way without giving offence'.[28] Finally, Sir Robert's twentieth-century biographer J. H. Plumb states that he could find no evidence that Sir Robert and Lady Walpole were in the same place, much less temporarily reconciled, nine months before Horace was born. Lady Walpole was, however, visiting near the Hervey estate in Norfolk around the time that her son was conceived.[29]

Nor does Lewis's negative evidence – that Sir Robert was never lampooned about this scandal – prove convincing. A satirist aims to disconcert his victims by exposing their secrets. But Horace's status as a Walpole was not a secret. Whatever Sir Robert knew or suspected about the infant's origin, he allowed him to be christened not only a 'Walpole' but also a 'Horatio', after his uncle and brother. (He did, after all, already have two undoubtedly legitimate sons.) Because Sir Robert was so publicly unconcerned about his wife's behaviour and apparently never questioned Horace's claim to the name Walpole, this bit of gossip could not have been of much use to his enemies. Finally, Lewis's assumption that Sir Robert would have been publicly disgraced for such peccadillos rests on a Victorian concept of political respectability. More than a century later in the 1890s, Charles Stuart Parnell, leader of the Irish party agitating for home rule, was indeed driven from office because of a sexual scandal.[30] But such an outcry would have been virtually unimaginable in Sir Robert Walpole's heyday. Those in the know – including Lady Mary – simply laughed good naturedly about it all.

But what about Horace's monument for his mother in Westminster Abbey? Lewis writes: 'Had any [rumours] reached him, I do not think that he would have made his mother and himself ridiculous by putting up this monument, which extolled her numerous virtues and was ornamented by the figure of "Modesty".'[31] Horace himself composed the inscription that concluded:

> She loved a private life,
> Though born to shine in public;
> And was an ornament to Courts,
> Untainted by them.

However, the monument *did* seem ridiculous to at least some of Horace's contemporaries. Lady Louisa recorded a friend's amazement upon first seeing the monument. Lady Anne Pitt was viewing the abbey with some foreign friends and there saw Walpole's inscription, at which 'she expressed her amazement with uplifted eyes and hands':

> How wonderful, she said, that a man of his taste and knowledge of the world should venture to set forth such a panegyric on a woman whose gallantries were so notorious! – and if it were possible that they could have altogether escaped his own knowledge, that was more wonderful still – she added much besides, concluding with – 'Why who ever believed Horace himself to be Sir Robert Walpole's son?'[32]

This monument, however, could have sprung from motives more complex than mere ignorance. Walpole's devotion to his mother was widely known. Perhaps he chose the memorial as a defiant gesture, saying in effect, 'You may have known her as a flagrantly unfaithful wife, but *this* is how I knew her'.

I believe it also points to a more significant, probably unconscious defence that illuminates much about Horace's turn of mind.
Freud observes that when a child begins to realize that his parents
are flawed, ordinary human beings, not the all-powerful, ideal
figures they once seemed, he turns to fantasy. He tells himself a
'family romance'. The child tells himself that these people are not
really his parents; his *true* progenitors are a king and queen.[33] This
fiction is a useful defence because it revises history into a more
acceptable and more gratifying version. Lady Walpole's monument
could also be read as just such an exercise in fantasy wish-fulfilment. In a culture where wealth and power depend on one's
'father' really *being* one's father, any uncertainty both imperils
one's place in the social hierarchy and imputes disgrace for the
mother who has violated the taboo against extramarital sex for
'good women'. According to the cultural rules, she is a 'fallen
woman'. One could, therefore, read his monument as his first
public exercise in rewriting history according to the contours of
his own desires, and it thus adumbrates Walpole's most characteristic strategy throughout his eccentric career, creating ersatz, but
emotionally gratifying, 'Gothic' structures in various media.

Whether one sides with W. S. Lewis or with Lady Mary on the
question of Horace's paternity, his manifold works testify to his
troubling anxieties about himself and his parents – the paradoxical good mother, who undoubtedly was his mother and yet was
'bad' according to cultural standards, and the equally paradoxical
'father' who was not his father and a monster besides, but who
had been good to him. Such fears would account for Horace's
lifelong obsession with the past, with genealogy, with family
secrets, with deceptive situations and with disguise and the counterfeit. It explains why the plot of *Otranto* turns on the exposure
of illegitimate succession. It explains Macaulay's sense that Walpole
was endlessly masquerading and Morris Brownell's observation
that what he feared most was to seem ridiculous.[34] It explains his
career, which may be seen as a lifelong drive to 'materialize'
'Horace Walpole'. And it explains why, in the 1760s, Horace
Walpole's cathartic Shakespearean Gothics concerned weak sons
doomed by their forefathers' sins, a wrongly maligned 'father' and
a 'virtuous' mother who was also an adulteress. The scandalmon-

gers of Sir Robert's generation may not have found the (open) secret of his birth interesting, but for Horace himself, it was a ghost he never entirely exorcized.

Sweetest Shakespeare, fancy's sire

If Horace Walpole was not Sir Robert's son, he was doomed at birth to a lifelong masquerade. English has no word for such a role. What does one call an illegitimate son acknowledged as a son by the not-father, who is living a very public lie? Although Sir Robert apparently never made the slightest gesture towards disowning Horace, the person playing 'Horace Walpole' must have heard or intuited something about the parlous nature of his identity.[35] All his life Horace flagrantly relished his role as the prime minister's son and, upon reaching adulthood, vigorously defended him against attackers. But, shortly after his putative father died, Horace also began to construct a persona defiantly distinct from Sir Robert's. The prime minister had transformed his country house Houghton Hall into a massive Palladian palace; Horace leased a small cottage (from a toy merchant) and created Strawberry Hill, a 'castle' that followed no rules but those of his 'Gothic' fantasies. He shunned Sir Robert's passion for politics and turned to literature and art. Brownell argues that Walpole created an identity for himself as 'The Prime Minister of Taste' in response to his father's very different sort of prime ministry.[36] He assumes that Horace experienced the usual Oedipal anxieties about a powerful father, and hence took 'taste' rather than politics as his private province. Horace, however, was in the habit of contrasting 'taste' with 'passion', and explicitly preferred 'passion'. But 'passion' needed a local habitation and a name. Walpole found both in Shakespeare.

Walpole's appropriation of Shakespeare has, until quite recently, evoked surprisingly little analysis.[37] His importance seemed obvious in the early days of Gothic criticism. Eino Railo's *The Haunted Castle* (1927) stated that Shakespeare was a seminal influence on early Gothic from Walpole onwards.[38] But Railo's argument about Shakespeare was quickly disavowed by critics

rushing to protect him and the high Romantics from any association with the disreputable Gothic. In 1934, Jess M. Stein published
'Horace Walpole and Shakespeare', arguing that while Walpole
was extremely familiar with England's greatest dramatist and
shared his culture's evaluation of him as the quintessential 'poet of
nature', Shakespeare's actual influence on Walpole was minimal:
'Various minor devices may have come from Shakespeare,
although one can more easily conceive of their coming from
contact with medieval ruins.'[39] He also quotes W. P. Harbeson's
'The Elizabethan influence on the tragedy of late eighteenth and
the early nineteenth centuries' (1921), which declared that 'the
influence of Elizabethan writers upon those of the late eighteenth and early nineteenth centuries was almost nil'.[40] Of *The
Mysterious Mother*, Stein writes, 'There seems to be no possible
parallel source in Shakespeare' for this 'filial relationship, tending
towards horror and repulsiveness'.[41]

However, Harold Bloom has shown us that literary influence has
its unconscious dimensions. It is clear that eighteenth-century
ideas about Shakespeare would have made him particularly
congenial to Walpole's unconscious needs. From Shakespeare he
sought something besides a powerful father to conquer; he needed
authority for expressing his own unauthorized realities. Instead of
Bloom's Oedipal 'anxiety of influence', Walpole appears to have
suffered more from the 'anxiety of authorship' that Gilbert and
Gubar ascribe to literary *daughters*, writers who as women feel
themselves positioned as 'illegitimate' successors of their literary
fathers.[42] And Shakespeare could play the role of a nurturing rather
than a threatening father. Far from appearing as a Bloomian
powerful precursor, Shakespeare was still something of an under-
dog in the literary hierarchy. For most of the century, the
national-poet-to-be was attacked and denigrated by the French
critics, who decried his barbarous ignorance of the rules. Thus, in
English eyes, Shakespeare might be seen as the victim of prejudice,
of injustice, of misplaced authority wielded blindly – that is, of
foreign tyranny. Indeed, Shakespeare might appear implicitly to be
an object of empathy for Walpole, who always sympathized with
the less fortunate. (Despite his own social position, he was harshly
critical of aristocratic follies, hypocrisies and imperialist adven-

tures.)[43] Ironically, Shakespeare could even be associated with that most pervasive marginalized class: women. Milton's memorable epithet in 'L'Allegro' would have been familiar: 'Sweetest Shakespeare, Fancy's Child, / Warbling his native wood-notes wild' (ll. 133–4). It is unlikely that Walpole consciously arrived at this feminist insight, but from his secret perspective as illegitimate inheritor, he might have felt empathy for Shakespearean 'otherness' of all kinds.

According to Milton, Shakespeare was an untaught, spontaneous, implicitly feminized child of nature, almost a damsel in distress. Certainly, the second preface to *Otranto* suggests a rescue fantasy. The idea that Shakespeare was 'the poet of nature' had originated in early comparisons with Ben Jonson, whom critics consistently aligned with 'art'.[44] Samuel Johnson was the most authoritative contemporary exponent of this idea: 'Shakespeare is above all writers, at least above all modern writers, the poet of nature, the poet that holds up to his readers a faithful mirror of manners and of life.'[45] At first glance, it may seem that here, at least, was one idea that Walpole and Johnson could agree about. (Horace distrusted the latter's piety and deplored his Tory politics.) But even on 'nature' they do not agree, for Walpole's conception of it was significantly broader than Johnson's. He adhered to the neoclassical conception of '*la belle nature*'– an idealized version of actuality – while Walpole embraces nature as he sees it, with its inconsistencies, irrationalities and serendipitous connections. Walpole's understanding of human nature implies what Freud would name 'the unconscious'.

Walpole found Shakespeare's most perceptive insights precisely in those elements neoclassical critics regarded as 'flaws'. He saw verisimilitude in his 'barbarous' mixtures of comedy and tragedy, prose and poetry, the living and the dead, and in his practice of showing aristocrats such as the prince of Denmark joking with 'low' characters such as the gravediggers. In Walpole's opinion, these mixtures were a positive virtue, for Shakespeare was not constrained by false, 'civilized' concepts such as 'good taste'. He associated such shibboleths with the critical standards that had created the world in which 'the great resources of fancy have been damned up' (*Otranto*, p. 9). As Walpole wrote to Robert

Jephson in February 1775, 'What French criticism can wound the ghosts of Hamlet or Banquo? Scorn rules, Sir, that cramp genius, and substitute delicacy to imagination in a barren language. Shall we not soar, because the French dare not rise from the ground?'[46] Indeed, Walpole admitted that Shakespeare's 'taste' was inferior to that of later writers but, since he had written in an age before English had been refined, he regarded this lack as inconsequential. As Walpole declared to Christopher Wren on 9 August 1764, 'It seems to me as if there was a sobriety in taste which would be a shackle on a genius ... One of the greatest geniuses that ever existed, Shakespeare, undoubtedly wanted taste'.[47]

In one of his most extended comments on Shakespeare, Walpole practises an implicitly psychoanalytic mode of criticism. After a performance of *Hamlet* directed by David Garrick, who, in a nod to French taste, had omitted the gravedigger scene, Walpole recorded an extended comment in his commonplace book. He argues for the scene's fidelity to human nature. He asserts that it should be performed because it offers so many insights into Hamlet and into humanity in general:

> Mirth itself, especially in the hands of such a genius as Shakespeare, may excite tears or laughter, and ought to do so. The grave-digger's account of Yorick's ludicrous behaviour is precisely an instance of that exquisite and matchless art, and furnishes an answer too to the last objection, that the humour of the grave-digger interrupts the interest of the action and weakens the purpose of Hamlet. Directly the contrary; the skull of Yorick and the accounts of his jests could have no effect but to recall fresh to the Prince's mind the happy days of his childhood, and the court of the King his father, and then make him [see] his uncle's reign in a comparative view that must have rendered the latter odious to him, and consequently the scene serves to whet his *almost blunted purpose*. Not to mention that the grave before him was destined to his love Ophelia – what incident in this scene but tends to work on his passions?[48]

This is an essentially Freudian insight, as is Walpole's recognition that this grisly scene is important because it reminds Hamlet of his happy childhood, when his good father, the rightful king, ruled. Such a memory, he argues, implicitly intensifies Hamlet's present disgust with Claudius as substitute father and usurping king. It bolsters the son's resolve to destroy his stepfather. This observation makes no sense without some intuition of unconscious motivation. Walpole also notes Shakespeare's juxtaposition of *eros* and *thanatos* (represented by the dead Yorick and Ophelia), perhaps the most powerful of Freudian paradoxes. In short, he sees that an accurate – a truly *natural* – representation of the human self can only be achieved by including its mysteries and inconsistencies. And these, he believes, must necessarily disturb any neoclassical rage for order. Fidelity to 'human nature' justifies – even demands – a 'Gothic' aesthetic.

Concluding his second preface to *Otranto*, Walpole writes that 'The result of all I have said is to shelter my own daring under the cannon [*sic*] of the brightest genius this country, at least, has produced' (p. 13). The Gothics that emerged from the crucible of Walpole's self-analysis are all, in Freudian terms, 'compromise formations', where the dream or the symptom permits unconscious fears and desires a coded expression in their manifest content. According to my reading, *Otranto* enabled Walpole to express in a displaced mode his 'knowledge' of his own illegitimacy. *Historic Doubts* and *The Mysterious Mother* then address two consequences of this insight. Even though his claim to be a 'Walpole' might be spurious, Horace nevertheless played the role of Sir Robert's son. Yet since this 'father', while powerful, was widely regarded as a corrupt monster, it may have seemed that fate had played a nasty trick on him. Obeying the logic of 'family romance', Walpole may have rewritten his own family history by transforming the bad king into a good one, and, incidentally, confronting Shakespeare.[49] Having successfully bested his precursor on the field of history rather than poetry, in *The Mysterious Mother* he is finally ready for his greatest challenge. Walpole both masquerades as Shakespeare and transforms a good mother into a guilty one. He portrays the Countess of Narbonne as a virtuous woman who finally confesses herself to be an incestuous adulteress. (Though Sir Robert did not become an earl until after his first wife's death, an earl's wife is a 'countess'. And Narbonne is a name that figures in *All's Well That Ends Well*, a play that turns on the bed-trick.) What did Walpole find in his Shakespearean disguises? In a word, legitimacy. *Otranto, Historic Doubts* and *The Mysterious Mother* all affirm that in the realm of art, Horace's *true* father was a Goth, and that he was, indeed, the rightful heir.

Hamlet's closet

One needs taste to be sensible of the beauties of Grecian architecture; one wants only passion to feel Gothic.

Horace Walpole, *Anecdotes of Painting* (1764)

'Fari quae sentiat'

Walpole's motto on the ceiling of his library
at Strawberry Hill (1754)

To this point, I have implied that in constructing Gothic romances – in patching together his Gothic masquerades – Horace Walpole was something of a *bricoleur*, Claude Lévi-Strauss's term for one who pieces together cultural artefacts from randomly available materials. But Walpole's selection of shreds and patches was far from random; all three of his Shakespearean Gothics are versions of *Hamlet*. The index of the Yale *Correspondence* reveals that he mentioned this play most frequently – fifty times (*Macbeth* is second with twenty-nine mentions). The gravedigger scene appears ten times.

Certainly, *Hamlet* portrays a world fraught with the same anxieties and the same cast of characters that peopled Walpole's own private psychodrama: a good and bad father; a good and bad mother; and an ambivalent son unable to live up to his dead father's demands. Although the usurper King Claudius *denies* that 'our state' is 'disjoint and out of frame' (1.2.20),[50] in his nephew/ stepson's mind, this is precisely the problem; Hamlet lives in a realm corrupted by the murder of his father, the good king, and by the murderer's incestuous marriage to his widow. In fact, these metaphors are literalized by two of *Otranto*'s significant supernatural events – the apparition of Alphonso's disjointed armour and the portrait of his usurping grandfather Ricardo, who steps out of the frame. Manfred addresses the walking likeness as Hamlet would have: 'Speak, infernal specter! ... Lead on! I will follow thee to the gulf of perdition!' (p. 25). Shakespeare's play also includes a character named 'Horatio', one of those Prufrockean 'attendant lords' who has a front-row seat on the action but barely participates in it. He is there, however, for two of the play's most Gothic moments: the appearance of the ghost in act 1 and the graveyard scene of act 5.

Walpole was so insistent that the gravedigger scene epitomized Shakespeare's genius that one is tempted to call it his Shakespearean 'primal scene', the fantasy of origin that, according to Freud, demarcates a psychic boundary, the point behind or beyond which the analysand's imagination cannot go. It usually concerns the child's observation of his parents having sex, which he interprets as violence inflicted by his father on his mother. The gravedigger scene hardly conforms to these Freudian expectations of Oedipal violence. But it does reveal the moment when Hamlet appeared on earth. The gravedigger tells him that he began digging graves on the day that Hamlet's late father slew the elder Fortinbras, which was also the day of Hamlet's birth. The mother is missing, replaced with a glimpse of masculine violence directed not at a woman but at another king, a situation that foreshadows Claudius's murder of his brother. But Walpole's language unconsciously reveals that this scene is less a primal scene than a primal *screen*. Walpole's fascination with the scene masks something even more disturbing. He writes that the gravedigger scene is necessary 'to whet [Hamlet's] *almost blunted purpose*' (italics in original). That phrase, however, belongs elsewhere. These words were spoken by the ghost of Hamlet's father, who reappeared as Hamlet confronted Gertrude in her closet (3.4).

Here we do find the more expected elements of a primal scene, though unconventionally configured. Hamlet kills a father, though not the one he intends to kill. Instead of trying to preserve the erotic bond with the mother, he plays the father's role, inflicting violence on her. But, as the ghost's appearance makes clear, Hamlet is acting on his father's instructions. He has gone to his mother's chamber in order to berate her for her sins. The ghost's imagery ('whetting' Hamlet's appetite) is appropriately phallic, since he demands that his son enforce the Law of the Father. For such a task, language is the appropriate weapon, for the father's ghost is patriarchy's superego, which unconsciously enforces the Law. Before entering Gertrude's chamber, Hamlet declares that he will be 'cruel, not unnatural' and 'will speak daggers to her, but use none' (3.2.365, 366). By accusing his mother of living '[i]n the rank sweat of an enseamèd bed, / Stewed in corruption, honeying and making love / Over the nasty sty' (3.4.82–4), Hamlet metaphorically kills her. She responds, 'These words like daggers enter in my ears' (l. 85) and 'O Hamlet, thou hast cleft my heart in twain!' (l. 147), to which he bitterly replies, 'O throw away the worser part of it / And live the purer with the other half' (ll. 158–9).

The gravedigger scene, including Hamlet's iconographic contemplation of Yorick's skull, is an extended memento mori. Whereas the closet scene reveals Hamlet's (and his father's) effort to impose and enforce the law, the gravedigger scene illustrates the futility of such efforts. Materiality cannot be controlled. All that culture can do is respond defensively, digging graves to bury the dead, joking about death, playing with words and playfully confronting the reality that human laws are not necessarily enforced, or enforceable. (The suicide Ophelia, for instance, is being buried in hallowed ground because she is a member of the court.) Most significantly, however, Gertrude reappears in this landscape of death in the guise of a virtuous woman, behaving conventionally, even sentimentally, when she eulogizes Ophelia as the one who should have been Hamlet's wife. Yorick's ironic 'resurrection' modulates between these two versions of Gertrude. Yorick is, for Hamlet, at once a man of wit, a memento mori and a mother figure ('He hath bore me on his back a thousand times … Here hung those lips that I have kiss'd I know not how oft' (5.1.172–5)). Hamlet's response to Yorick thus fuses affection and abjection, like a musical modulation that takes us back to the tonic major key. Gertrude as ideal mother is back on stage.

Thus, Walpole's fascination with the gravedigger scene begins to make sense as being highly overdetermined. Publicly and consciously, it permits Walpole to endorse ostentatiously the eccentric, the passionate and the English, all in the person of

Shakespeare. Unconsciously, it masks that other scene in *Hamlet* in which the tragic anti-hero expresses rage and disgust toward Gertrude. Such feelings appear to have been unthinkable in Walpole's experience of his own mother. But, from the design of Lady Walpole's monument until he finished *The Mysterious Mother*, Walpole was unconsciously struggling, like Hamlet, to live with the paradox that his mother was both good to him and (in others' eyes) irreparably corrupt. Hamlet declared that Gertrude's sin is 'Such an act / That blurs the blush and grace of modesty' (3.4.39–40). Can it be coincidental that Horace chose 'Modesty' to adorn his mother's cenotaph?

As several critics have observed, a strain of misogyny is incongruously mixed, in Walpole's writing, with his documented fondness for dowagers such as the Marquise du Duffand and much younger women such as the Berry sisters or Lady Diana Beauclerc. His relationships with women of his own age were strictly social. He apparently never even considered marriage.[51] But he spent his life attempting to reconcile his own experiences of Lady Walpole with her cultural definition as a 'fallen' (abject?) woman that followed from his own knowledge of illegitimacy. Like Hamlet, who could be read as an allegory of the Kristevan speaking subject caught on the border between the semiotic and the symbolic, Walpole was a legitimate/illegitimate son who did not conform to his culture's notion of manliness and hence was implicitly consigned to the cultural margins. Just as Walpole unconsciously masked the closet scene with that of the gravediggers, masking the bad mother with a good one, in *The Mysterious Mother* he dared to portray a good mother – the virtuous and charitable countess – who is ultimately unmasked as a bad one. This *un*masking, however indirect, nevertheless comes close to expressing the reality that appears to have so desperately troubled Horace Walpole. When the countess confesses that she had betrayed her husband with her son, she kills herself with a dagger. In this way, Walpole's play literalizes Hamlet's daggers, which are words. As she dies, she says to her distraught Edmund (whose name echoes that of the villainous bastard in *King Lear*): 'Peace, and control our shame – quick, frame some legend –'.[52] Such 'framing' was, I believe, Horace Walpole's lifelong work.

Notes

1.   This phrase, which Ketton-Cremer declares was the Walpole family motto, quotes Horace's epistle to Tibullus, *Sapere and fari quae sentiat* (Robert Wyndham Ketton-Cremer, *Horace Walpole: A Biography* (3rd edn; Ithaca: Cornell University Press, 1966), p. 129).

2.   Harold Bloom, *The Anxiety of Influence* (1973; reprint, New Haven: Yale University Press, 1997).

3.   Kristina Bedford, '"This castle hath a pleasant seat": Shakespearean allusion in *The Castle of Otranto*', *English Studies in Canada*, 14, 4 (December 1988), 415; E. L. Burney, 'Shakespeare in *Otranto*', *Manchester Review*, 12 (1972), 62–3.

4.   Horace Walpole, *Historic Doubts on the Life and Reign of King Richard III* (Dublin: G. Faulkner, A. Leathley and W. and W. Smith, 1768), p. 9.

5.   E. J. Clery, 'Horace Walpole's *The Mysterious Mother* and the impossibility of female desire', in Fred Botting (ed.), *The Gothic* (Cambridge: Brewer, 2001), pp. 38–41.

6.   Horace Walpole, *The Yale Edition of Horace Walpole's Correspondence*, ed. W. S. Lewis et al. (48 vols; New Haven: Yale University Press, 1937–1983), vol. 1, p. 88.

7.   Horace Walpole, *The Castle of Otranto*, Michael Gamer (ed.) (New York: Penguin, 2001), p. 9. Further references to *Otranto* will be to this edition and will be included in the body of the text.

8.   Horace Walpole, *A Description of the Villa of Mr Horace Walpole* (1784; reprint, London: The Gregg Press Limited, 1964), p. iv.

9.   Strawberry leaves traditionally appear on the coronets of earls, marquesses and dukes.

10.   At the ground level of Strawberry Hill, Walpole constructed a series of peaked arches (about eighteen inches tall) furnished with iron bars to signal that Strawberry Hill had a dungeon.

11.   Max Fincher points out that the term 'homosexual' is, these days, shunned by theorists as it forms part of a hierarchical binary with 'heterosexual', implicitly granting normative status to the latter (Max Fincher, *Queering Romanticism in the Romantic Age: The Penetrating Eye* (New York and London: Palgrave, 2007), pp. 12–13).

12.   William Guthrie, *A Reply to the Counter-Address & etc.* (London: W. Nicoll, 1764), p. 7.

13.   Samuel Taylor Coleridge, *Table Talk*, in Peter Sabor (ed.), *Horace Walpole: The Critical Heritage* (London and New York: Routledge & Kegan Paul, 1987), p. 148.

14.   Thomas Babington Macaulay, 'Letters of Horace Walpole', *Edinburgh Review*, October 1833, in Sabor, *Horace Walpole*, p. 312.

15.   Walpole, *The Yale Edition of Horace Walpole's Correspondence*, vol. 30, p. 43.

16.   Timothy Mowl, *Horace Walpole: The Great Outsider* (London: John Murray, 1996), p. 2.

[17]   See, for instance, George Haggerty's *Men in Love: Masculinity and Sexuality in the Eighteenth Century* (New York and London: Columbia University Press, 1999); and 'Queering Horace Walpole', *Studies in English Literature*, 46, 3 (summer 2006), 543–62.

[18]   Cited by Sabor, *Horace Walpole*, p. 319.

[19]   J. H. Plumb, *Sir Robert Walpole* (2 vols; London: Cresset Press, 1956–60), vol. 1, p. 258.

[20]   Robert Halsband, 'Walpole versus Lady Mary', in Warren Smith (ed.), *Horace Walpole: Writer, Politician and Connoisseur: Essays on the 250th Anniversary of Walpole's Birth* (New Haven: Yale University Press, 1967), p. 215.

[21]   As Walpole wrote to Lord Lincoln, he 'did not imagine that she would try to [claim the relationship] by making you of her blood; of her poxed, foul, malicious black blood!' (quoted in Halsband, 'Walpole versus Lady Mary', p. 219).

[22]   Ibid., p. 216.

[23]   Horace's use of counterfeit and travesty (papier-mâché fan vaulting) in Strawberry Hill may unconsciously reflect his sense of himself as somehow inauthentic.

[24]   See, for instance, *The Rival Wives: Or, the Greeting of Clarissa to Skirra in the Elysian Shades* (London: Printed for W. Lloyd, 1738); and *The Rival Wives Answer'd: or, Skirra to Clarissa* (London: Printed for W. Lloyd, 1738).

[25]   Alexander Pope, 'Epilogue to the Satires', (2, ll. 133–5); italics added.

[26]   See Sabor, *Horace Walpole*, p. 328.

[27]   See Ibid., p. 310.

[28]   Quoted in Ketton-Cremer, *A Biography*, p. 11.

[29]   Plumb, *Sir Robert Walpole*, pp. 258–9.

[30]   When it emerged that Parnell had had a long-standing affair, and several children, with Katherine O'Shea, wife of one of his colleagues, Parnell was driven from his position as head of the Irish Parliamentary Party. After marrying Maria, Walpole succeeded in having her received by the queen, annoying some sticklers of etiquette.

[31]   Wilmarth Sheldon Lewis, *Horace Walpole*, A. W. Mellon Lectures in the Fine Arts (London: Rupert Hart Davis, 1961), pp. 14–15.

[32]   Quoted in Sabor, *Horace Walpole*, p. 330.

[33]   Sigmund Freud, 'On family romances', in Peter Gay (ed.), *The Freud Reader* (New York: Norton, 1989), pp. 297–300.

[34]   Morris R. Brownell, *The Prime Minister of Taste: A Portrait of Horace Walpole* (New Haven and London: Yale University Press, 2001), p. 317.

[35]   We will probably never know the reason for Walpole and Gray's serious quarrel toward the end of their Grand Tour, for Walpole destroyed the relevant letters. Mowl speculates that the cause was a lovers' quarrel, occasioned by the arrival of Lord Lincoln. I think it more likely that Gray brought up the old rumour of Walpole's illegitimacy.

[36]   Brownell, *The Prime Minister*, p. 323.

[37]   But see E. J. Clery's discussion in *The Rise of Supernatural Fiction* (New York:

Cambridge University Press, 1995), pp. 42–9; and Jerrold E. Hogle, 'The ghost of the counterfeit in the genesis of the Gothic', in Allan Lloyd Smith and William Hughes (eds), *Gothick Origins and Innovations* (Amsterdam and Atlanta: Rodopi, 1994), pp. 28–31.

38 Eino Railo, *The Haunted Castle: A Study of the Elements of English Romanticism* (New York: E. P. Dutton and Sons, 1927).

39 Jess M. Stein, 'Horace Walpole and Shakespeare', *Studies in Philology*, 31 (1934), 65.

40 W. B. Harbeson, 'The Elizabethan influence on the tragedy of the late eighteenth and the early nineteenth centuries', Ph.D. dissertation, University of Pennsylvania, 1921, quoted by Stein, 'Walpole and Shakespeare', 51.

41 Stein, 'Walpole and Shakespeare', 65.

42 Sandra Gilbert and Susan Gubar, *The Madwoman in the Attic: The Woman Writer and the Nineteenth-Century Literary Imagination* (New Haven and London: Yale University Press, 1978), pp. 45–92.

43 W. S. Lewis makes the same point less concretely on several occasions.

44 Gary Taylor, *Reinventing Shakespeare: A Cultural History, from the Restoration to the Present* (Oxford: Clarendon, 1993), pp. 382–3.

45 Samuel Johnson, *Johnson on Shakespeare*, in Arthur Sherbo (ed.), vols 7 and 8 of *The Yale Edition of the Works of Samuel Johnson* (New Haven: Yale University Press, 1968), vol. 8, p. 62.

46 Walpole, *The Yale Edition of Horace Walpole's Correspondence*, vol. 41, p. 297.

47 Ibid., vol. 40, p. 352.

48 Wilmarth Sheldon Lewis (ed.), 'Notes by Horace Walpole on several characters of Shakespeare', *Miscellaneous Antiquities* (Windham, CT: Hawthorne House, 1940), pp. 5–7; italics in original.

49 That Horace's drive to debunk the myths of Richard III's monstrosity reflects his feelings about Sir Robert has been suggested by W. S. Lewis (*Horace Walpole*, p. 165), and Betsy Perteit Harfst, *Horace Walpole and the Unconscious: An Experiment in Freudian Analysis* (New York: Arno Press, 1980), pp. 142–3. Neither considers that he may have doubted the relationship itself.

50 William Shakespeare, *Hamlet*, in *The Norton Shakespeare*, ed. Stephen Greenblatt et al. (New York: Norton, 1997). Further references will be included in the body of the text.

51 Ketton-Cremer, *A Biography*, pp. 29–31.

52 Horace Walpole, *The Mysterious Mother*, in *The Castle of Otranto and The Mysterious Mother*, ed. Frederick S. Frank (New York: Broadview Literary Texts, 2002), 5.6.84–5.

2

Ann Radcliffe, 'The Shakespeare of Romance Writers'

RICTOR NORTON

᧖

In 1798, the critic Nathan Drake called Ann Radcliffe 'the Shakespeare of Romance Writers'.[1] He was not alone; some critics judged Radcliffe to be the equal of Shakespeare, or even his superior. Drake's epithet alluded to Radcliffe's practice of heading chapters in her novels with a quotation from Shakespeare, and her modelling of some of her most striking tableaux on scenes from *Hamlet, Macbeth, The Tempest* and *A Midsummer Night's Dream*. In this chapter, I examine what Radcliffe's Shakespearean sources were; how she employed Shakespearean themes and images in her novels and poetry; her critical contribution to the understanding of Shakespeare's technique; her personal identification with Shakespeare; and the importance of the Shakespearean associations to her own lasting fame as a writer.

Radcliffe's understanding of Shakespeare's technique is explicit in her posthumous essay 'On the supernatural in poetry', probably written between 1811 and 1815 but not published until 1826. It originally was part of a conversation between two English travellers in Shakespeare's native county of Warwickshire that constituted Radcliffe's long introduction to her romance *Gaston de Blondeville* (written in 1802–3 and published in 1826).[2] Henry Colborn wisely decided to publish this section as a stand-alone essay in his *New Monthly Magazine* in 1826, a teaser to stir up interest in his forthcoming publication of the posthumous romance. The essay reveals both Radcliffe's own techniques for creating a sense of the supernatural in her novels and how important Shakespeare was for her.

The chief lesson Radcliffe learned from Shakespeare is that characters are coterminous with circumstances, that everything in a work of imagination will be more or less a projection of the passions of the characters. This view moves away from the pretence that stories are non-fictional histories and frankly acknowledges the central importance of the creative artist, who endeavours to create a unified world. The traveller, who represents Mrs Radcliffe herself, is seen 'following Shakspeare [*sic*] into unknown regions':

> 'Where is now the undying spirit', said he, 'that could so exquisitely perceive and feel? that could inspire itself with the various characters of this world, and create worlds of its own; to which the grand and the beautiful, the gloomy and the sublime of visible Nature, up-called not only corresponding feelings, but passions; which seemed to perceive a soul in every thing ...'
>
> ('On the supernatural in poetry', p. 163)

The storm in Shakespeare's *Julius Caesar*, which parallels the passions of the conspirators in the porch of Pompey's theatre, is cited as an example of this 'correspondence' of 'attendant circumstances':

> 'These appalling circumstances, with others of supernatural import, attended the fall of the conqueror of the world – a man, whose power Cassius represents to be dreadful as this night, when the sheeted dead were seen in the lightning to glide along the streets of Rome. How much does the sublimity of these attendant circumstances heighten our idea of the power of Caesar, of the terrific grandeur of his character, and prepare and interest us for his fate. The whole soul is roused and fixed, in the full energy of attention, upon the progress of the conspiracy against him; and, had not Shakespeare wisely withdrawn him from our view, there would have been no balance of our passions.'
>
> (pp. 163–4)

Although Radcliffe is describing *Julius Caesar*, act 1, scene 3 – 'When the most mighty gods by tokens send / ... dreadful heralds to astonish us', such as 'gliding ghosts', and 'this dreadful night / ... thunders, lightens, opens graves, and roars' (1.3.55–6, 63, 73)[3] – she is simultaneously thinking of Horatio's description of the same event in *Hamlet*:

> A little ere the mightiest Julius fell,
> The graves stood tenantless, and the sheeted dead
> Did squeak and gibber in the Roman streets.
> ...
> And even the like precurse of fierce events,
> As harbingers preceding still the fates
> And prologue to the omen coming on.
>
> (1.1.106.7–9, 106.14–16)

The ghost scene in *Hamlet* affected Radcliffe so powerfully that Shakespeare's other plays were sometimes filtered through its lens. Radcliffe also praises other such scenes in *Cymbeline*:

> How finely such circumstances are made use of, to awaken, at once, solemn expectation and tenderness, and, by recalling the softened remembrance of a sorrow long past, to prepare the mind to melt at one that was approaching, mingling at the same time, by means of a mysterious occurrence, a slight tremor of awe with our pity.
>
> ('Of the supernatural in poetry', p. 165)

Radcliffe describes here the moment when Belarius and Arviragus are searching for Fidele (Imogen disguised as a page), and 'solemn music is heard from the cave, sounded by that harp of which Guiderius says, "*Since the death of my dearest mother, it did not speak before. All solemn things should answer solemn accidents*". Immediately, Arviragus enters with Fidele senseless in his arms' (p. 164; italics in original).[4] *Macbeth* similarly 'shows, by many instances, how much Shakspeare delighted to heighten the effect of his characters and his story by correspondent scenery: there the desolate heath, the troubled elements, assist the mis-chief of his malignant beings' (p. 164). And, finally, Radcliffe comes to *Hamlet*:

Above every ideal being is the ghost of Hamlet, with all its attendant incidents of time and place. The dark watch upon the remote
platform, the dreary aspect of the night, the very expression of the
officer on guard, 'the air bites shrewdly; it is very cold'; the recollection of a star, an unknown world, are all circumstances which
excite forlorn, melancholy and solemn feelings, and dispose us to
welcome, with trembling curiosity, the awful being that draws
near; and to indulge in that strange mixture of horror, pity and
indignation, produced by the tale it reveals. Every minute circumstance of the scene between those watching on the platform, and
of that between them and Horatio, preceding the entrance of the
apparition, contributes to excite some feeling of dreariness, or
melancholy, or solemnity, or expectation, in unison with and
leading on toward that high curiosity and thrilling awe with which
we witness the conclusion of the scene.

(p. 166)

Then follows a detailed analysis of the first scene of the play on
the watchtower, when the audience's expectation of seeing the
ghost is prepared for by the dialogue between Horatio and
Bernardo:

Oh, I should never be weary of dwelling on the perfection of
Shakespeare, in his management of every scene connected with
that most solemn and mysterious being, which takes such entire
possession of the imagination, that we hardly seem conscious we
are beings of this world while we contemplate 'the extravagant and
erring spirit'.

(p. 167)

Radcliffe insists that even minor details should correspond to the
work's passion or mood:

In the scene where Horatio breaks his secret to Hamlet Shakspeare,
still true to the touch of circumstances, makes the time evening,
and marks it by the very words of Hamlet, 'Good even, sir', which
Hammer [*sic*] and Warburton changed without any reason, to 'good
morning', thus making Horatio relate his most interesting and
solemn story by the clear light of the cheerfullest part of the day.

(p. 168)

Radcliffe feels that 'accordant circumstances' should serve to intensify a mood and to anticipate an event, and hence that they should share the same quality as that emotion or event, rather than contrast sharply with it. Thus, although she acknowledges that 'objects of terror sometimes strike us very forcibly, when introduced into scenes of gaiety and splendour, as, for instance, in the Banquet scene in *Macbeth'*, she feels that the effect of sharp contrasts is 'transient', unlike 'the deep and solemn feelings excited under more accordant circumstances, and left long upon the mind'. Although 'deep pity mingles with our surprise and horror' at the appearance of Banquo's ghost, it does not arouse 'the gloomy and sublime kind of terror' that the ghost of Hamlet's father calls forth (p. 168).

Radcliffe was almost certainly familiar with Elizabeth Montagu's famous *Essay on the Writings and Genius of Shakespeare* (1769), which pointed out, among other things, the 'correspondence' between the wandering star and the appearance of the ghost in *Hamlet*, and which defended Shakespeare's use of 'praeternatural beings' on the grounds that superstitions were part of national folklore.[5] Radcliffe's theory of 'correspondent scenery' or 'accordant circumstances' derives from the mid-eighteenth-century critical theory of 'association', which characterizes any type of writing that parallels a psychological mood without directly describing it. For example, in a poem quoted in *The Romance of the Forest*, Cawthorn speaks of the 'according music' with which Handel matches the emotions of his characters.[6] Radcliffe consciously adopted this technique in all of her novels, even in her earliest novel, *The Castles of Athlin and Dunbayne* (1789), when Mary wanders through a wood 'whose awful glooms so well accorded with the pensive tone of her mind'.[7] Music and sound, in particular, always accord with the moods of Radcliffe's characters.

Radcliffe's distinct contribution to this theory of correspondence was her insistence on devising associations that would excite feelings of fear and dreadful anticipation; most of her accordant circumstances were directed towards just one object, terror or the sublime: 'The union of grandeur and obscurity, which Mr Burke describes as a sort of tranquillity tinged with terror, and which causes the sublime, is to be found only in *Hamlet*; or in scenes where circumstances of the same kind prevail.' This statement refers to Edmund Burke's influential essay, *A Philosophical Enquiry into the Origin of Our Ideas of the Sublime and Beautiful* (1757),[8] and it leads on to the passage most frequently quoted from Radcliffe's essay:

> Terror and horror are so far opposite, that the first expands the soul, and awakens the faculties to a high degree of life; the other contracts, freezes and nearly annihilates them. I apprehend, that neither Shakspeare nor Milton by their fictions, nor Mr Burke by his reasoning, anywhere looked to positive horror as a source of the sublime, though they all agree that terror is a very high one ...
>
> ('Of the supernatural in poetry', p. 168)

Burke, surprisingly, does not discuss Shakespeare in his *Enquiry*. Radcliffe must have found him deficient in this respect, but she makes amends by elevating Shakespeare as the supreme master of sublimity; at the potent bidding of 'those great masters of the imagination', Shakespeare and Milton,

> the passions have been awakened from their sleep, and by [their] magic a crowded Theatre has been changed to a lonely shore, to a witch's cave, to an enchanted island, to a murderer's castle, to the ramparts of an usurper, to the battle, to the midnight carousal of the camp or the tavern, to every various scene of the living world.
>
> (p. 169)

Verse epigraphs contribute most of the fundamental accordances or correspondences in Radcliffe's novels, anticipating the mysteries that will occur in each chapter. In these epigraphs, Shakespeare's works are cited many times. Warren Hunting Smith, in a survey of nineteen Gothic romances by fifteen authors, counted 561 poetical quotations used in the chapter headings: 157 from Shakespeare, thirty-seven from James Thomson in second place, thirty from Milton in third place, nineteen from Collins in fourth place, nine from Ariosto, seven from Spenser, five from Tasso and a smattering from others.[9] One reason for this distribution is that Smith includes three novels by Radcliffe: *The Romance of the Forest, The Mysteries of Udolpho* and *The Italian*.[10] Most of the novels that Smith surveyed post-date Radcliffe's work and bear her influence. Hence, it is not so much a matter of Radcliffe following the Gothic novel tradition of quoting Shakespeare, as a matter of Gothic novelists emulating Radcliffe. The frequency and distribution of authors quoted in Radcliffe's novels is virtually identical: fifty-one from Shakespeare, eighteen from Thomson, fourteen from Milton, fourteen from Collins, twelve from Beattie, ten from Mason and a scattering from Pope, Macpherson, Dryden, Goldsmith, Gray, Young, James Cawthorn, Walpole, Warton and others. Most of the quotations from Shakespeare come from those plays with supernatural elements: *Hamlet, Macbeth, The Tempest* and *A Midsummer Night's Dream*, and from references to ghostly happenings in *Julius Caesar*.

The revival of interest in Shakespeare during Ann Ward Radcliffe's childhood had a profound impact on her novels. The most distinctive characteristics of Radcliffe's work, namely the conjoint influence of Shakespeare and Burke's sublime, are present from her very first novel, *The Castles of Athlin and Dunbayne* (1789). Although it contains no chapter epigraphs, by the end of the first twenty pages the reader realizes that the tale parallels Hamlet's attempt to avenge the death of his father. Radcliffe's Matilda, like Hamlet's mother, 'sunk lifeless in her chair' when Osbert informs her of his resolve.[11] Later, as in *Hamlet*, we shiver at 'the dismal note of a watch-bell'.[12] It is equally clear that Radcliffe must have already read Burke, for Osbert 'delighted in the terrible and the grand, more than in the softer landscape; and wrapt in the bright visions of fancy, would often lose himself in awful solitudes'.[13]

Radcliffe's first direct quotation of Shakespeare appears in the epigraph to *A Sicilian Romance* (1790): 'I could a Tale unfold!' Readers would recognize the lines spoken by the ghost of Hamlet's father, a tale 'whose lightest word / Would harrow up thy soul ...' (*Hamlet*, 1.5.15–16).[14] *The Romance of the Forest* (1791) contains a sudden burst of poetic epigraphs, one (sometimes even two) for each chapter. There are about fourteen quotations from or allusions to Shakespeare throughout the romance, beginning with the epigraph repeated on the title page for each volume:

> Ere the bat hath flown
> His cloister'd flight; ere to black Hecate's summons,
> The shard-born beetle, with his drowsy hums,
> Hath rung night's yawning peal, there shall be done
> A deed of dreadful note.
>
> (*Macbeth*, 3.2.41–5)

It may be that Radcliffe and her imitators used popular anthologies, such as William Dodd's *The Beauties of Shakespeare, Regularly Selected from Each Play* (published in 1752 and frequently reprinted).[15] Five more quotations used in *The Romance of the Forest* also appear as 'beauties' in Dodd's collection: the five-line epigraph for chapter 3, from *As You Like It*; the brief allusion to 'melancholy boughs' in chapter 3, also from *As You Like It*; the epigraph for chapter 6 – 'Hence, horrible shadow! / Unreal mockery, hence!' – addressed by Macbeth to Banquo's ghost in *Macbeth* (3.4.105–6); and the *two* epigraphs for chapter 14, both from *King John*. However, the novel also contains other quotations from Shakespeare that are *not* duplicated by Dodd: the epigraph for chapter 7, from *Macbeth*; the epigraph for chapter 8, from *Julius Caesar*; the epigraph for chapter 10, from *King Lear*; and an allusion to 'music such as charmeth sleep' in chapter 10, from *A Midsummer Night's Dream* (4.1.80).

Moreover, the epigraph for chapter 4, 'My May of life / Is fall'n into the sear, the yellow leaf' (from *Macbeth*, 5.3.23–4), is rendered as 'My *way* of life' by Dodd, so *The Beauties of Shakespeare* cannot be reductively identified as *the* 'source' for Radcliffe's quotations. For this particular quotation, Radcliffe is clearly following Dr Johnson, who argued that 'As there is no relation between the *Way of Life*, and *fallen into sere*, I am inclined to think, that the *W* is only an *M* inverted, and that it was originally written – My *May* of Life'.[16] Johnson's note on this line was first published in 1745 in his *Miscellaneous Observations on the Tragedy of Macbeth*, but it was frequently reprinted in other collections more accessible to Radcliffe. Radcliffe briefly refers to Johnson's *Prefaces to Shakespeare* in *A Journey Made in the Summer of 1794* (1795),[17] so she was familiar with Johnson's opinion and may have owned the 1771 edition of *The Works of Shakespeare, with Dr Johnson's Prefaces*.

Johnson's emendation has not been accepted by modern editors, but was widely influential in many early editions of *Macbeth* and was quoted in works by other critics – for example, by Charles Dibdin in his study *A Complete History of the English Stage* (1800).[18]

Although we cannot pin down the exact 'source' of Radcliffe's Shakespeare, nevertheless the habit of collecting 'the beauties of Shakespeare' is relevant to Radcliffe's practice. Contemporary critics have complained that because Dodd's collection consisted almost entirely of verse extracts lifted from the plays rather than any of the prose dialogue, it produced a model of Shakespeare the poet rather than Shakespeare the playwright. The resulting emphasis on Shakespeare's poetic imagination or 'fancy' is often seen in Radcliffe's own works and is in keeping with her own appreciation of Shakespeare more as a conjuror-poet than as a dramatist. As Radcliffe flexed her talent in *The Romance of the Forest*, particularly her talent for poetry, it was natural for her to invoke the name of Shakespeare, who for her was the icon of the Romantic imagination. Thus, one of Adeline's own poems, 'Morning, on the sea shore' (in chapter 18), contains echoes from *A Midsummer Night's Dream* and *The Tempest*, and the long poem 'Titania to her love' was written by Adeline 'after having read that rich effusion of Shakespeare's genius, "A Midsummer Night's Dream"'. Thus, Radcliffe presents 'Shakespeare's genius' as being poetical rather than dramatic, and we should note that Adeline's poem is written after she has *read* the play, rather than after having *seen a performance* of it. Radcliffe's imitations of Shakespeare were successful: Anna Laetitia Barbauld felt that Radcliffe's poems 'Song to a spirit', 'The sea nymph' and 'Down, down, a hundred fathom deep!' 'might be sung by Shakespeare's Ariel'.[19]

The poet and critic Charles Bucke, who dined with Mrs Radcliffe, noted that '[h]er favourite tragedy was *Macbeth* … her favourite poets, after Shakespeare, Tasso, Spenser and Milton'.[20] This group of poets was virtually a literary trope. For instance, Joseph Warton, in *An Essay on the Writings and Genius of Pope* (1756 and 1782), placed Spenser, Shakespeare and Milton, whom he categorized as 'sublime and pathetic', in the highest class of poets.[21] The *locus classicus* for this grouping is Richard Hurd's *Letters on Chivalry and Romance* (1762):

> The greatest geniuses of our own and foreign countries, such as
> Ariosto and Tasso in Italy, and Spenser and Milton in England,
> were seduced by these barbarities of their forefathers; were even
> charmed by the Gothic Romances. Was this caprice an absurdity in
> them? Or, may there not be something in the Gothic Romance
> peculiarly suited to the views of a genius, and to the ends of
> poetry?

Hurd then gives high praise to 'Shakespeare's wild sublimity'.[22]
Thus, Shakespeare is firmly placed among the epic poets rather
than the dramatists.

The Mysteries of Udolpho (1794) contains even more poetry than
The Romance of the Forest.[23] In addition to the chapter epigraphs,
there are about seventy-five quotations and eighteen complete
poems composed by the characters themselves. Twenty-two of
the chapter epigraphs come from Shakespeare (five from *Macbeth*,
four from *Julius Caesar*, three each from *Hamlet* and *A Midsummer
Night's Dream*, and one each from *Antony and Cleopatra, Romeo and
Juliet, King John, Measure for Measure, Richard II, The Tempest* and
Titus Andronicus). Again, in *The Italian* (1797),[24] each chapter has a
verse epigraph, including eleven from Shakespeare (one each
from *Twelfth Night, Romeo and Juliet, Hamlet, Merchant of Venice,
Othello, Macbeth, King John, Richard III* and *As You Like It* and two
each from *Julius Caesar* and *King Lear*).

Radcliffe's epigraphs and quotations are so systematic and so
conspicuous that they clearly serve a meta–narrative function. It
seems likely that Radcliffe cultivated the 'epic poets' as a kind of
imprimatur to align her work with high culture. The verse that
embellishes Radcliffe's romances demonstrates that they are not
mere novels, but works of literature. The children in Madame de
Genlis's *Adelaide and Theodore; or Letters on Education* (1783) do
not read fairy tales, but they do read Milton, Tasso, Ariosto,
Shakespeare, Corneille and Voltaire.[25] Such a list – excluding
Corneille and Voltaire! – would be used by Radcliffe to demonstrate her taste and even to suggest that she herself belonged
among them. In this respect, Radcliffe was overwhelmingly
successful. Her publishers Hookham and Carpenter even marketed
her as a Shakespearean property; in their advertisement for the

fourth edition of *The Romance of the Forest* in *The Courier, and Evening Gazette* for Saturday, 10 May 1794, they give two quotations from *Macbeth*. In France, even before the publication of her most famous novel, Radcliffe's energetic tableaux had been singled out by Marie-Joseph de Chénier as 'les vrais coups de théâtre, et même quelques tons de Shakespeare' (dramatic and even Shakespearean turns of events).[26] The *Critical Review* for August 1794 begins similarly by praising Radcliffe and *Udolpho* in the highest possible terms:

> 'Thine too these golden keys, immortal boy!
> This can unlock the gates of joy,
> Of horror, that and thrilling fears,
> Or ope the sacred source of sympathetic tears.'

> Such were the presents of the Muse to the infant Shakspeare [*sic*], and though perhaps to no other mortal has she been so lavish of her gifts, the keys referring to the third line Mrs Radcliffe must be allowed to be completely in possession of.[27]

The lines of verse, which come from Gray's *Progress of Poesy* (3, ll. 9–12), describe the prophetic birth of Shakespeare.

Radcliffe's canonization was complete when, in the 1797 edition of *The Pursuits of Literature*, Thomas James Mathias, respected scholar, editor of Gray and librarian to Buckingham Palace, labelled her

> the mighty magician of *The Mysteries of Udolpho*, bred and nourished by the Florentine Muses in their sacred solitary caverns, amid the paler shrines of Gothic superstition and in all the dreariness of inchantment: a poetess whom Ariosto would with rapture have acknowledged, as the

> La nudrita
> Damigella Trivulzia al sacro speco. O.F. c. 46.[28]

The quotation, from Ariosto's *Orlando Furioso*, refers to a virgin whose youthful marks of poetic genius suggest that she was bred in the cave of Apollo – thus clinching Radcliffe's reputation as an

enchantress-poet. Nathan Drake – who would become a compe-
tent Shakespearean critic – was prompted to write two Gothic
tales after reading *The Italian*. When he described Radcliffe as
'The Shakespeare of Romance Writers' in 1798, he cited in
support of this commendation the passage about Radcliffe from
the seventh edition of *The Pursuits of Literature*.[29] Sir Walter Scott,
in his 'Prefatory memoir to Mrs Ann Radcliffe' for *The Novels of
Mrs Ann Radcliffe* in Ballantyne's Novelist's Library (1824), also
quoted Mathias's praise of the 'mighty magician'.[30]

Thereafter, virtually every extended comment on Radcliffe
echoed the passage via Scott. The English traveller Jane Waldie
recalled that, while standing on the Rialto bridge in Venice, she
naturally thought not only of Shakespeare's *The Merchant of Venice,*
but also of Radcliffe's romances:

> This is not the only spot at Venice which recalls fiction, poetry, and
> romance, to the mind. Shakespeare, Otway and – in spite of many
> inaccuracies – Mrs Radcliffe, rise up every where in the shape of
> their heroes and heroines. The very situation of the city – the very
> names of the surrounding objects, constantly recall them.[31]

Waldie was probably recalling a similar judgement by Byron:

> I loved [Venice] from my boyhood; she to me
> Was as a fairy city of the heart,
> Rising like water columns from the sea,
> Of joy the sojourn, and of wealth the mart;
> And Otway, Radcliffe, Schiller, Shakespeare's art,
> Had stamped her image in me.

> (*Childe Harold's Pilgrimage*, Canto 4 [1818], ll. 154–9)

In 1816 another English traveller, John Sheppard, observed that
the name of Venice 'is fraught with an indefineable charm, were
it only for the associations linked with it by our Shakespeare, and
by the "mighty magician of Udolpho"'.[32]

As this body of praise suggests, the Shakespearean magic that
Radcliffe conjured up was perceived primarily as the magic of

poetry. Nevertheless, contemporary critics generally praised Radcliffe's characterization, at least beginning with *The Romance of the Forest*. Her comic characters come from the same stable as Shakespeare's Mistress Quickly, or the Nurse in *Romeo and Juliet* or the rustics in *A Midsummer Night's Dream* – for example, the rather tedious Peter in *The Romance of the Forest*, the passably amusing faithful servant Annette in *The Mysteries of Udolpho*, and her only really successful comic character, Paolo in *The Italian*, who is modelled partly on Shakespeare's Puck. Beginning with La Motte in *The Romance of the Forest*, Radcliffe nevertheless did create believable characters within the sublime mould; and nearly all critics agreed that the Abbess and the monk Schedoni in *The Italian* were finely drawn, with conflicting emotions coexisting in the same breast.

Anna Laetitia Barbauld, in her biographical-critical preface for the 1810 reprints of Radcliffe's novels in Rivington's inexpensive edition of *The British Novelists*, expressed her special admiration for the characterization of La Motte in *The Romance of the Forest*, even suggesting that Radcliffe's technique, in this instance, was superior to Shakespeare's:

> There is a scene between [La Motte] and the more hardened Marquis, who is tempting him to commit murder, which has far more nature and truth than the admired scene between King John and Hubert, in which the writer's imagination has led him rather to represent the action to which the King is endeavouring to work his instrument, as it would be seen by a person who had a great horror of its guilt, than in the manner in which he ought to represent it in order to win him to his purpose:
>
> > '— If the midnight bell
> > Did with his iron tongue, and brazen mouth,
> > Sound one unto the drowsy ear of night;
> > If this same were a churchyard where we stand,
> > And thou possessed with a thousand wrongs;
> > — if thou could'st see me without eyes,
> > Hear me without thine ears, and make reply
> > Without a tongue', &c. [*King John*, 3.3.37–44]

What must be the effect of such imagery but to infuse into the mind of Hubert that horror of the crime with which the spectator views the deed, and which it was the business, indeed, of Shake-speare to impress upon the mind of the spectator, but not of King John to impress upon Hubert. In the scene referred to, on the other hand, the Marquis, whose aim is to tempt La Motte to the commis-sion of murder, begins by attempting to lower his sense of virtue, by representing it as the effect of prejudices imbided in early youth, reminds him that in many countries the stiletto is resorted to without scruple; treats as trivial his former deviations from integrity; and, by lulling his conscience and awakening his cupidity, draws him to his purpose.[33]

This piece of astute criticism was quoted verbatim in the obit-uary of Mrs Radcliffe that was published in the *Annual Biography and Obituary* for the year 1824, part of whose aim was to consoli-date her reputation as 'The Shakespeare of Romance Writers'.[34]

Radcliffe's appreciation of Shakespeare came primarily from reading him on the printed page, rather than seeing him per-formed on stage. Nevertheless, from her essay 'On the super-natural in poetry' we know that she saw performances of *Hamlet* and *Macbeth*. The ghost scene in *Hamlet* was her great touchstone, but she felt 'no little vexation in seeing the ghost of Hamlet *played*' (italics in original). She also complained about a produc-tion of *Macbeth*:

But who, after hearing Macbeth's thrilling question —

> — 'What are these,
> So withered and so wild in their attire,
> That look not like the inhabitants o' the earth,
> And yet are on't?'

who would have thought of reducing them to mere human beings, by attiring them not only like the inhabitants of the earth, but in the dress of a particular country, and making them downright Scotch-women – thus not only contradicting the very words of Macbeth, but withdrawing from these cruel agents of the passions all that strange and supernatural air which had made them so affecting to the imagination, and which was entirely suitable to the solemn and important events they were foretelling and accomplishing.

(pp. 164–5)

For Radcliffe, who was not superstitious, 'the only real witch [is] the witch of the poet', and to depict these figures realistically was to lessen their power over the imagination and destroy the illusion:

So vexatious is the effect of the stage-witches upon my mind, that I should probably have left the theatre when they appeared, had not the fascination of Mrs Siddons's influence so spread itself over the whole play, as to overcome my disgust, and to make me forget even Shakspeare [*sic*] himself.

(p. 165)

We can deduce that Radcliffe attended performances at the Little Theatre in the Haymarket and Covent Garden.[35] In his authorized memoir, Thomas Noon Talfourd says that she frequently went to the opera and, more rarely, accompanied her husband to the theatre; and that she warmly admired Mrs Siddons, and spoke with pleasure at seeing her with her son Henry going to church in Bath.[36] F. W. Price has pointed out that Mrs Siddons performed the character of Hamlet at the Bath–Bristol Theatre Royal on 27 June 1781, when Ann Ward 'was twelve days short of seventeen years of age and perhaps living in Bath'.[37] Price allows us to infer that Radcliffe saw Mrs Siddons then. But although this was Siddons's first appearance as Hamlet in Bath, she had appeared as Hamlet on five previous occasions, the first of which was in Liverpool, in March 1778. There is thus a possibility that the fourteen-year-old Ann Ward may have seen Siddons in an earlier performance in Liverpool, in the company of her uncle Thomas Bentley on one of his business trips to that city. (It is almost certainly the case that Ann Ward did not live with her parents in Bath, but with her uncle Bentley in Turnham Green, London.[38] Bentley, the partner of Josiah Wedgwood, was originally a Liverpool merchant, and he regularly made trips to that city. He was also a theatregoer, whereas Ann's parents were not.) However, Bentley died in November 1780, so Ann Ward would indeed have been with her parents in Bath in June 1781. The year 1781 also seems a likely date for Ann Ward to have seen Mrs Siddons going to church with her son Henry, who was born in October 1774.

In 'On the supernatural in poetry', Radcliffe suggests that Mrs Siddons would have been better in the role of Hamlet than her brother John Philip Kemble:

> I should suppose she would be the finest Hamlet that ever appeared, excelling even her own brother in that character; she would more fully preserve the tender and refined melancholy, the deep sensibility, which are the peculiar charm of Hamlet, and which appear not only in the ardour, but in the occasional irresolution and weakness of his character – the secret spring that reconciles all his inconsistencies ... Her brother's firmness, incapable of being always subdued, does not so fully enhance, as her tenderness would, this part of the character.
>
> (pp. 165–6)

This passage suggests that Radcliffe saw Kemble rather than Mrs Siddons in the role of Hamlet, but the raising of the possibility of a female Hamlet does suggest that it had a special meaning for Radcliffe. Perhaps she simply remembered seeing advertisements for Siddons's 1781 performance or hearing people discuss the notable event.

Radcliffe shared her contemporaries' estimation of Mrs Siddons as the Tragic Muse. Siddons's performance as Lady Macbeth in a benefit at Drury Lane on 2 February 1785 was a triumph, and was repeated by royal command on 7 February.[39] She had so successfully penetrated the mystery of Lady Macbeth that from 1785 the role became her exclusive property. The Drury Lane season of 1784–5 included performances of *Hamlet* and *The Tempest*; in 1785–6, Mrs Siddons performed as Ophelia; in 1786–7, she played the role of Imogen in *Cymbeline*, which was remarked for its affecting scene in a cave (the scene Radcliffe analysed in her essay on the supernatural); on 10 March 1788, Mrs Siddons performed again as Lady Macbeth, and in the winter of 1788 her brother John Philip Kemble joined her on stage as Macbeth.[40] Ann Ward married William Radcliffe in January 1787, and it was probably during their courtship and first year of marriage that Mrs Radcliffe most frequently attended the theatre and would have had the opportunity to see Mrs Siddons. Her essay 'On the supernatural in poetry' certainly confirms that she saw Kemble and Siddons perform in *Macbeth*, when her disgust at the all-too-human Scotch witches was overcome by the genius of Siddons's performance: 'Mrs Siddons, like Shakspeare [*sic*], always disappears in the character she represents, and throws an illusion over the whole scene around her, that conceals many defects in the arrangements of the theatre' (p. 165). Mrs Siddons portrayed Lady Macbeth as a 'sublime' figure, virtually the female equivalent of Milton's Satan; as Hazlitt commented in *Characters of Shakespear's Plays* (1817):

> [W]e can conceive of nothing grander ... it seemed almost as if a being of a superior order had dropped from a higher sphere to awe the world with the majesty of her appearance. Power was seated on her brow, passion emanated from her breast as from a shrine; she was tragedy personified ... She glided on and off the stage like an apparition. To have seen her in that character was an event in every one's life, not to be forgotten.[41]

It is against this background that we will best appreciate Radcliffe's supreme characterization of sublime terror in *The Italian*. It was specifically the character of Schedoni that prompted Nathan Drake's praise of Radcliffe:

> [E]very nerve vibrates with pity and terror ... every word, every action of the shocked and self-accusing Confessor, whose character is marked with traits almost super-human, appal yet delight the reader, and it is difficult to ascertain whether ardent curiosity, intense commiseration, or apprehension that suspends almost the faculty of breathing, be, in the progress of this well-written story, most powerfully excited.[42]

Dunlop's evaluation of *The Italian* is no less valid today than it was in 1814: that part of the novel that begins with Ellena's arrival at the desolate house on the seashore and ends with Schedoni conducting her home 'is in the first style of excellence, and has neither been exceeded in dramatic nor romantic fiction. The terror … is raised by a delineation of guilt, horror and remorse, which, if Shakespeare has equalled, he has not surpassed.'[43] The most powerful *coup de théâtre* in the novel is the scene in which Schedoni, with his hired assassin Spalatro, are advancing through a corridor to murder Ellena when they are suddenly confronted by the apparition of a beckoning bloody hand, which is clearly inspired by the vision of the bloody dagger in Shakespeare's *Macbeth*. The epigraph for this chapter of *The Italian* is: 'I am settled, and bend up / Each corporal agent to this terrible feat.'[44] These lines come from *Macbeth* (1.7.79–80), indicating Macbeth's final determination to fall in with Lady Macbeth's demand that he assassinate Duncan.

Radcliffe does not merely employ Shakespearean allusions in an artificial stylistic manner; she also interacts creatively with the dramatic structures she finds in Shakespeare. Schedoni's near murder of Ellena is modelled upon the murder of Duncan in *Macbeth*, but with sex changes: the sleeping Ellena takes on the role of the sleeping Duncan; Spalatro, like Macbeth, sees the equivalent of the bloody 'dagger of the mind' (2.1.38); and Schedoni plays Lady Macbeth: 'Give me the dagger, then', says the Confessor (referring to *Macbeth*, 2.2.51). Or, to be more accurate, Schedoni plays the role of Mrs Siddons playing the role of the 'unsex'd female' (1.5.39), Lady Macbeth.

Any view that Radcliffe employed Shakespeare in a purely calculated, professional manner is undermined by much evidence that she had a very strong personal response to Shakespeare. In her posthumously published poems, forests, cliffs and seashores invariably remind her of *A Midsummer Night's Dream* or *The Tempest*.[45] On returning to Dover after her only trip abroad, she delighted in seeing once again 'Shakespeare's cliff, bolder still and sublime as the eternal name it bears'.[46] Radcliffe collected 'picturesque' scenes for her novels during her travels. She often took notes on 'Shakespearean' scenes, carefully recording the 'accordant circumstances'. During her holiday tour in July 1800, while approaching Hastings one night she observed

> no moon; starlight; milky-way very lucid; seemed to rise out of the sea. Solemn and pleasing night-scene. Glow-worms, in great numbers, shone silently and faintly on the dewy banks, like something supernatural. Judgement of Shakespeare in selecting this image to assist the terrific impression in his ghost-scene.[47]

During her autumn 1800 tour, 'Three miles of continual ascent, or descent of almost tremendous hills, long and steep opening to vast distances, now obscured in ruin, but sublime in their obscurity' remind her of a quotation: '"These high, wild hills and rough uneven roads, / Drag out our miles and make them wearisome." Cymbeline.'[48] These lines, however, come not from *Cymbeline*, but from *Richard II* (2.3.4–5). Radcliffe relied on memory in these journals and was occasionally liable to misquote.

Radcliffe was also highly sensitive to what she called 'picturesque sounds',[49] which she often associated with Shakespeare. For example, in October 1811, after returning to the inn at Steephill on the Isle of Wight, she mused:

> How sweet is the cadence of the distant surge! It seemed, as we sat at our inn, as if a faint peal of far-off bells mingled with the sounds on shore, sometimes heard, sometimes lost: the first note of the beginning, and last of the falling peal, seeming always the most distinct. This resounding of the distant surge on a rocky shore might have given Shakspeare [*sic*] his idea when he makes Ferdinand, in the *Tempest*, hear, amidst the storm, bells ringing his father's dirge; a music which Ariel also commemorates, together with the sea-wave: —

> > 'Sea-nymphs hourly ring his knell,
> > Ding, dong, bell!'[50]

This poetic passage could easily have fit into one of Radcliffe's novels. Similarly, during a midnight visit to Warwick Castle in 1802, 'there arose a strain (like French horns), as if commanded by

Shakespeare's wand', evoking 'the sweet sound, that breathes upon a bank of violets' (*Twelfth Night*, 1.1.5–6).[51] But it is to the ghost scene in *Hamlet* that Radcliffe constantly recurs:

> Near the summit [of one of the towers of Warwick Castle is] an embattled overhanging gallery, where formerly, no doubt, sentinels used to pace during the night, looked down upon the walls of the Castle, the rivers and the country far and wide, received the watch-word from the sentinel, perched in the little watch-tower, higher still and seeing farther into the moonlight, and repeated it to the soldiers on guard on the walks and gates below. Before those great gates and underneath these towers, Shakespeare's ghost might have walked; they are in the very character and spirit of such an apparition, grand and wild and strange; there should, however, have been more extent. Stayed before these grey towers till the last twilight.[52]

Radcliffe may have suffered from clinical depression in 1802–3 and again in 1810–11. She lived in retirement at Windsor from 1812 to 1815, probably recuperating from a nervous break-down.[53] There, she spent much time rambling through Windsor Forest and pacing the terraces of Windsor Castle late at night, perhaps wrestling with her own ghosts:

> The massy tower at the end of the east terrace stood up high in shade; but immediately from behind it the moonlight spread, and showed the flat line of wall at the end of that terrace, with the figure of a sentinel moving against the light, as well as a profile of the dark precipice below ... No sound but the faint clinking of the soldier's accoutrements, as he paced on watch, and the remote voices of people turning the end of the east terrace, appearing for a moment in the light there and vanishing. In a high window of the tower a light. Why is it so sublime to stand at the foot of a dark tower, and look up its height to the sky and the stars? ... It was on this terrace, surely, that Shakespeare received the first hint of the time for the appearance of his ghost. —
>
> > 'Last night of all,
> > When yon same star that westward from the Pole

Had made his course to illume that part of heaven
Where now it burns, Marcellus and myself,
The bell then beating one —.'[54]

This passage from the travel journal was reused in the introduction to *Gaston de Blondeville* that was printed separately in Radcliffe's essay, 'On the supernatural in poetry'. Ultimately, we are left with the non-literary issue of personal psychology, and Radcliffe's unanswerable question: 'Why is it so sublime to stand at the foot of a dark tower, and look up its height to the sky and the stars?'

Notes

[1] Nathan Drake, *Literary Hours: or Sketches Critical, Narrative and Poetical* (3rd edn; 3 vols; London: T. Cadell and W. Davies, 1804), vol. 1, p. 361.

[2] Ann Radcliffe, 'On the supernatural in poetry', *New Monthly Magazine*, 16 (1826), 145–52, reprinted in E. J. Clery and Robert Miles (eds), *Gothic Documents: A Sourcebook, 1700–1800* (Manchester: Manchester University Press, 2000), pp. 163–72; Ann Radcliffe, *Gaston de Blondeville* (4 vols; London: Henry Colburn, 1826). For the complicated history of the writing of *Gaston de Blondeville* and its introduction, see Rictor Norton, *Mistress of Udolpho: The Life of Ann Radcliffe* (London and New York: Leceister University Press, 1999), chapter 14. Further references to 'On the supernatural in poetry' will be to the reprint and will be incorporated into the body of the text.

[3] All references to Shakespeare's works are to *The Norton Shakespeare*, Stephen Greenblatt et al. (eds) (New York: W. W. Norton, 1997). Shakespeare references will be incorporated into the body of the text.

[4] The scene from *Cymbeline* to which Radcliffe refers is 4.2.

[5] Elizabeth Montagu, *An Essay on the Writings and Genius of Shakspeare* (London: Printed for J. Dodsley, J. Walter, T. Cadell and J. Wilkie, 1769).

[6] James Cawthorn, 'Life unhappy, because we use it improperly', ll. 165–76, quoted in Ann Radcliffe, *The Romance of the Forest* (4th edn; 3 vols; London: T. Hookham and J. Carpenter, 1794), ch. 16.

[7] Ann Radcliffe, *The Castles of Athlin and Dunbayne: A Highland Story* (London: T. Hookham, 1789), p. 42.

[8] Edmund Burke, *A Philosophical Enquiry into the Origin of Our Ideas of the Sublime and Beautiful* (London: R. and J. Dodsley, 1757).

[9] Warren Hunting Smith, *Architecture in English Fiction* (New Haven: Yale University Press, 1934), especially pp. 55–8.

[10] The other novels Smith reviews are M. G. Lewis's *The Monk*, Charlotte

---

Smith's *The Old Manor House* and *The Banished Man*, Regina Maria Roche's *Clermont* and *The Children of the Abbey*, Eleanor Sleath's *The Orphan of the Rhine*, Francis Lathom's *The Midnight Bell* and nine lesser-known works.

[11] Radcliffe, *Castles of Athlin and Dunbayne*, p. 20. The reference is to *Hamlet*, 3.4.33–5:

> Peace, sit you down,
> And let me wring your heart, for so I shall
> If it be made of penetrable stuff.

[12] Radcliffe, *Castles of Athlin and Dunbayne*, p. 25. The reference is to *Hamlet*, 1.1.5.

[13] Radcliffe, *Castles of Athlin and Dunbayne*, pp. 8–9.

[14] Ann Radcliffe, *A Sicilian Romance* (2 vols; London: T. Hookham, 1790).

[15] William Dodd, *The Beauties of Shakespeare, Regularly Selected from Each Play* (London: T. Waller, 1752).

[16] Samuel Johnson, *Miscellaneous Observations on the Tragedy of Macbeth* (London: E. Cave, 1745), p. 56; italics in original.

[17] Ann Radcliffe, *A Journey Made in the Summer of 1794, through Holland and the Western Frontier of Germany, with a Return Down the Rhine* (London: G. G. and J. Robinson, 1795), p. 135.

[18] Charles Dibdin, *A Complete History of the English Stage* (London: Printed for the author, 1800).

[19] Anna Laetitia Barbauld, 'Mrs Radcliffe', biographical preface to *The Romance of the Forest*, vol. 43 of *The British Novelists* (London: Rivington, 1810), pp. vi–vii.

[20] Charles Bucke, *On the Beauties, Harmonies and Sublimities of Nature* (new edn; 3 vols; London: T. Tegg and Sons, 1837), vol. 2, p. 123.

[21] Joseph Warton, *An Essay on the Writings and Genius of Pope* (2 vols; London: M. Cooper, 1756–1782), vol. 1, pp. x and xi.

[22] Richard Hurd, *Letters on Chivalry and Romance* (London: A. Millar, W. Thurlbourn and J. Woodyer, 1762), pp. 4 and 60.

[23] Ann Radcliffe, *The Mysteries of Udolpho, A Romance* (4 vols; London: G. G. and J. Robinson, 1794).

[24] Ann Radcliffe, *The Italian, or The Confessional of the Black Penitents* (3 vols; London: T. Cadell and W. Davies, 1797).

[25] Stéphanie Félicité Ducrest de St-Aubin, Countess of Genlis, *Adelaide and Theodore; or Letters on Education* (3 vols; London: T. Cadell, 1783), vol. 1, p. 71.

[26] Marie-Joseph de Chénier, *Tableau historique de l'état et des progrès de la littérature française, depuis 1789* (Paris, 1816), p. 229.

[27] Review of *The Mysteries of Udolpho*, *Critical Review*, 11 (August 1794), 361. This review is commonly, but mistakenly, attributed to Coleridge; see Norton, *Mistress of Udolpho*, pp. 105–6.

[28] Thomas James Mathias, *The Pursuits of Literature, or What You Will* (London: J. Owen, 1794). *The Pursuits of Literature* first appeared in 1794, but the reference to Mrs Radcliffe did not appear until the revised third edition (1797), p. 14.

---

29 Drake, *Literary Hours*, vol. 1, p. 361.

30 Sir Walter Scott, 'Prefatory memoir to Mrs Ann Radcliffe', *The Novels of Mrs Ann Radcliffe*, vol. 10 of Ballantyne's Novelist's Library (Edinburgh: James Ballantyne, 1824), p. vii.

31 Jane Waldie, *Sketches Descriptive of Italy in the Years 1816 and 1817* (4 vols; London, 1820), vol. 4, pp. 163–4.

32 John Sheppard, *Letters, Descriptive of a Tour through some parts of France, Italy, Switzerland, and German, in 1816* (2 vols; Edinburgh: Printed for Oliphant, Waugh & Innes, 1817), vol. 2, p. 438.

33 Barbauld, 'Mrs Radcliffe', pp. vi–vii.

34 'Ann Radcliffe', *Annual Biography and Obituary*, 8 (1824), 91.

35 She compared these theatres to the Frankfurt Theatre in *A Journey Made in the Summer of 1794*, p. 233.

36 Thomas Noon Talfourd, 'Memoir of the life and writings of Mrs Radcliffe', prefixed to Ann Radcliffe, *Gaston de Blondeville*, vol. 1, pp. 99–100.

37 F. W. Price, 'Ann Radcliffe, Mrs Siddons and the character of Hamlet', *Notes and Queries*, n.s., 23, 4 (April 1976), 164–7.

38 See Norton, *Mistress of Udolpho*, ch. 3.

39 James Boaden, *Memoirs of the Life of John Philip Kemble* (2 vols; London: Longman, Hurst, Rees, Orme, Brown and Green, 1825), vol. 1, pp. 242–3, 248.

40 Ibid., vol. 1, pp. 250, 268; 328–30; 343; 415–19.

41 William Hazlitt, *Characters of Shakespear's Plays* (2nd edn; London: Taylor and Hessey, 1818), pp. 21–2.

42 Drake, *Literary Hours*, vol. 1, pp. 361–2.

43 John Dunlop, *The History of Fiction* (3 vols; London: Longman, Hurst, Rees, Orme, Brown and Green, 1814), vol. 3, p. 396.

44 Radcliffe, *The Italian*, vol. 2, ch. 9.

45 Radcliffe, *Gaston de Blondeville*, 'In the new forest', vol. 4, p. 179; *Gaston de Blondeville*, 'Shakspeare's [sic] Cliff', vol. 4, p. 169.

46 Radcliffe, *A Journey*, p. 369.

47 Talfourd, 'Memory', vol. 1, p. 43; the reference is to *Hamlet*, 1.5.89–91.

48 Talfourd, 'Memory', vol. 1, pp. 43–4.

49 Radcliffe invented this phrase in *The Mysteries of Udolpho*; it occurs at the beginning of vol. 1, ch. 7.

50 Talfourd, 'Memoir', vol. 1, p. 79.

51 Ibid., vol. 1, p. 71.

52 Ibid., vol. 1, p. 60.

53 Norton, *Mistress of Udolpho*, ch. 16.

54 Talfourd, 'Memoir', vol. 1, pp. 97–8, quoting *Hamlet*, 1.1.33–7.

3

The Curse of Shakespeare

JEFFREY KAHAN

Beside yon Charnel House, lie shrin'd those bones,
Which e'en the bard of sacrilege wou'd spare;
A dream anathema enshields the stones;
To brave the Curse of Shakspeare; who would dare?
W. H. Ireland, 'Monody on Shakespeare' (1833)[1]

In 1799, W. H. Ireland – or 'Shakespeare Ireland', as he was dubbed – recalled the how and why of his turn from forging Shakespearean drama to writing Gothic novels. About to enter his house, the doorknob in his hand, he had overheard two 'gents' talking about him. One affirmed that Ireland was the author of the Shakespeare forgery, *Vortigern*, which had occupied much of literary England for the past eighteen months. 'I will maintain', said the other, 'that he is *not* the author.'[2]

The Tragedy of Vortigern was, perhaps, the most controversial Shakespearean production of the entire eighteenth century. The play was staged on 2 April 1796 at the Theatre Royal Drury Lane, with some of the greatest Shakespearean actors of the day. The play was only one of nearly two dozen 'recently discovered' Shakespeare documents – collectively known as the 'Shakspeare Papers' – which included legal papers, love letters, lost poems, portraits, correspondence between Shakespeare and Leicester, Shakespeare and Southampton, Shakespeare and Queen Elizabeth and Shakespeare and his printer, signed and annotated books from Shakespeare's library, the original manuscript of *King Lear* and a fragment of *Hamlet*, both with significant variants – even a lock of Shakespeare's hair. Key members of the cast, including the principal lead, John Philip Kemble, were dead set against the 'lost' Shakespeare, much of the audience was hostile and Drury Lane pulled the play after a single performance. Kemble's half-hearted acting contributed to the fall of *Vortigern*, but many saw Kemble as merely a henchman of the Shakespeare scholar Edmond Malone. Malone himself had not been idle. The day before the play premiered, he released a 424-page harangue against Ireland and his work, the *Inquiry into the Authenticity of Certain Miscellaneous Papers* (1796).

In the case of *Vortigern* and the 'Shakspeare Papers', the question of authorship was a complex issue. Even after Ireland had come forward and admitted that he had forged the Shakespearean play, most people, including his own father, refused to believe him. Some affirmed that the play was genuine; others admitted that the play was a forgery but insisted that Ireland was merely a messenger boy. There was talk that Ireland's father, Samuel, was the actual author; still others suspected the impish Shakespeare editor George Steevens.[3] Thus, Ireland was put in the odd position of having to prove that he was the author of his own forgeries. To the two 'gents', and anyone else within earshot, Ireland declared: 'Before all the world I have said, that I *was*, and before all the world I am ready to repeat, that I *am*, the author of those Papers' (*The Abbess*, vol. 1, p. ix; italics in original).

The discovery of the 'Shakspeare Papers'

Ireland's own account of the forgeries runs as follows: in 1793, Samuel Ireland, a collectibles dealer and travel writer who was obsessed with William Shakespeare, journeyed to Stratford-upon-Avon in order to search for documents pertaining to the playwright. Accompanying Samuel was his apparently dim-witted son, William Henry. Father and son knocked on doors and asked if any old papers were about. They failed, bought a few worthless trinkets and departed, the father crushed by his lack of success.

Soon after their return from Stratford, however, William Henry Ireland informed his father that he had met a gentleman, whom he referred to as 'Mr H.'. This 'gent' had some old papers in a trunk. Some apparently bore Shakespeare's signature. The gent had wanted to come forward with the discoveries himself, but as the papers made clear, his great-great-grandfather, or one of the great-great-grandfather's close friends, had stolen the documents from Shakespeare. To avoid scandal to his family name, it was essential that Mr H.'s true identity remain unknown. Thus, he was willing to allow Ireland to take the papers, which, no doubt, would yield important secrets concerning Shakespeare's life and artistry.

Not long after this supposed encounter, W. H. Ireland returned home with one of the documents and gave it to his father, who then had it inspected. The document was validated as having a legitimate Shakespearean signature, making it a find of tremendous significance and monetary value. Samuel Ireland then ordered his boy to retrieve yet more papers from the trunk. William set off for the gent's house and returned hours later with a profession of faith, Shakespeare's signed adherence to Protestantism. It, too, was examined and validated. The scholarly world took notice. The son was sent back once again to search the trunk. This time he unearthed a letter from Shakespeare to Anne Hathaway. Accompanying the letter was a love poem and a lock of Shakespeare's hair. Amazingly, hair, letter and poem were all validated. On his next search, yet more documents were found. Again, each was accepted as a lost Shakespeare document. Days later, Ireland 'discovered' a handwritten version of *King Lear* and a fragment of *Hamlet*. On 3 January 1795, W. H. Ireland announced that he had discovered an unknown Shakespeare play called *Vortigern*.

Filiation and forgery: The Castle of Otranto *and* Vortigern

Previous studies of Ireland's forgeries usually see the trunk convention as a homage to Chatterton, who had framed his forgeries with a similar narrative.[4] But, in many ways, it was Horace Walpole, not Chatterton, who was W. H. Ireland's literary father. Walpole's most famous forgery was, of course, his Gothic novel, *The Castle of Otranto* (1764), which, Walpole said, he had discovered 'in the library of an ancient Catholic family in the north of *England*'.[5] Walpole posed as the translator of the work – the 'original', he informed his readers, was in Italian. In the second edition, however, the narrator admitted that there was no discovered manuscript and, thus, no translation. Walpole's name – and, thus, the identity of the true author – remained a mystery, though he did add a sonnet, which he signed cryptically as 'H. W.'.

Aside from passing off *Otranto* as a lost manuscript, Walpole also counterfeited a letter from Frederick the Great, inviting Rousseau, whom he hated, to spend his exile in Austria. On another occasion, he forged documents in an effort to blackmail a man who was charging his brother with buggery.[6] Even his contemporaries warned readers to judge Walpole's statements of fact 'with extreme caution and doubt';[7] a later biographer went so far as to write: 'If literary forgery were the capital offence, the same gallows should have sufficed for Walpole and Chatterton.'[8] Further, in Ireland's *Confessions* (1805), the author makes clear that his admiration of Chatterton grew out of a love for Walpole's *The Castle of Otranto*. Ireland states that he spent many a night with his mind 'entirely riveted' by imaginings of himself as a character in Walpole's Gothic novel: 'Thus was my bedchamber a regular armoury; and on many occasions, when the moon has shone upon a full suit, I have sat upright in my bed, and pictured scenes from my lord Orford's Castle of Otranto.'[9] This armour is significant; in Walpole's novel, a ghost of a murdered man (Alfonso the Good) appears in armour, just as the ghost does in *Hamlet*. John Collick is convinced that here Walpole was following *Hamlet*, and Walpole himself made no bones about his influence, saying, 'Shakespeare was the model I copied'.[10] We may further add that if Walpole copied Shakespeare, Ireland copied Walpole. Note Ireland's interplay of Walpole's 'H. W.' and Ireland's 'Mr H.': 'H. W.' turned upside down and reversed becomes 'M. H.' or 'Mr H.'.

Moreover, Walpole was not just a name on a book spine but also a business associate of the forger's father, who met Walpole often when the latter was in London. On occasion, Samuel Ireland actually visited Strawberry Hill.[11] It is very possible that the forger himself accompanied his father on these trips. Certainly, the boy would have wanted to meet his literary hero, and Ireland, by his own admission, 'became a collector of helmets, breastplates, gorgets, cuisses, &c.; and any part of the suit which was deficient, I … made up … with pasteboard' (*Confessions*, p. 10). The use of pasteboard is an intriguing detail, as Walpole himself stated that in order to create the effect of battlements on his Strawberry Hill house, 'he nailed cardboard on the framework of the cottage'.[12]

Putting W. H. Ireland within earshot of Walpole certainly has its advantages, especially in terms of understanding *Vortigern's* aesthetics. Walpole's views about Shakespeare were a common theme of his dinners and discussions. He even collected his thoughts for eventual publication, which were sought after by Edmond Malone, who was putting together his 1790 edition of Shakespeare. Walpole declined Malone's invitation to have his notes added to the edition. Nonetheless, Walpole's notes survive and shed light on the subjects of his Shakespearean conversations. One of Walpole's irritations, for instance, was that Shakespeare had been faulted for not following neoclassical rules. Reversing this logic, Walpole mused whether playwrights might not abandon writing 'correct' plays in favour of 'incorrect' Shakespearean plays:

> Is it not amazing that as all rules are drawn from the *conduct* of great geniuses … nobody should have thought of drawing up rules from Shakespeare's plays, rather than of wishing they had been written from rules collected from such subaltern genius's [*sic*] as Euripides and Sophocles? I maintain that it was likely we should have had finer tragedies, if Shakespeare's daring had been laid down for a rule of venturing, than by pointing out his irregularities as faults.[13]

Walpole even suggested that it was only a matter of time before new Shakespearean documents – that is to say, documents by or pertaining to Shakespeare – would come to light.[14] Writing on the reign of Richard III, Walpole argued that Shakespeare's own sources were corrupted by the forging pen of 'impostors' who were 'the only persons who attempted to write history'. Modern scholars, he argued, were therefore duty bound to reject the falsehoods of existing histories in favour of other documents that were sure to be discovered as 'time brings new materials to light'.[15]

The subplots: a bastard, a damsel and the ghost of Shakespeare

If such pronouncements aesthetically paved the way for Ireland's fraud, Walpole never associated the 'Shakspeare Papers' with his own artistic activities. But others did: *The Gentleman's Magazine* noted the recent forgeries by Ireland and traced their roots to Walpole's *Castle of Otranto*, 'the archetype of all that miserable trash' that now deludes the press; and *The Monthly Mirror* for May 1803 contextualized Ireland's recent 'impositions upon the public' as part of a literary tradition that began when the 'Earl of Orford first gave to the world his "Castle of Otranto"'.[16] But Ireland, rather than downplaying his connection to Walpole's novel, encouraged the association by writing actual letters to his family and forging letters to himself with yet more Gothic motifs: an illegitimate bantling raised among unloving strangers, a story of missing identity, a fallen woman and even a damsel in distress.

To begin with the problem of paternity: W. H. Ireland was haunted by the thought that he was not really the son of Samuel Ireland. This subplot came to a head in a letter dated 3 January 1797, in which he demanded of Samuel point-blank: 'If you are really my Father I appeal to your feelings as a Parent.'[17] If Ireland doubted the identity of his father, he was certain who his mother was; he was the bastard child of Samuel's housekeeper, Mrs Freeman, who was, herself, the former mistress of the earl of Sandwich – hence, the possibility that Ireland was the bastard offspring of a licentious aristocrat who had been pawned off on Samuel Ireland, a man who showed no real affection for his 'son'.[18]

While Ireland was busily writing letters to his father concerning the dark secret of his illegitimacy, he also created a set of letters from a woman who was the prisoner of a sensuous scoundrel. In the first letter, signed merely 'Incognita', she begs W. H. Ireland to meet her 'alone in the Parish ... as a clue to my person I have very long Flaxen Hair'. This light lady also refers to our forger as a 'Man of *Honour*' and goes on to hint of her undying love for him.[19] Apparently, Incognita did not keep the meeting, for in a second letter, dated 27 October 1796, she apologizes for breaking the appointment with Ireland: she had been sick. On top of that, she now says that she has been forced into an engagement with a man she does not love. If only William Henry Ireland can save her! This time she signs off as 'Seraphina'. She also mentions that these letters are not to be shown to Samuel Ireland, as he is acquainted with her guardian. Seraphina also has a flare for poetry. 'She' begins one of her letters to Ireland thus:

> Dull languor sad and irksome care
> The frequent sigh, the falling tear
> Intrusive guests – my hours employ
> And rob them of their wonted joy:
> Ah Lifes [*sic*] gay prospects all are tain
> The gilded pleasures end in pain.[20]

What was Ireland's model for these subplots? Why, Walpole, of course! The forger's narratives concerning Samuel Ireland, Mrs Freeman and Lord Sandwich bear an uncanny resemblance to *The Castle of Otranto*, in which Manfred, the unloving father, decides to put off his wife and marry his son's intended, Isabella, who is eventually saved by Theodore, the true heir of Otranto. Defeated, Manfred confesses that he has killed Theodore's father and that the will declaring him legal heir of the title was forged. Ireland's forgery even has its own ghost, conveniently supplied not by Ireland himself but by William Bland Burgess, who wrote the prologue to *Vortigern*. The piece calls for actor James Whitfield to assume the guise of 'immortal Shakspeare' and demand that his audience accept this lost play as 'the favour'd relics of your Shakspeare's hand'. As we shall see, Ireland, always with an eye towards appropriating a good thing, would make use of both Shakespeare and ghosts when writing his Gothics.

What's in a name?

Ireland not only fictionalized his life but also became his own
ghostwriter, forging and reforging his identity with ever changing
noms de plumes: As 'Cervantes', he wrote a pantomime for
George III's daughter Elizabeth that was performed at Frogmore
Fete; as 'Charles Clifford', he wrote a poem celebrating fishing
and the great outdoors; as 'Satiricus Sculptor' and 'Ben Block', he
satirized subjects ranging from pornography to 'Nicknackatarian
Mania'; as 'H. C.', he wrote long narrative poems infused with
political commentary; as Anne-Jean-Marie-René Savary, duc de
Rovigo, he wrote the *Memoirs of the Duke of Rovigo, M. Savary*; as
Thomas Fielding, Esq., he jotted *Proverbs of All Nations: Illustrated
with Notes and Comments*; as Pauline Adélaide Alexandre Panam,
he composed *Memoirs of a Young Greek Lady*; as Henry Boyle, he
recorded *The Universal Chronologist, and Historical Register, From the
Creation to the Close of the Year 1825*; sometimes as Frances
Twysden Villiers Jersey, sometimes as Lady Anne, he penned
The Death-Bed Confessions of the Late Countess of Guernsey; as
Baron Karlo Excelmans, he published a *Life of Napoleon*; as
Richard Fenton, he put to paper *Tour in Quest of Genealogy,
Through Several Parts of Wales, Somersetshire and Wiltshire*. When
Ireland's publisher asked why he often wrote under a variety of
pseudonyms, our man of a thousand names replied that his
implacable enemies would do anything to ruin his career: if 'I
should be ... suspected ... as the writer ... I know my men [read:
my enemies] & many of them if they could would give 500 that
it [his writing] should not appear.'[21]

If Ireland actually felt that his enemies would block the publication of his work, why did he not also use pseudonyms for his
Gothics? The answer may be found in the reactions of those two
'gents' that Ireland cites as his inspiration for writing his Gothics.
After swearing, 'I *was*, and before all the world I am ready to
repeat, that I *am*, the author of those papers', Ireland noted that
one of the men called him a rapscallion and stormed off. The
other double-dared him to repeat his genius: 'Ireland', said one of
them, 'there is one thing in which you must agree with me. If you
have been able to write, you still *are* ... I would lay any wager, that

some even think you cannot read. Now, suppose you were to write something – were it but a Novel ... Could you do such a thing?' 'Why not?' Ireland answered after musing some minutes, 'I will try a Novel' (*The Abbess*, p. xii; italics in original).

The Abbess was a huge success, not only in England but also in America. A second American edition was issued in 1802 and a third in 1834. In 1822, a Spanish translation appeared, with yet another edition coming out in 1836; in 1824, it was translated into German. Ireland's publishers were so pleased that when Ireland wrote another Gothic a year later, they made sure that audiences now associated Ireland's name with *The Abbess* rather than with *Vortigern*. The title page of this second Gothic novel reads: *Rimualdo: or the Castle of Badajos. A Romance. By W. H. Ireland, author of 'The Abbess', &c. &c. In Four Volumes. Rimualdo* sold less well than *The Abbess*, though a French translation was issued in 1823.

Ireland's Gothic as confession and apology for the 'Shakspeare Papers'

Ireland's *Vortigern* was less suited to the neoclassical stage than it was to the Gothic page. Significantly, only one year before *Vortigern* failed to win audiences, John Philip Kemble mounted a highly successful production of *King Lear* – not Shakespeare's *King Lear*, but Tate's, *sans* Lear's and Cordelia's deaths, *sans* the fool, *sans* sad ending. *Vortigern* reversed this winnowing process by mixing and matching dark elements from Shakespeare's tragedies with comic mottlings from his cross-dressing comedies. It is not that Ireland's play is unShakespearean; it is that his play is determinedly unlike any Shakespeare on the Georgian stage. The 'discovery' of *Vortigern* proved that Shakespeare was, like Ireland himself, a Gothic writer, his art a crowded hotchpotch of genre and convention.[22]

Because *Vortigern* was modelled upon the tastes of Gothic readers, Ireland had every reason to believe that writing Shakespearean Gothics would bring him rewards. However, Ireland had little reason to believe those rewards would be financial. As Devendra P. Varma, who greatly admired *The Abbess*, unhappily admits: 'Actual purchase of these novels was exceptional: confidential maids got them from Lane's or other libraries, and regular borrowing and library circulation soon reduced the few copies to scraps. And as they were more or less transient entertainment no one cared about their survival.' Furthermore, because 'the reading of novels was despised as a waste of time by serious-minded persons', Ireland could not have expected that writing even a stellar Gothic, in and of itself, would redeem his literary reputation.[23] Gothic writers themselves often admitted that the genre was a dumping ground for ideas that were rejected by the more legitimate medium of the theatre.

If the Gothic, although traditionally allied with elements of Shakespeare, was hardly the literary form to convince critics of his genius, why, then, did Ireland choose it? Had Ireland simply miscalculated? While this is possible, it is unlikely. Ireland was a meticulous and calculating forger who had fooled London's literati for over a year. It is hard to imagine that he would have planned his next move so poorly or, having miscalculated, would then persevere in that miscalculation by writing five more Gothic novels over a nine-year span: *The Abbess* (1799), *Rimualdo* (1800), *Gondez, the Monk* (1805), *The Catholic* (1807) and *Rizzio* (composed *c.*1808 and published 1849, with additions by Ireland and G. P. R. James). What, then, was his plan?

That Ireland often hid his identity, but did not do so with his Gothic novels, suggests that they were created specifically to rehabilitate his literary reputation. This process can be glimpsed in his romances, as well. In *A Woman of Feeling* (1804), Ireland introduces a chapter on the subject of lying, which he associates with both high Romantic thoughts and common hackwork:

> [N]othing gives us so much pleasure as downright impossibilities; and as the race of authors must consult public taste, whether plain common sense or the high varnish of romance please the public, so to each of these must the author fashion his production, in order to procure present fame, and the more substantial benefit of present food and cloathing.[24]

Ireland goes on to state, however, that sometimes lying can perpetuate more lies, until the author, caught in his own fiction, has no escape but full confession: 'the constant practice of deceit becomes in a short time absolutely necessary to cover former falsehoods; and if there be one link in this chain broken, it is then a man's character becomes truly developed, and he is an object for the fingers of scorn to point at' (*A Woman of Feeling*, vol. 3, p. 210). The last volume of the novel includes what seems to be a personal confession in which the author looks into the mirror and declares:

> [N]ever, perhaps, was mortal more calculated to fall into the constant commission of error than myself, and never, perhaps, appeared an individual on the theatre of life whose actions were, not only to say more erroneous, but often more culpable than my own. I, notwithstanding, avow, that I do not mean to destroy or order these papers to be destroyed unperused after my death. No they shall stand the test of my own survivors. My virtues and vices shall be placed in the scale of severest scrutiny, and let them who dare cast at me the '*first stone*'.
>
> (vol. 4, pp. 33–4; italics in original)

The book's title page, however, complicates this seeming confession and avowal of his work's lasting value. Ireland's name is nowhere to be found; rather, *A Woman of Feeling* is attributed to 'Paul Persius'.

Ireland's fictional martyrdoms

Of course, we cannot read *The Abbess*, *The Monk* or *The Catholic* – or any work that calls itself a 'confession' and warns against casting the 'first stone' – without recognizing a theological metonymy. Was Ireland comparing himself to Christ? Hitherto, critics have merely noted his anti-Catholicism. Discussing *The Abbess*, Benjamin Franklin Fisher, IV, states that: 'Ireland never missed a chance to play on the anti-Catholic emotions of his readers, and, no doubt taking his cue from [Matthew Lewis's] *The Monk*, he attempted to pander to such prejudice.'[25] Ireland was very keen on defending Shakespeare from the charge of Catholicism and forged a document to prove the poet was a Protestant:

Having the most rooted antipathy to every thing like superstition and bigotry, and having heard it very frequently surmised that our great poet, like his father, was no protestant ... I determined, if possible, to decide the point on the other hand, by making the profession of faith appear to be written by a sincere votary of the protestant religion.

(*Confessions*, p. 57)

Furthermore, Ireland often depicted his own foes as staunch papists. By his own account, when the forger asked James Boaden why the scholarly community continued to persecute him, Boaden replied: 'You must be aware, sir, of the enormous crime you committed against the divinity of Shakspeare. Why, the act, sir, was nothing short of sacrilege; it was precisely the same thing as taking the holy chalice from the altar, and ★★★★★★★ therein!!!!.'[26]

The anti-Catholicism of Ireland's Gothics also operates to rehabilitate his reputation. After all, if Ireland had committed literary sacrilege, it was necessary that he be punished but also absolved and, ultimately, like Prospero in *The Tempest*, set free.[27] In the last chapter of *A Woman of Feeling*, Ireland, or rather 'Paul Persius', writes: 'I know that my avowing myself is sailing under false colours; but I may just as well sign myself Paul Persius as John Thompson, the one being as interesting to the reader as the other' (vol. 4, pp. 252–3). He asserts, however, that the author's identity matters very much. Were anyone to know it, he has no doubt that he would 'pass his judgement on me, and either *commit my pages to the oblivion of the flames, or bring me to the public ordeal of the press*' (vol. 4, p. 254; italics added). For those who have read Ireland's critics, the reference to fire is plain enough. In *An Inquiry in the Authenticity of Certain Miscellaneous Papers*, Edmond Malone recommended that Ireland be burned as a heretic and that his work be cast into 'a proper fire ... of the most baleful and noxious weeds'.[28] The 'ordeal of the press' suggests not only the fourth estate but also a common method of torture, which consisted of pressing a heavy weight on a man's chest. When the weight was lifted, the man, gasping for air, was asked if he wanted to confess. If he refused, the process continued.

It is not merely the fear of torture that is repeated in Ireland's work. Were that the case, Ireland's heroes would be no different than Matthew Lewis's monk Ambrosio, who 'suffered the most excruciating pangs that ever were invented by human cruelty ... his dislocated limbs, the nails torn from under his hands and feet, and his fingers mashed and broken by the pressure of screws'.[29] In Ireland's novels, by contrast, torture is used as a test of integrity. The typical Ireland hero does not run from punishment; instead, he gleefully embraces it. In Ireland's first Gothic, *The Abbess* (1799), we meet the Conte Marcello Porta, who falls in love with the beautiful Maddelena Rosa. The story turns on a *Measure for Measure* bed-trick in which the monk Ubaldo leads Porta into a room for a midnight rendezvous with Rosa. To emphasize the association, chapter 5 begins with two passages from Shakespeare's play:

> This outward sainted deputy,
> Whose settled visage and deliberate word,
> Nips youth in the head, and follies doth [enew],
> As falcons doth the fowl, is yet a devil.
> MEASURE FOR MEASURE [referring to 3.1.88–91][30]

> I have begun,
> And now I give my sensual race the rein:
> Fit thy consent to my sharp appetite;
> Lay by all nicety, and prolixious blushes
> That banish what they sue for.
> MEASURE FOR MEASURE [referring to 2.4.159–63]

In the midst of his midnight encounter, a veiled woman makes Porta swear on a Bible never to reveal the secret of their affair. Porta swears and then falls to his knees, promising eternal devotion. He then discovers that he has made a pact not with his beloved Rosa but with Vittoria Bracciano, the mother superior of the convent, who is appropriately named for the title character of John Webster's *The White Devil*. When the Inquisition learns that Porta has visited a woman in the convent, he is arrested and threatened with torture but refuses to break his vow:

[Y]ou now assert my guilt in peremptory terms; you alledge proofs, and flagrant ones, against me … but, you forget to expatiate on the theme of honour, that rigid sentiment, which alone restrains me from a confession. The passion, which holds dominion over my heart, no powers of the most fertile imagination can describe.

(*The Abbess*, vol. 4, p. 18)

A grim sadist racks Porta until his body begins to break, but our hero remains steadfast. He is then taken to an infirmary, where he receives medical attention until his body is well enough to endure yet more pain. In the end, Porta, punished beyond any reasonable measure for his oath, is given pardon and absolution.

False confessions

Did Ireland see himself as the martyr/hero of his own novel? Might this not explain why he used pseudonyms for his other writings but used his own name when penning and publishing his Gothics? Surely, there is some similarity between Ireland's heroes who are unfairly tortured and Ireland, at least as he portrayed himself in his expanded apology, *The Confessions of William-Henry Ireland* (1805):

Whatever has been my fault, my judges unquestionably have not been lenient, nor did they justly weigh the motive and inducement before they decided on the act … It is time I should cease to endure the blighting censure of Malignity rather than the mild and convincing reproof of Truth.

(p. 300)

But if Ireland's 'factual' confessions are doubted, how can we accept as truthful his 'fictional' penances? Even if we could accept that Ireland's heroes do somehow engage the reader with the crisis of their author, we still have a problem: Ireland's heroic characters undergo torture but do not always make full or truthful confession, and neither do his villains. To begin with a notable exception: in Ireland's third novel, *Gondez the Monk* (1805), the vice-ridden Gondez is brought before the Inquisition on charges of heresy, parricide and murder; he denies them all. The ghost of one of his victims then appears before the monk, demanding confession, but he persists in his claim of innocence, leaving the Inquisitors no choice but to rack Gondez lustily:

> During three successive nights did the guilty Gondez endure the tortures inflicted upon his person; in vain too, had every stratagem been put into effect during each day, by pretended commiserating friends who visited him, to draw forth an unfeigned confession; nought availed; the Abbot continued obdurate, when as the last recourse, an order was given for the infliction of the extremest torture.

We never learn what the exact nature of this 'extremest' torture is, but Gondez does finally 'make a full confession of every crime which had tainted his soul'.[31]

More commonly, however, the guilty evade confession or manipulate confession to their own ends. In *The Abbess*, for instance, despite enduring horrific tortures, Ubaldo never confesses to his crimes. This pattern recurs in Ireland's *The Catholic* (1807), which tells the story of Moor O'Mara, a religious zealot implicated in the Gunpowder Plot. Eventually, O'Mara is captured and taken to a room where 'new devices were to be resorted to in order that a full confession might be drawn from me'.[32] Due to his religious constancy, this murderous conspirator does not break and remains 'in full belief of redemption' (vol. 3, p. 303). O'Mara does, however, write his own memoir, a declaration and affirmation of his crimes, which he leaves behind for his child. In the memoir, he remains unrepentant for trying to blow up King James and his counsellors. There are, furthermore, problems even with the worst of Ireland's villains, the diabolical Vittoria, who confesses her crimes only to avoid further punishment, not because she feels any remorse:

> After the infliction of the first and second torture, her pride, every consideration yielded to the corporeal anguish she endured, and Vittoria, in a convulsed tone, requested to be heard. – The

Inquisitor stayed the familiars; but it was not until the question had
been several times repeated, and the torturers were again ordered to
do their duty, that she could be prevailed upon to divulge the truth.

(*The Abbess*, vol. 4, pp. 90–1)

Nonetheless, the sincerity of Vittoria's confession is not only
accepted but is turned into a sort of cant whereby, rueful or not,
it will be accepted as a sincere and candid confession, if only by
sheer dint of repetition. As punishment, Vittoria is stripped of her
office and ordered to walk barefoot to Rome, where she will be
whipped on the first Friday of the month and made to eat
publicly off the pavement, abstain from animal food and, in the
presence of the whole community, 'pronounce aloud the guilty
deed' (vol. 4, p. 93). Given this motif of staged confession, could
we conclude that in writing his own confessions, Ireland did so
without genuine penance?

There is yet another problem. It is not only the villains in
Ireland's novels who refuse to confess or who make unapologetic,
and perhaps even counterfeit confessions. On two occasions, the
virtuous hero does (or offers to do) the same. In *The Abbess*, Porta
remains impervious to torture until his beloved Rosa is threatened with the rack. Only then does he promise to confess to
crimes he has not committed: '*I will annul my oath – I will make a
full confession*' (vol. 4, p. 46; italics in original). Vittoria is exposed
before he can do so; still, our hero was willing to confess, if only
to save another person. Ireland's *Rizzio* follows the same pattern:
Riccio, refusing to admit his crimes, is tortured. Mary, like Rosa
in *The Abbess*, is forced to watch and then is herself threatened
with physical abuse, at which point Riccio, re-enacting the role
of Porta, confesses. Since both heroes are innocent, their confessions are recognized as patently false by the reader.

An elaborate hoax? The Abbess *and Ireland's feigning art*

What, then, are we to make of such conflicting confessions, at
least as they appertain to Ireland? Should we reject some or all of
them? Can we trust anything Ireland writes under his own name,

much less a confession written under a pseudonym, appearing in a novel? And what of those two gentlemen Ireland describes in the Preface to *The Abbess*? Are they real, or were they invented to justify Ireland's fictional forays? Certainly, for Ireland, as an author and forger, the related issues of authorship and authenticity further complicate his narrative art. Here, we do not have a Walpolean editor claiming that fiction is fact. Instead, we have a fiction claiming that its author is not a charlatan. The twin issues of authenticity and authorship were neatly encompassed by the *Morning Chronicle*, which noted: 'W. H. Ireland has come forward and announced himself author of the papers attributed by him to Shakspeare; which, if *true*, proves him to be a *liar*' (quoted in *Confessions*, p. 269; italics in original).

If we can read Ireland's Gothics in relation to his confessions, it may be argued that Ireland, despite confessing and re-confessing, was merely telling his readers what they wanted to hear. Indeed, these various, seemingly interconnected confessions might be one elaborate joke or, perhaps, more subversively, a tacit defence – or even extension – of the 'Shakspeare Papers'. While I have already quoted from *The Abbess*, I have not yet mentioned that the title page of that novel also contains a quotation, which reads:

> Let Modest Matrons at thy mention start,
> And blushing Virgins, when they read our annals,
> Skip o'er the guilty page.
>
> SHAKSPEARE

Superficially, these lines seem to be yet another sign of contrition; Ireland uses Shakespeare to ask us, when reading his 'annals' – that is to say, his histories or confessions – to ignore his 'guilty pages'. Some of my readers, who are well versed in Shakespeare, might be scratching their heads, and for good reason. These lines are *not* by Shakespeare. They come, instead, from John Dryden's 1679 rewrite of *Troilus and Cressida*.[33] More intriguingly, the prologue to Dryden's *Troilus and Cressida* was echoed in the Prologue to Ireland's own *Vortigern*. Ireland's play, we recall, began with William Bland Burgess's prologue, in which an actor playing the ghost of Shakespeare demands that its audience accept *Vortigern* as a lost Shakespeare play. Dryden's prologue has an actor playing the ghost of Shakespeare who demands still more Shakespeare: 'Now, where are the Successours to my name? / What bring they to fill out a Poets [*sic*] fame?'[34] Ireland may have read Dryden's poem as a permission slip of sorts, a license to forge. If this was the case, Ireland's title page to his first Shakespearean Gothic declares his intent to continue to forge Shakespeare.

Not surprisingly, *The Abbess* also contains a number of forged lines. In volume 1, Ireland faked some verse 'by' Sir Charles Sedley (1639–1701), a dramatist of some note who had crafted a number of Shakespeare imitations, including *Antony and Cleopatra* (1677).[35] When writing volume 1, Ireland also quoted from the Shakespeare adapter Naham Tate. Nothing wrong in this per se, except that Ireland changed a line in the quotation to read 'Till they resent my wrongs' rather than the correct 'Till they resent the wrongs'. Obviously, Ireland wanted to use Tate's verse to re-direct the reader to his own plight as literary outcast. Similarly, in volume 2, he adds the pronoun 'My' to a quotation by Nathaniel Lee to suggest his own literary crimes: '*My* plot grows full of death … / My fancy's great in mischief' (italics added). Volume 3 begins with Ireland's 'quoting' from two lines of Dryden's *Virgil* that do not exist, at least in Dryden's poem.

Given these various literary misdemeanours in *The Abbess*, we can now say with some certainty that it was no accident that the publication of Ireland's Shakespeare forgery *Vortigern* in 1799 coincided with his first novel, *The Abbess*. *The Abbess* does not attempt to expunge the literary crime of forgery; instead, the novel justifies it. Even twenty-five years after his first Shakespeare forgery, Ireland continued to tease and entice his readers with the same claptrap that he used in his forgeries. In the following passage from *The Death-Bed Confessions of the Late Countess of Guernsey* (1821), Ireland, playing the familiar role of literary go-between, tells his readers that the manuscript before him came from a mysterious source, then suggests that he would like to tell us where he found it but that the secret must never be divulged. Indeed, *The Death-Bed Confessions* works as an aide-memoire to his earlier tell-alls, *An Authentic Account of the Shaksperian Manuscripts* (1796) and *The Confessions of William-Henry Ireland* (1805):

The important document which we are about to introduce to the public teems with matter of such vital interest to the most exalted personages, elucidating a series of transactions hitherto either veiled in obscurity or represented through the medium of blind and erring prejudice, that it will be naturally asked how came it into our possession? To this we are bound to reply, that, at present, *the seal of secrecy is on our lips* – more we dare not say; but we feel assured that, to the mind of the attentive reader, no circumstance can possibly operate against the *authenticity* and genuineness of the following 'CONFESSIONS'.[36]

At the very least, these various cross-references prove that Ireland was, in fact, the author of the 'Shakspeare Papers'. In this regard, his use of pseudonyms ultimately frustrated the ability of his readers to make these seemingly obvious interconnections. Ireland, who turned identity theft into a literary art form, became a victim of his own artistic process. Remarkably, even when he forged new documents in front of eyewitnesses, many remained unconvinced; Ireland might have been a copyist, but who, asked one reporter, 'composed the play he Copied[?]'[37] Even fifty years later, the notion persisted that W. H. Ireland was only a cog in a forgery machine. C. M. Ingleby, who exposed the forger Collier, wrote with assurance in *The Shakspeare Fabrications* (1859) that it was Samuel who had masterminded the forgeries: the daughters had written the text; W. H. Ireland merely copied it into Shakespeare's hand. Ingleby was right in thinking that Ireland did not write *Vortigern* alone: his entire family participated in the revision of the play for the stage. However, their revisions were undertaken in the mistaken belief that the papers were genuine. Ironically, the youthful forger himself was not allowed to revise his own play because his family assumed that he was the worst writer among them.[38] Ireland's later writings, including the Gothics, were dismissed as the work of an 'ignoramus', one 'deficient in grammar and unable to write a correct sentence'.[39] Facets of this thinking continue to affect adversely Ireland's artistic standing. Today, most assume that Ireland was the sole author of the 'Shakspeare Papers', but this has done little to enhance his reputation. The highly respected F. E. Halliday suggests that

Ireland 'might have made an honourable name for himself as a contemporary of Coleridge and the other Romantic writers, for he had undoubted talent', but that 'it is scarcely to be wondered at that nobody took an impostor seriously as a writer'.[40]

Rather than contest these charges, it may be more useful to note that after the scandal of Ireland's 'Shakspeare Papers', questioning the identity and function of the author became increasingly common, especially in reference to Gothic and romance novels. Elizabeth R. Napier has gone so far as to suggest that the term 'Gothic' was used interchangeably in the early nineteenth century with such unflattering descriptors as 'unoriginal' and 'repetitious'.[41] Indeed, the Gothic, even at the peak of its popularity, was often associated with plagiarism. In 1821, Sir Walter Scott was accused of having stolen the plot-lines for his works or of having acted merely as a front man for the real author or authors.[42] In 1845, Gilbert Abbott A'Beckett (most likely a pseudonym) wrote *Timour, the Cream of All Tartars* (1845), a work that burlesqued Matthew Lewis's *Timour the Tartar* (1811). 'Beckett''s play demonstrated, as all good burlesque does, how easily a capable writer can undermine the concept of a distinctive, authorial voice. Similarly, while no one doubted that Ann Radcliffe wrote her novels, it became increasingly common to ascribe other, no less Radcliffean, novels to her – among them, Ireland's *The Abbess*, which, when translated into German in 1824, was attributed to 'Anna Radcliff'.[43]

Authorial confusion in the Gothic is common because literary appropriation is one of the genre's distinguishing features. Nick Groom, explaining the literary interconnections of forgery to 'the machinery of the Gothic novel', observes that the *Waverley* novels of Sir Walter Scott were based in large measure upon the forgeries of Macpherson, which were, in turn, based upon a variety of earlier sources that the author/discoverer reworked or newly forged. Groom further notes that Chatterton, yet another forger, indirectly inspired such Gothic classics as *Frankenstein* (1818). Chatterton had, in turn, borrowed from Milton, who had borrowed from Shakespeare, who had borrowed from others before him.[44] And Ireland? Well, he borrowed from Shakespeare, Milton, Chatterton, Macpherson, Walpole and who knows who else. Perhaps this was Walpole's point when he wrote rather vaguely that 'All of the houses of forgery are relations'.[45] We may further state that literary appropriation is not distinct to the architecture of the Gothic. Indeed, *all* genres, by their very definition, are based upon non-proprietary literary convention: nobody owns the love story or the ghost story, or the happy ending. All writers may strive for literary independence, but they are still part of an extended fraternity of prose. Thus, it makes little sense to think of authorship, particularly Gothic authorship, in terms of originality or autonomy. Given the fact that Gothic literature is so heavily laden with convention, no writer of the genre can claim to be the single, original author of his or her work – heaven to a writer like Ireland, whose art consisted in reforging the ideas and even the phrases of others.

I might now conclude triumphantly that Ireland, who had famously impersonated the talents of Shakespeare; Ireland, whose literary pen-names defied boundaries of class, nationality and even gender; Ireland, whose identity vanished into his fiction and even into his confessional writing, was responsible for (or was, at least, agent provocateur, if not author, of) what is called the 'Authorial Fallacy'. Yet making that assertion implies that Ireland was a unique artist and that original ideas could come from his or any other pen – a contradiction in terms, since Ireland's craft was dedicated to the collapse of any distinctions between originality, conventionality and authorial intent. Ireland's sacrilege was that he made Shakespeare imitable; his curse was that no one believed him.

Notes

[1] Folger Shakespeare Library MS D.a.54. This unpublished poem was written for Miss Clara Fisher, who, according to Ireland, was to have performed the piece on the American stage. If it was performed, no date is given. The poem accompanies a letter dated 20 January 1833, in which Ireland confesses his poor health.

[2] William Henry Ireland, *The Abbess* (4 vols; London: Earle and Hemet, 1798), p. xiii. Further references to all works by William Henry Ireland will be included in the body of the text and indicated by short title.

[3] Jeffrey Kahan, *Reforging Shakespeare* (Bethlehem, PA: Lehigh University Press, 1998), pp. 108–23.

4   According to Ian Haywood, Defoe's *A Journal of the Plague Year* (1722) was
    the first work of fiction to employ the 'lost' manuscript as a literary device
    (*The Making of History: A Study of the Literary Forgeries of James Macpherson and
    Thomas Chatterton in Relation to Eighteenth-Century Ideas of History and Fiction*
    (Rutherford, NJ: Fairleigh Dickinson University Press, 1986), pp. 67–9.

5   Horace Walpole, 'Preface to the first edition', *The Castle of Otranto: A Gothic
    Story* (3rd edn; London: William Bathoe, 1766), p. v; italics in original.

6   Paul Baines, *The House of Forgery in Eighteenth-Century Britain* (Aldershot:
    Ashgate, 1999), p. 164.

7   *Quarterly Review*, July 1822, cited in John Henry Ingram, *The True Chatterton:
    A New Study from Original Documents* (London: T. Fisher Unwin, 1910),
    p. 307.

8   Daniel Wilson, *Chatterton: A Biographical Study* (London: Macmillan, 1869),
    cited in Charles Edward Russell, *Thomas Chatterton, the Marvelous Boy:
    The Story of a Strange Life, 1752–1770* (New York: Moffat, Yard and Co.,
    1908), p. 243.

9   William Henry Ireland, *The Confessions of William-Henry Ireland* (New York:
    Burt Franklin, 1805), pp. 10–11.

10 John Collick, *Shakespeare, Cinema and Society* (Manchester: Manchester
    University Press, 1989), p. 138. See also Walpole, 'Preface to the second
    edition', *The Castle of Otranto*, p. xvii.

11 The relationship broke down briefly after Samuel Ireland bribed one of
    Walpole's other engravers to get a copy of the frontispiece for *Noble Authors*,
    which he then had pirated, printed and sold (Horace Walpole, *The Yale
    Edition of Horace Walpole's Correspondence*, ed. W. S. Lewis et al. (48 vols; New
    Haven: Yale University Press, 1937–1983), vol. 42, p. 120 and 175; vol. 33,
    p. 575).

12 E. F. Bleiler, 'Horace Walpole and *The Castle of Otranto*', in *Three Gothic
    Novels* (New York: Dover, 1966), pp. viii–ix.

13 W. S. Lewis (ed.), 'Notes by Horace Walpole on several characters of
    Shakespeare', *Miscellaneous Antiquities* (Windham, CT: Hawthorne House,
    1940), p. 7; italics in original.

14 The forger must have been surprised by Walpole's certainty that the
    'Shakspeare Papers' were fakes: 'I am not surprised at any new lie that
    Ireland tacks to his legend; were he to coin himself into a grandson of
    Shakespear, with his ignorance of all probabilities, it would be but an addi-
    tion to his head-roll of incredibilities' (Walpole, *The Yale Edition of Horace
    Walpole's Correspondence*, vol. 15, p. 271).

15 Horace Walpole, *Historic Doubts on the Life and Reign of King Richard III*
    (Dublin: G. Faulkner, A. Leathley and W. and W. Smith, 1768), pp. viii and 2.
    Ireland was also an apologist for Richard III, arguing that Shakespeare was
    to blame for the 'odium generally attached to the king's character'
    ('Introduction' to W. H. Ireland and G. P. R. James, *Rizzio; or, Scenes in Europe
    During the Sixteenth Century* (3 vols; London: T. C. Newby, 1849), vol. 1,
    p. 28.

16 Obituary for Horace Walpole, *The Gentleman's Magazine* (March 1797),
    pp. 258–9; 'Literary Forgeries', *The Monthly Mirror* (May 1803), 294.

17 William Henry Ireland, Correspondences and press clippings, 1777–1835, BL MS 30346.

18 Robert Miles, 'Forging a Romantic identity: Herbert Croft's *Love and Madness* and W. H. Ireland's Shakespeare Ms', *Eighteenth-Century Fiction*, 17, 4 (July 2005), 599–627. See also Nick Groom, *The Forger's Shadow: How Forgery Changed the Course of Literature* (London: Picador, 2002), pp. 217–55.

19 The letter is dated Thursday night, 13 October 1796, four months after Ireland had actually married the less romantically named Alice Crudge. The character of the letter writer may have been inspired by William Congreve's novel, *Incognita: Or, Love and Duty Reconciled: A Novel* (1692), which is often cited as a forerunner of the Gothic.

20 Ireland, Correspondences and press clippings, British Library MS 30347.

21 Ireland, Correspondences and press clippings, Bodleian MS, Montagu e 5, fo. I am grateful to Nick Groom for the Bodleian transcriptions of Ireland's correspondences.

22 The full plot of *Vortigern* is summarized in Kahan, *Reforging Shakespeare*, pp. 17–19.

23 Devendra P. Varma, *The Gothic Flame* (London: Arthur Barker, 1957), p. 6.

24 [William Henry Ireland], *A Woman of Feeling* (4 vols; London: D. N. Shury, 1804), vol. 3, pp. 208–9.

25 *The Abbess* (4 vols, 1799); facsimile with Introduction by Benjamin Franklin Fisher, IV (ed.) (New York: Arno, 1974), vol. 1, p. xxiii. On Ireland's anti-Catholicism, see also Sister Mary Muriel Tarr, *Catholicism in Gothic Fiction* (Washington, DC: Catholic University of America Press, 1946), pp. 108–9.

26 Preface to *Vortigern; An Historical Play, With An Original Preface . . .* (London: J. Thomas, 1832), p. xiii.

27 G. P. R. James anticipates aspects of my analysis when he writes that Ireland's foes were motivated by 'Petty and Malevolent *passions* [that] directed *the scourge* that *chastised* him; and the object evidently was *to punish* and to crush rather than to correct and guide' (Ireland and James, *Rizzio*, vol. 1, p. 25; italics added).

28 Edmond Malone, *Inquiry into the Authenticity of Certain Miscellaneous Papers* (London: W. Baldwin, 1796), p. 361.

29 M. G. Lewis, *The Monk*, ed. Dennis Wheatley (London: Sphere Books Ltd., 1974), p. 337.

30 Ireland is following the folio spelling 'emmew', which generally is emended as 'enew'. References to lines numbers for Shakespeare's plays are to *The Riverside Shakespeare*, ed. G. Blakemore Evans et al. (2nd edn; Boston: Houghton Mifflin, 1997); Ireland's spelling is retained.

31 William Henry Ireland, *Gondez, the Monk: A Romance* (4 vols; London: W. Earle and J. W. Hucklebridge, 1805), vol. 4, p. 132.

32 William Henry Ireland, *The Catholic, An Historical Romance* (3 vols; London: W. Earle, 1807), vol. 3, p. 294.

33 John Dryden, *Troilus and Cressida*, in vol. 13 of *The Works of John Dryden*, ed. Alan Roper and Vinton A. Dearing (20 vols; Berkeley: University of California Press, 1956–1984), 4.2.388–90.

34 John Dryden, 'Prologue' to the April 1679 performance of *Troilus and Cressida, or Truth Found Too Late,* in Pierre Danchin (ed.), *The Prologues and Epilogues of the Restoration, 1660–1700* (Nancy: Presses Universitaires de Nancy, 1978), part 2.3, pp. 157–8, ll. 17–18.

35 Sir Charles Sedley, *Antony and Cleopatra* (London: Jacob Tonson, 1677). Ireland's quotation cannot be found in any of Sedley's works. Another 'Charles Sedley' penned the following novels: *The Barouche Driver and His Wife* (1807), *Asmodeus* (1808), *The Faro Table* (1808) and *A Winter in Dublin* (1808). Given Ireland's love of pseudonyms, he may have adopted Sedley's name here and in later works.

36 [William Henry Ireland], *The Death-Bed Confessions of the Late Countess of Guernsey* (London: J. Fairburn, [1821]), p. 1; italics in original.

37 Copy of article, *Gazetteer*, 27 December 1796, in Correspondences and press clippings, 1777–1835, British Library MS 30349.

38 C. M. Ingleby, *The Shakespeare Fabrications* (London: J. R. Smith, 1859), appendix I, p. 102. On the various hands involved in the rewriting of *Vortigern*, see Kahan, *Reforging Shakespeare*, pp. 134–40.

39 Zoltan Haraszti, *The Shakespeare Forgeries of William-Henry Ireland: The Story of a Famous Literary Fraud* (Boston: Trustees of the Public Library, 1934), p. 8.

40 F. E. Halliday, *The Cult of Shakespeare* (London: Gerald Duckworth & Co., Ltd., 1957), pp. 108–9.

41 Elizabeth R. Napier, *The Failure of Gothic: Problems of Disjunction in an Eighteenth-Century Literary Form* (Oxford: Clarendon, 1987), p. x.

42 J.[ohn] L.[eycester] Adolphus, *Letters to Richard Heber, Esq., Containing Critical Remarks on the Series of Novels Beginning with 'Waverley', and an Attempt to Ascertain Their Author* (London: Rodwell and Martin, 1821). The charge was renewed in 1856, with Gilbert French arguing that Scott's brother Thomas and his wife were the genuine authors of the earlier *Waverley* novels. See *An Enquiry into the Origin of the Authorship of Some of the Earlier Waverley Novels* (Bolton: J. Hudsmith, 1856), p. 3.

43 A. A. S. Wieten, *Mrs Radcliffe: Her Relation Towards Romanticism; with An Appendix on the Novels Falsely Ascribed to Her* (Amsterdam: H. J. Paris, 1926).

44 Groom, 'Forger's Shadow', pp. 109–113; see also p. 132.

45 E. H. W. Meyerstein, *Thomas Chatterton* (London: Ingpen and Grant, 1930), p. 277.

PART II

Rewriting Shakespeare's Plays and Characters

4

Shakespearean Shadows' Parodic Haunting of Thomas Love Peacock's Nightmare Abbey *and Jane Austen's* Northanger Abbey

MARJEAN D. PURINTON
and MARLISS C. DESENS

෨

While critical analyses of Thomas Love Peacock's *Nightmare Abbey* (1818) and Jane Austen's *Northanger Abbey* (1818) have exposed their complex satirical relations with contemporary writers, the novels' parodic interconnection with William Shakespeare's *Hamlet* has not been recognized. By 1818, Shakespeare not only had become the paradigmatic figure of English literary authority but also had been increasingly 'Gothicized' in readings of the page and performances on the stage – a model for those who wished to deploy the supernatural and the superstitious or who wished to ignore the rational boundaries imposed by neoclassical 'rules'. *Hamlet* had taken centre stage, both as a model of exemplary hauntings and as a quintessential source of that peculiarly 'English' identity with which Gothic writers wished to align themselves, and that familiarity made *Hamlet* available for parody.

Like Shakespeare and the Gothic, parody and satire were themselves being transformed in the late eighteenth century. They were becoming more dialogical than neoclassical parody, establishing

relationships not only between their sources and immediate historical circumstances but also between the reader and the original
text. In other words, parody had become a two-way channel
between the model text and the satire.[1] The Shakespearean
shadows of *Hamlet* surface in two principal ways in *Nightmare
Abbey* and *Northanger Abbey*. First, Gothic Shakespeare bubbles up
in the characterization and relational dynamics deployed by both
novelists, whose gender-bending and gender-role inversions are
informed by the shadows of a 'Gothicized' but parodied *Hamlet*.
Secondly, Austen and Peacock appropriate the performative and
spectacular elements popular in Georgian Shakespeare. The abbeys
of both novels become stages on which a Shakespearean landscape
is recast and satirized in order to mediate not only the conflicts in
the novels but also the social and political instabilities of the early
nineteenth century.

Gothic characterization

In the *Morning Chronicle* (14 March 1814), William Hazlitt asserts
that what distinguishes Shakespeare from all other dramatists is
'the wonderful variety and perfect individuality of his characters'.[2] For Samuel Taylor Coleridge, writing in *Table Talk* (1827),
Hamlet's character was 'the prevalence of the abstracting and
generalizing habit over the practical'.[3] From these two respected
theatre critics of the early nineteenth century, it would seem that
Shakespeare's characters could be at once individualized and
generalized, a chameleon quality that could therefore be modelled
and molded by novelists intent on audience recognition of, and
reverence for, Shakespearean dramatization in Gothic fiction.
Howard Mills's reading of *Nightmare Abbey* argues that its characters are abstractions, with ideas satirized and literary traditions
mocked, while Carl Dawson reads Peacock's satire as Menippean,
his caricatures as 'embodied classifications' with particular literary
associations.[4] The prevailing scholarly position on Peacock and
Austen views the satire as localized, but we are suggesting that
satire in these two works functions in a more complex and global
manner. The satire relies on the recognition of embedded

Shakespearean drama, so that Gothic conventions undergo a 'sea-change / Into something rich and strange' (*The Tempest*, 1.2.401–2).[5]

Peacock's novel is set at Nightmare Abbey, a dilapidated mansion in the Fens owned by the Glowry family. Young Scythrop Glowry, disapointed in love, has turned to melancholy and metaphysics of a very Shelleyan order. Eccentric visitors to the abbey are satiric portraits of Coleridge, Byron and Southey, while Scythrop's beloved Marionetta reminds us of both Harriet Shelley and Mary Godwin. The relational dynamics between Ophelia and Hamlet are recontextualized in the novel's characterization of Scythrop and Marionetta. An early scene in the novel sets the stage for the couple's satiric association with the lovers of Shakespeare's play:

> 'For heaven's sake, indeed!' said Scythrop, springing from the table; 'for your sake, Marionetta, and you are my heaven – distraction is the matter. I adore you, Marionetta, and your cruelty drives me mad'. He threw himself at her knees, devoured her hand with kisses, and breathed a thousand vows in the most passionate language of romance.
>
> Maronietta listened a long time in silence, till her lover had exhausted his eloquence and paused for a reply. She then said, with a very arch look, 'I prithee deliver thyself like a man of this world'. The levity of this quotation, and of the manner in which it was delivered, jarred so discordantly on the high wrought enthusiasm of the romantic inamorato that he sprang upon his feet, and beat his forehead with his clenched fists.[6]

The sense of dramatic enactment, the use of archaic language and a pithy quotation (drawn from *2 Henry IV*, 5.3.97–8) here invoke a Shakespearean milieu that encourages further associations with the Hamlet–Ophelia dynamic. As in Hamlet's distorted perception of Ophelia, Marionetta torments Scythrop, whom she keeps 'in a perpetual fever' (*Nightmare Abbey*, p. 23); importantly, Marionetta torments Scythrop deliberately, whereas Hamlet simply attributes such behaviour to Ophelia. Superficially, Ophelia, who on her father's orders has denied Hamlet access to her and who, at the start of their encounter in the nunnery scene, suddenly returns 'remembrances' of his because, she says, 'Rich gifts wax poor when givers prove unkind' (*Hamlet*, 3.1.92, 100), does appear to reject Hamlet and place the blame on him, just as Marionetta rejects Scythrop. The Shakespearean audience, however, knows that Ophelia, shrivelling under Hamlet's wrath, is controlled by her father, whereas Marionetta not only actively resists Scythrop's attempt to script her as the cruel, cold woman but paradoxically realizes his intent and turns it back upon him. When Scythrop retreats into the secrecy of his tower or reads Dante, however, Marionetta attempts to uncover his secrets. Hamlet also suspects Ophelia of spying on him – he obviously realizes in the nunnery scene that there are eavesdroppers – although we know that she is her father's and the king's puppet. Earlier, Ophelia had obeyed her father and 'did repel his letters, and denied / His access to me' (2.1.106–7). Hamlet had responded by appearing to her in an encounter that she describes to her father as a farewell (1.2.174–97). Polonius then decides that they must uncover this secret, which leads to the nunnery scene.

In *Nightmare Abbey*, Marionetta acts and Sythrop reacts. Marionetta makes several ineffectual attempts to extract from Scythrop his vexing mystery. According to the narrator, 'Scythrop grew every day more reserved, mysterious and *distrait*; and gradually lengthened the duration of his diurnal seclusions in his tower' (*Nightmare Abbey*, p. 52). Rarely speaking, Scythrop vainly attempts to comfort Marionetta, who tearfully claims that he is 'ungrateful, cruel, cold-hearted' (p. 53). Again, Marionetta throws back at Scythrop his own identification of her as a cold, unfeeling woman, an undercutting of the Petrarchan approach that Shakespeare similarly satirizes in his sonnets and plays. Elements of the relationship between Hamlet and his mother also appear to be parodied in the Scythrop–Marionetta relationship, perhaps in part because Hamlet collapses his mother and Ophelia into a single category: woman. Scythrop's mother is (conveniently) long dead, while Hamlet's mother disrupts his idealized views about male–female relationships and, like Marionetta with Scythrop, attempts to pry out the secret behind his increasingly bizarre behaviour. 'I say we will have no moe marriage', exclaims Hamlet in the nunnery scene, but Scythrop, with equal desperation, seeks exactly the opposite (*Hamlet*, 3.1.147). When Mr Glowry hints that Marionetta should leave Nightmare Abbey, Scythrop snatches his ancestor's skull, fills it with Madeira and threatens suicide if she does not remain, a parody of Hamlet's order to Ophelia to 'Get thee to a nunnery' (l. 140) and of the play's poisoned wine. Faced with this suicide threat, the parents agree to the marriage.

Thus, both Hamlet and Scythrop are idealists who fit uncomfortably into the real world. Scythrop's scheme for human social regeneration preoccupies him, as does Hamlet's desire to avenge his father's murder, although Hamlet's project might actually have a chance of success. Both Scythrop and Hamlet meditate, indeed brood, upon their tasks but are loathe to act. Hamlet engages the travelling troupe of players to enact *The Mouse-Trap*, complete with a 'speech of some dozen or sixteen lines, which I would set down and insert in't' (*Hamlet*, 2.2.541–2), in order to verify the truth of his father's death but declines the opportunity to kill Claudius immediately after *The Mouse-Trap* performance; Scythrop determines to write a tragedy, based on the German model, in order to transform mankind, then laments to Glowry that he will sit forever. Scythrop throws himself into his armchair, assuming 'the Hamlet pose' and announces: 'The crisis of my fate is come: the world is a stage, and my direction is *exit*' (*Nightmare Abbey*, p. 89; italics in original). We hear echoes of Hamlet's exclamation of 'My fate cries out' (1.4.81) as he shakes off his friends and follows the ghost of his father. We hear, too, his final resolution before the fencing match with Laertes:

> There is special providence in the fall of a sparrow. If it be [now], 'tis not to come; if it be not to come, it will be now; if it be not now, yet it [will] come – the readiness is all. Since no man, of aught he leaves, knows what is't to leave betimes, let be.
>
> (5.2.219–24)

Ironically, Scythrop has cast himself as Hamlet in his own little drama, a parody of Shakespeare's play within the play but also a parody of the theatrical metaphor that is central to Shakespeare's *Hamlet*.

Like *Nightmare Abbey*, *Northanger Abbey* (completed around 1798 but not published until 1818) uses the all too familiar conventions of Radcliffean Gothic to satirize the incompatibility of literature and life, as well as the social practices that both feed young women with 'heroinical' fantasies and restrict severely their actions. The life-as-theatre metaphor so central to *Nightmare Abbey* informs Jane Austen's *Northanger Abbey* when Henry Tilney stages a little Gothic play, in which he parodies *The Mouse-Trap* from *Hamlet* to expose Catherine Morland as a failed heroine within a drama of her own construction. *Hamlet* was, of course, a play familiar to English audiences. According to John Genest, for instance, Drury Lane or Covent Garden performed *Hamlet* every year from 1778 to 1814, the year that Austen is last known to have attended a theatre. These years also included multiple productions of *Hamlet* in Bath and Bristol.[7] As Penny Gay points out, Austen's life also coincided with the heyday of the Gothic drama that was performed at Bath-Royal Theatre in Orchard Street (1799–1805).[8] Thus, for Austen, *Hamlet* and the Gothic are easily linked together.

For Catherine Morland, as well, familiarity with drama makes her receptive to Gothic plots and atmosphere. From volume 1 of the novel, we learn that Catherine has an interest in fashionable drama and an inclination towards the dramatic. When she and the Tilneys go to the theatre in Bath, Catherine knows that they are accustomed to the finer performances of the London stage, which render everything else, she is told by Isabella, 'quite horrid'.[9] But the real drama for Catherine happens not on the Bath stage but in the boxes, where Henry Tilney and his father join a party, and 'the stage could no longer excite genuine merriment – no longer keep her whole attention' (*Northanger Abbey*, p. 108). As with the performance of *The Mouse-Trap*, the more interesting play occurs offstage. Catherine finds Henry's performance enigmatic, being uncertain about how to read his visual presence and his encoded speech. Darryl Jones points out as well that Henry exerts a kind of destabilized masculinity in his willingness to cross over into the female sphere of fashion and novels, in stark contrast to John Thorpe's normative form of masculinity.[10]

Such gender-bending reflects on issues raised within *Hamlet* itself. In contrast to Henry's condescension toward females, Hamlet's comments on the female sphere are harsh: 'I have heard of your paintings, well enough. God hath given you one face, and you make yourselves another. You jig and amble, and you [lisp], you nickname God's creatures and make your wantonness [your] ignorance' (*Hamlet*, 3.2.142–6). Austen's parody of Shakespeare may take shape, as John Wiltshire points out, not on the surface of the plot but within the structure of Austen's dramatic conflict, her capacity for generating moral and psychological sets of similarities within differences, her sense of an 'integrated world' in her novels, something that could only occur in her internalization of 'Shakespeare'.[11] Catherine's adventures in Bath thus become a series of pseudo-dramatic scenes: the visit to Blaize Castle, her brother's engagement, her conversations with Isabella Thorpe and Henry Tilney; and, just when it seems that this domestic play is about to end, General Tilney invites Catherine to visit Gloucestershire and Northanger Abbey, thrilling words that 'wound up Catherine's feeling to the highest point of extasy' (*Northanger Abbey*, p. 146).

The 'mouse-trap' into which Catherine steps in volume 2 is the private theatrical constructed by Henry Tilney, which Marilyn Butler identifies as a 'burlesque Gothic story'.[12] Although Catherine assures Henry that she will not be frightened at the abbey, he teases her that she will be lodged apart from the rest of the family, 'along many gloomy passages, into an apartment never used since some cousin or kin died in it about twenty years before', 'with only the feeble rays of a single lamp to take in its size – its walls hung with tapestry exhibiting figures as large as life, and the bed, of dark green stuff or purple velvet, presenting even a funereal appearance' (*Northanger Abbey*, p. 161). Henry describes how the housekeeper will hint 'that the part of the abbey [she] inhabit[s] is undoubtedly haunted, and informs [her] that [she] will not have a single domestic within call' (p. 161). According to Henry's script, her door will have no lock, and Catherine will have such 'unconquerable' horror that she will barely sleep. A violent storm will occur on the third night:

Peals of thunder so loud as to seem to shake the edifice to its foundation will roll round the neighbouring mountains – and during
the frightful gusts of wind which accompany it, you will probably
think you discern (for your lamp is now extinguished) one part of
the landing more violently agitated than the rest.

(p. 162)

Despite these Gothic circumstances, Henry claims, Catherine will
be unable to repress her curiosity and become intent on solving a
mystery:

After a very short search, you will discover a division in the tapestry
so artfully constructed as to defy the minutest inspection, and on
opening it, a door will immediately appear – which door being
only secured by massy bars and a padlock, you will, after a few
efforts, succeed in opening – and with your lamp in your hand, will
pass through it into a small vaulted room.

(p. 162)

This room, in turn, leads to the chapel of St Anthony, where
'perhaps there may be a dagger', 'a few drops of blood, perhaps
the remains of some instrument of torture' and a 'large, old-
fashioned cabinet of ebony and gold' containing a 'secret spring
opening an inner compartment', in which may be found the
manuscript memoirs of 'the wretched Matilda' (pp. 162–3). These
Gothic 'stage directions' may well be inspired by productions of
Shakespeare that it is likely Austen saw and recontextualized as
Gothic fiction.[13]

Catherine, who recognizes the Gothic conventions, laughs at
Henry's script but nonetheless internalizes it as her role once she
is at Northanger Abbey. In a more heavy-handed manner,
Shakespeare's Ophelia also is constantly scripted by the males in
her life. When we first see her in *Hamlet*, act 1, scene 3, Laertes is
detailing a script of her seduction by Hamlet, although in deference to her feelings, he employs euphemisms; Polonius, however,
constructs the script in cruder terms. Hamlet likewise scripts the
scene in Ophelia's closet, an encounter unseen by the audience
but described by Ophelia (*Hamlet*, 2.1.74–97). Hamlet, as

Thompson and Taylor note in their Arden edition of the play, evokes the conventions of a languishing lover driven mad (p. 234). Polonius, at whom the performance is also directed, exclaims, 'Mad for thy love?' Ophelia replies, 'My lord, I do not know, / But truly I do fear it' (2.1.82–3). Thus Ophelia, internalizing the role of the desperately beloved, will be shattered in the nunnery scene, in which she also appears as part of Polonius' script, a performance that collapses as Hamlet moves to take over and redirect the 'play'. Ophelia will be less willing to be scripted in her next encounter with Hamlet, which occurs just prior to the performance of *The Mouse-Trap*, even as Hamlet uses sexual double entendre in an attempt to rewrite the encounter as one between lovers, perhaps as a continued performance for Polonius, who calls it to the king's attention when Hamlet rejects his mother's invitation for 'metal more attractive': 'O ho, do you mark that?' (3.2.109, 111), comments Polonius. In the end, Ophelia's resistance proves futile.

Henry's script similarly engulfs Catherine. As a storm rages on the first night of her visit, Catherine, in her chamber, spies an old-fashioned, large, oriental cabinet and determines that it is the basis of a mystery she must solve. Although rationally she has nothing to fear, the sounds of the storm 'brought to her recollection a countless variety of dreadful situations and horrid scenes, which such a building had witnessed, and such storms ushered in' (*Northanger Abbey*, p. 169). Agitated by curiosity but unable to turn the key in the cabinet door, Catherine imagines how the storm 'seemed to speak the awfulness of her situation' (p. 170). When Catherine extinguishes her candle, she is petrified with horror, and a cold sweat appears on her forehead: 'Darkness impenetrable and immovable filled the room. A violent gust of wind, rising with sudden fury, added fresh horror to the moment' (p. 171). Catherine believes that the curtains move, that someone attempts the lock on her door; 'hollow murmurs seemed to creep along the gallery, and more than once her blood was chilled by the sound of distant moans' (p. 172). When Catherine does extricate a roll of paper from the cabinet's cavity, she discovers an inventory of linen – a washing bill from a previous guest – which becomes the culminating point in Austen's parody of *Hamlet's Mouse-Trap*.

Catherine's failures, while they parallel those of Ophelia, are also similar to those of Hamlet who, according to Coleridge, is guilty of 'running into long reasonings while waiting for the ghost, carrying off the impatience and uneasy feelings of expectations by running away from the *particular* in[to] the *general*. This aversion to personal, individual concerns, and escape to generalizations and general reasonings [is] a most important characteristic' of Hamlet (italics in original).[14] Catherine therefore acts as a feminized Hamlet. In a discussion of the evolving critical response to *Hamlet*, R. A. Foakes notes the emergence in the later nineteenth century of an image of Hamlet as 'exquisite, weak, feminine and delicate'.[15] Marjorie Garber, in *Shakespeare After All*, also notes that Hamlet 'seemed to behave in ways that some observers in the late nineteenth century regarded as unmanly'.[16] Is Austen perhaps anticipating, in a more nuanced manner, those late nineteenth-century critics' gendered responses? Austen is, after all, writing during the cultural transition between the Restoration and Victorian periods, so it would not be unusual for her to speak to the ambivalence of her society's attitudes toward gender dichotomies.

In addition, there were, at the time, female Hamlets on the stage. Thompson and Taylor, citing a forthcoming work by Tony Howard, note that Sarah Siddons, sister of John Philip Kemble, 'whose Hamlet dominated the stage between 1783 and 1817', herself 'was an early female Hamlet, performing the role in Birmingham, Bristol, Liverpool and Manchester in the 1780s and reviving it in Dublin in 1802'.[17] We also know from Genest's dramatic records that although Siddons played Hamlet on 27 June 1781 in a Bristol production for one night only, this was the sixth time she had performed the role rather than her customary assignment as Queen Gertrude.[18] Whether or not Austen had the opportunity to see Siddons as Hamlet, she surely would have known of the theatrical cross-dressing that often placed women in this role.[19] Within Austen's own family, there was also a tradition of family theatricals, in which parts were assigned not by gender but by who was present.[20] It is an intriguing possibility that Austen may have known of this and other female Hamlets, but even if she did not, she was certainly capable of recognizing that, just as women are scripted into narrow gender roles, Hamlet is also being scripted into a role that he resists. As Garber notes, many actresses are attracted to the role: 'Women, from Sarah Bernhardt on, have often aspired to be Hamlet rather than Gertrude or Ophelia – not because Hamlet is a woman, but because "mankind" is Hamlet.'[21]

Neither Ophelia nor Catherine can succeed in the script into which the males have inscribed them. Ophelia, in many ways, is a failed comic heroine in that, unlike the heroines of Shakespearean comedy, she listens to her father and places him before the man she loves, and ends by losing both.[22] Catherine, as a failed heroine specifically within the Gothic genre, also does not learn sufficiently from her drama. Instead, she fantasizes about how General Tilney has either dispatched his wife or incarcerated her within the old section of the abbey. Catherine's conjectures are heightened in her mind by the general's reluctance to show her a narrow passage and winding staircase leading to a room, where, she rationalizes, Mrs Tilney probably died or is still incarcerated, 'receiving from the pitiless hands of her husband a nightly supply of coarse food' (*Northanger Abbey*, p. 186). The Shakespearean version of this Gothic plot is, of course, Gertrude's presumed complicity in the murder of her husband Hamlet, king of Denmark; her sin has been to 'kill a king and marry with his brother', Hamlet says (3.4.29), and although Gertrude's bewilderment suggests she was not directly involved, she is nevertheless guilty of an 'o'erhasty marriage' (2.2.57) that, belatedly, she recognizes has traumatized her son. Catherine, in the same vein, muses on the general's supposed behaviour: 'She could remember dozens who had persevered in every possible vice, going on from crime to crime, murdering whomsoever they chose, without any feeling of humanity or remorse; till a violent death or a religious retirement closed their black career' (*Northanger Abbey*, p. 188). Catherine therefore determines to discover proof of the general's crime, perhaps in his wife's fragmented journal.

Austen's Gothic casts aristocratic cruelty as the male exercise of gender prerogative. Like Shakespeare's play within the play, the little drama embedded in *Northanger Abbey* can be read as one that exposes a class and gender privilege sanctioned by the society that the general represents. The general did not torture or kill his wife, but he could have done so, just as he is legally and culturally legitimate in his dismissal of Catherine from Northanger Abbey after he discovers her not to be as rich as he had thought. Like his son, Henry, the general has scripted Catherine into a particular role, and he becomes enraged when she cannot fulfill it, much as Polonius tries to script and control Ophelia. Polonius worries that his daughter might embarrass him politically by making him appear to be a social climber who wishes to marry his daughter to the heir to the throne, or embarrass him personally by presenting him with a child born out of wedlock ('tender me a fool' (1.3.109)). Indeed, General Tilney is exposed as a Polonius, here trying to manipulate a financially advantageous marriage for his son, who is another effeminate male. The general's character thus exposes the misogyny inherent in Gothic, a misogyny also present in *Hamlet* but often left unrecognized in romanticized depictions of the prince of Denmark. Coleridge's description of Polonius may be applied with accuracy to General Tilney, who as 'the skeleton of his own former skill and statecraft, hunts the trail of policy at a dead scent, supplied by the weak fever-smell in his own nostril' (*Northanger Abbey*, p. 148). Polonius himself proclaims:

> Hath there been such a time – I would fain know that –
> That I have positively said, 'Tis so',
> When it proved otherwise?
> …
> If circumstances lead me, I will find
> Where truth is hid, though it were hid indeed
> Within the centre.
>
> (*Hamlet*, 2.2.153–5, 157–9)

Perhaps Austen perceived in this appropriation of Shakespeare the moral instruction that Charles Lamb recognized in *Hamlet*, as a play that 'abounds in maxims and reflections beyond any other'.[23] Catherine gets caught up in a fiction that does not exist, and Henry misreads her reading of the Gothic conventions.

The peformative Gothic

The titles *Northanger Abbey* and *Nightmare Abbey* signify places as settings but could also point to states of mind, narratological borrowings from the dramatic spaces of Denmark and Elsinore Castle in *Hamlet*. Austen's Bath is fictionalized as the 'real' world, in contrast to the imaginative 'other' world of Northanger Abbey, where, as we have seen, a Gothic play is improvised by Henry Tilney to test Catherine Morland's mental capabilities and her imaginative proclivities. In Peacock's novel, Scythrop's abbey is fictionalized as an interiorized space in which characters debate contemporary issues, but it could also symbolize a mental landscape or a dream. Pointing to the performative nature and imaginative settings of Shakespeare's plays in 'The four ages of poetry', Peacock asserts how 'picturesque' Shakespeare's drama is, varied in costume, action and character, 'a picture of nothing that ever was seen on earth, except a Venetian carnival'.[24] Peacock's assertions tell us something about the theatricality of the performances he was seeing at the theatre. Certainly, *Hamlet* opens on a bleak scene, with choppy, nervous dialogue. Instead of the sentinel challenging the man who approaches, that startled replacement cries out, 'Who's there?' and has to be reminded, 'Nay, answer me' (*Hamlet*, 1.1.1–2). It is 'bitter cold' in these very early hours, and the sentinel feels 'sick at heart' (ll. 8–9). As Barnardo begins his tale of 'this thing' (1.21), this 'dreaded sight' (1.25), this 'apparition' (1.28) over the past two nights, the ghost (the thing they cannot bring themselves to name) suddenly interrupts them. The men nervously attempt to question it, but it stalks off. The ensuing discussion of what the ghost's appearance might mean sets up the audience for the shock of its reappearance. The ghost seems at the point of speaking when the cock crows and, as a creature of the night, it must depart. Shakespeare's theatre relied heavily on verbal effects, as well as dramatic suspense, to create the eeriness and jumpiness of this opening scene, but performances on the late eighteenth-century stage could rely on special effects and scenery to create the Gothic picturesque that had come to be associated with Shakespeare. Jane Moody points out how Covent Garden productions of *Hamlet* included scenery, designed by

William Capon, that was modelled on specimens of the Gothic in England, and she notes how this scenery evoked the dramatic world of the Gothic sublime. John Philip Kemble's productions also exploited the visual trappings of Gothic mystery.[25] The Romantic stage effectively Gothicized Shakespeare through its scenery and machinery and its spectacles of sublimity and the picturesque.

We see this predilection for the picturesque in Catherine's passion for ancient edifices, especially castles and abbeys. Her luck makes it possible for her to be on the scene of Northanger Abbey, with its 'long, damp passages, in narrow cells and ruined chapel', and she hopes that she can uncover 'some traditional legends, some awful memorials of an injured and ill-fated nun' (*Northanger Abbey*, p. 147), conventions that invoke Duncan's murder in his host's castle or a sleepwalking Lady Macbeth. Like Macbeth's castle, or more especially the haunted Elsinore Castle of *Hamlet*, Northanger Abbey is painted as a spectacular stage upon which natural and supernatural events unfold. We learn that Northanger Abbey, nestled low in a valley and sheltered from the north and east by woods, had been a richly endowed convent at the time of the Reformation, that it had fallen into the hands of Tilney's ancestors upon its dissolution and that a large portion of the ancient building remained, despite its decay.[26] It is the kind of building that Catherine has read about, one in which she may encounter horrors such as sliding panels and tapestry.

The spectacle Catherine imagines of Northanger Abbey is not unlike that which she mentally creates for Blaize Castle near Bristol in volume 1. When John Thorpe invites Catherine to visit this old castle, Catherine immediately inquires about the edifice's 'towers and long galleries' (*Northanger Abbey*, p. 101), and she enthusiastically anticipates visiting every staircase, every room, every hole and corner of the castle. In reality, as Claire Grogan notes, Blaize Castle was known to readers as a sham, for it was built in 1766 for Bristol sugar merchant Thomas Farr. The castle façade included large circular rooms with three small towers, the tower being Catherine's favourite Gothic feature (p. 101). As with the visitation to Northanger Abbey, which was preconditioned in Catherine's expectations by Henry Tilnery's Gothic prelude, the proposed Blaize Castle visit is set by John Thorpe, who promises that the excursion will include 'broken arches, phaetons and false hangings, Tilneys and trap-doors' (p. 103). Here, the Tilneys are thrown into the setting as Gothic trappings. Catherine conjures 'a long suite of lofty rooms, exhibiting the remains of magnificent furniture, though now for many years deserted ... winding vaults, by a low, grated door ... their only lamp, extinguished by a sudden gust of wind', leaving her 'in total darkness' (p. 104).

Similarly, Peacock's narrator interiorizes all the action of his novel within the mysterious Gothic Nightmare Abbey, in Scythrop's tower study, with its various haunted chambers. According to Robert Kiernan, the mansion in rural Lincolnshire is positioned between the sea and the fens, recognizable symbols of melancholy.[27] As in the Gothicizing of Northanger Abbey, we find that outside the tower of Nightmare Abbey the rolling sound of thunder emanates, thereby creating a theatrical special effect with which a staged *Hamlet* could have begun, as prompt books of productions suggest. We know from eighteenth-century prompt books, for example, that in David Garrick's productions of *Hamlet* Garrick as Hamlet starts, staggers and stares when the ghost enters 'cas'd in canvass', and then, in melodramatic fashion, rises, kicks over his chair and poses in Garrick's characteristic stance, with 'one hand struck out before him and the other brought up close to his body as if to ward off the spectre'.[28] Garrick also introduced doorway entrances and exits for the ghost rather than using the traps located on the floor of the stage. Dramaticus, in the *Gentleman's Magazine* (May 1789), declared it more appropriate for ghosts and aerial spirits to dissolve into plastered walls and wainscot panels than to disappear 'through the gaping mouths of noisy trap-doors, as if spectres resided always in the bowels of the earth'.[29] James Boaden, on the other hand, reports his disdain for Kemble's staging of King Hamlet's ghost in full armour as a tasteless stage exhibition, noting how the great writing and charm of Shakespeare are Gothicized and 'dispelled by the heavy, bulky, creaking substantiality of the spirit instead of looking as if it were collected from the surrounding air and ready to melt into "thin air" again when its impression should be made'.[30]

In Peacock's novel, narratological interiorization is further developed through the characters' perceptions of ghost sightings, and its Gothic setting is inhabited by ghosts that come to symbolize the unspoken fears and repressed knowledge that lie beneath its society's surface. Here, the shadow of the ghost of King Hamlet is specifically signalled by Mr Hilary, who tells the misanthropic group gathered at the abbey – Toobad, Listless, Flosky, Scythrop, Glowry and Cypress – that evidence of the highest genius resides with Shakespeare and Socrates, even as their discussion turns to the subject of apparitions. Listless professes that he has never seen a ghost and hopes that he never will. He insists that they share no more ghost stories, and he adds:

> For though I do not believe in such things, yet, when one is apt, if one thinks of them, to have fancies that give one a kind of a chill, particularly if one opens one's eyes suddenly on one's dressing gown, hanging in the moonlight, between the bed and the window.
>
> (*Nightmare Abbey*, p. 74)

In contrast to Listless's material explanation for the presence of ghosts, Flosky theorizes that most people who claim to see ghosts are deluded by stage trickery: 'In the latter case, a ghost is a *deceptio visus*, an ocular spectrum, an idea with the force of sensation. I have seen many ghosts myself. I dare say there are few in this company who have seen a ghost' (p. 75). For the Reverend Mr Larynx, ghosts are a matter of spiritual understanding, such as the spectres that appeared to the Egyptians during the darkness with which Moses covered Egypt, or the witch of Endor that raised the ghost of Samuel. Mr Hilary asserts a medical explanation, the hallucination of a body compromised in mind and physique, for spectral sightings: 'Persons of feeble, nervous, melancholy temperament, exhausted by fever, by labour, or by spare diet, will readily conjure up, in the magic ring of their own phantasy, spectres, gorgons, chimaeras and all the objects of their hatred and their love' (p. 77).

While the learned conversation emphasizes these supernatural sources of danger, it fails to recognize the real dangers of patriarchal authority and filial transgression that its society shares with Shakespeare's tragedies. As in Shakespeare, scepticism about the 'reality' of ghosts is theatricalized in Gothic fiction, yet ghosts in both works also carry an unspoken and real danger. In *Hamlet*, Horatio scoffs at the report of a ghost sighting – until he sees it with his own eyes. In addressing the ghost, Horatio lists some of the conventional reasons that a ghost walks: needing some action that 'may do thee ease and grace to me', thereby completing what the spirit left undone on earth; 'being privy to thy country's fate' and so coming to warn it of impending attack; or having 'extorted treasure in the womb of earth', and thus needing to break this earthly connection by passing that wealth on to the living (1.1.130–7). What Horatio avoids mentioning is the most obvious reason that a ghost would walk: the person was murdered. When that person was the king, then it becomes an issue of political assassination and, indeed, of treason. Ghosts thus become Gothicized signifiers for the unacknowledged and unspoken dangers that truly threaten these societies.

Flosky and company struggle to grasp the meanings of the Gothicized signifiers that they integrate into their own writing, and so they turn to Shakespeare. Another theatricalized scene occurs in *Nightmare Abbey* when Scythrop's and Glowry's conversation in the tower study is interrupted by a loud noise behind the bookcase, which mysteriously moves to reveal an interior apartment in which Stella (in reality, Toobad's daughter Celinda) has been hiding. During his many hours of study, Scythrop has seen Stella, cloaked as a Gothic, feminine stranger sitting at his writing table, and when he inquires as to her name, she quotes Shakespeare: 'What is a name?' (*Nightmare Abbey*, p. 60, referring to *Romeo and Juliet*, 2.2.43). Thomas Schmid points out how important 'naming' is to the novel and, specifically, how it functions as Glowry's way of Gothicizing the world.[31] This scene parallels an earlier one in the novel in which Flosky sat in the study in a dazed frenzy, turning his gaze on Marionetta 'as if she had been the ghostly ladie of magical vision' (p. 60). She inspires his writing of a ballad, all mystery and indebted to Shakespeare's *The Tempest*, for it will be 'such stuff / As dreams are made on' (p. 49, referring to 4.1.155–6). Like Bottom's 'most rare vision' of *A Midsummer Night's Dream* (5.1.205), Flosky's ballad will be a product of his reverie and have no foundation, or 'bottom' (p. 49); the ballad cannot be explicated or explained logically, for it is beyond words. In these two scenes, Peacock's narrator raises the very question posed by Hamlet at the beginning of his tragedy: is the ghost real or merely a result of his imagination and grief? The key to the parody in *Nightmare Abbey* is mystery, what Flosky calls the 'mental element' (p. 7). Do readers, such as Flosky, Scythrop and Hamlet, live in the midst of a visionary world in which, as Flosky says, quoting Shakespeare, 'nothing is / But what is not' (p. 7, referring to *Macbeth*, 1.4.141–2), and where we dream with our eyes open?

The performance of reading, and of opening eyes and minds, was an act of legitimization surrounded by considerable controversy during the late eighteenth century. Anxieties about a reading bourgeoisie and critically thinking women comprise some of the shadows haunting *Nightmare Abbey* and *Northanger Abbey*. Flosky admonishes his colleagues in *Nightmare Abbey* that the current rage for 'novelty' is the bane of literature, perhaps offering Peacock's self-reflexive statement about his own novel. Flosky's observations reflect his misogyny, and he asserts that British literature is hag ridden, suggesting that it is being infiltrated by writers like Jane Austen:

> That part of the *reading public* which shuns the solid food of reason for the light diet of fiction, requires a perpetual adhibition of *sauce piquante* to the palate of its depraved imagination. It lived upon ghosts, goblins and skeletons … till even the devil himself … became too base, common, and popular, for its surfeited appetite.
>
> (*Nightmare Abbey*, p. 33; italics in original)

If, as Diane Hoeveler suggests, Austen has refined the Gothic so as to expose the false premises and inadequate stereotypes upon which the genre was based, she has enlisted Shakespeare in her project of legitimatization. Gothic readers were, Michael Gamer reminds us, as likely to be men as women and to be from various educational backgrounds.[32]

Peacock's and Austen's approach to the issue of the legitimization of the Gothic yet again invokes Shakespeare's *Hamlet*. At the time when this play was first acted, the adult companies were facing a challenge from the children's companies. These private theatres, with more exclusive audiences, cultivated a new, sharply satiric drama that often got them, and sometimes the adult companies, into trouble with the political authorities. In a society in which discussions of the legitimacy of the theatre were ongoing and where the ability to perform rested on official sanction, crossing the line could have political and national consequences. Hamlet asks Rosencrantz why the players are travelling, since performing at the home theatre would be more profitable. He is told of the 'aery of children, little eyases, that cry out on the top of question, [and] are most tyrannically clapp'd for't. These are now the fashion and so [berattle] the common stages – so they call them – that many wearing rapiers are afraid of goose-quills, and dare scarce come thither' (2.2.339–44). And yet, theatre history shows that the challenge to the adult stage by the boys' companies revitalized the drama.[33] Long after the boys' companies ceased to exist – very likely the reason why these lines appear in the second quarto but not the folio text of *Hamlet*, when they were no longer relevant – more cutting-edge satire had become legitimated on the stage. Shakespeare, like Peacock and Austen, knew that literature grows when it absorbs what is popular, even faddish, and reinvents it.

Much criticism has been proffered about the Gothic novels Catherine Morland and Isabella Thorpe enjoy reading in *Northanger Abbey*, an activity that the novel's narrator admonishes as 'performance' and in parodic terms:

> For I will not adopt that ungenerous and impolitic custom so common with novel writers, of degrading by their contemptuous censure the very performances, to the number of which they are themselves adding – joining with their greatest enemies in bestowing the harshest epithets on such works, and scarcely ever permitting them to be read by their own heroine, who, if she accidentally takes up a novel, is sure to turn over its insipid pages with disgust.
>
> (*Northanger Abbey*, pp. 59–60)

Isabella Thorpe, Eleanor Tilney, and Catherine Morland, we learn, are not the only avid readers of Gothic novels, for Henry Tilney confesses to having read Ann Radcliffe's *The Mysteries of Uldopho* and other popular Gothic fiction, which he justifies with the claim that he, unlike female readers, can ascertain the fine differences between history and fable, between discussions of the picturesque and dramatizations of the spectacular, between coquettish teasing and earnest reporting: 'Perhaps the abilities of women are neither sound nor acute – neither vigorous nor deep. Perhaps they may want observation, discernment, judgement, fire, genius, wit' (p. 126). Austen suggests here that three female readers and one male reader can discern distinctly different meanings in Gothic fiction. And, indeed, Catherine's reading skills are exposed for their inability to discern 'novel' crises from actual political threats, her conflation of instruction with torture. She sees the world as a stage and its players through the lens of fiction, and that is what makes her such a malleable performer for Henry's own Gothic theatrical at Northanger Abbey.

For Jacqueline Pearson, Austen betrays her awareness of the cultural politics that presented women's reading as a dangerous act.[34] Reading the national Bard's plays, as both Catherine and Austen suggest, requires the same kind of critical and discerning eye as reading a Gothic novel. At the end of *Northanger Abbey*, Catherine recognizes that her critical facilities have been influenced by the kind of reading that she has been doing, and she vows to 'act' with better judgement and good sense in the future, to become a 'resisting reader' – although she will continue to enjoy a good mystery, even a Gothic now and then, as the narrator remarks: '*She* could allow, that an occasional memento of past folly, however painful, might not be without use' (*Northanger Abbey*, p. 197; italics in original).

Northanger Abbey, like *Nightmare Abbey*, invites readers to consider the values that they bring to their reading, as Bharat Tandon points out, but we would add that these two Gothic parodies achieve self-awareness through their satires of work with 'national' significance and recognition. Tandon notes that Austen's placement of Catherine's largely misquoted snippets of Shakespeare makes performative fun of the quotations as detachable, portable qualities and, similarly, that her references to the 'horrid novels' of the Gothic are reduced to fantastic episodes out of context.[35] Part of the playfulness of *Nightmare Abbey* and *Northanger Abbey* occurs in the recognition of the Shakespearean shadows to which Gothic fiction is indebted. The Bard's presence testifies to the complexity of the Gothic fiction that, through parody, appropriated his work as a stage upon which late eighteenth-century social anxieties could be performed.

Notes

[1] Steven E. Jones, 'Introduction: forms of satire in the Romantic period', in Steven E. Jones (ed.), *The Satiric Eye: Forms of Satire in the Romantic Period* (New York: Palgrave Macmillan, 2003), pp. 1–9, asserts that satire marks a place outside of Romanticism from which to access its construction, while Kyle Grimes, 'Verbal jujitsu: William Hone and the tactics of satirical conflict', in ibid., pp. 173–84, points out that parody opens a channel between a model text and the parody that operates dialogically. Marshall Brown, *The Gothic Text* (Stanford: Stanford University Press, 2005) argues that Gothic novels are speculative constructs built upon supernatural devices in Shakespearean, Restoration and eighteenth-century tragedy (pp. 34–43).

[2] William Hazlitt, 'Mr Kean's Hamlet', in William Archer and Robert Lowe (eds), *Hazlitt on Theatre* (New York: Hill and Wang, 1957), p. 9.

[3] Samuel Taylor Coleridge, *Table Talk*, in Terence Hawkes (ed.), *Coleridge's Writings on Shakespeare: A Selection of the Essays, Notes and Lectures of Samuel Taylor Coleridge on the Poems and Plays of Shakespeare* (New York: Capricorn Books, 1959), p. 139.

[4] Howard Mills, *Peacock: His Circle and His Age* (Cambridge: Cambridge University Press, 1969), pp. 137–8; Carl Dawson, *Thomas Love Peacock* (London: Routledge and Kegan Paul, 1968), pp. 50–94. Julia M. Wright, 'Peacock's early parody of Thomas Moore in *Nightmare Abbey*', *English Language Notes*, 30 (1993), 31–8, identifies the Reverend Mr Larynx with Thomas Moore as well as with Peacock himself. Most readings of *Nightmare Abbey* associate Flosky with Coleridge and Scythrop with P. B. Shelley.

[5] All references to Shakespeare's works are to *The Riverside Shakespeare*, ed. G. Blakemore Evans et al. (2nd edn; Boston: Houghton Mifflin, 1997). Further references will be incorporated into the body of the text.

[6] Thomas Love Peacock, *Nightmare Abbey* (London: Hamish Hamilton, 1947), p. 16. Further references will be incorporated into the body of the text.

[7] John Genest, *Some Account of the English Stage from the Restoration in 1660 to 1830* (10 vols; Bath: H. E. Carrington, 1832), records a production of *Hamlet*

every season from 1778–1814; see volumes 6–8. According to Paula Byrne, Austen last attended the theatre on 28 November 1814 (*Jane Austen and the Theatre* (London: Hambledon and London, 2002), p. 46).

8   Penny Gay, *Jane Austen and the Theatre* (Cambridge: Cambridge University Press, 2002), pp. 52–3.

9   Jane Austen, *Northanger Abbey*, ed. Claire Grogan (Peterborough, Ont: Broadview Literary Texts, 1996), p. 108. Further references will be incorporated into the body of the text.

10   Darryl Jones, *Critical Issues: Jane Austen* (Houndmills: Palgrave Macmillan, 2004), pp. 45–6.

11   John Wiltshire, *Recreating Jane Austen* (Cambridge: Cambridge University Press, 2001), pp. 62–75.

12   Marilyn Butler, *Jane Austen and the War of Ideas* (1975; reprint, Oxford: Oxford University Press, 1987), p. 175.

13   Most stage directions either are added by editors of Shakespeare or created by performers, causing a stage history to evolve independent of the text. Whether they are 'Shakespeare' or not, such stage directions influence audience reception of the play. See Margaret Jane Kidnie, 'Where is *Hamlet*? Text, performance and adaptation', in Barbara Hodgdon and W. B. Worthen (eds), *A Companion to Shakespeare and Performance* (Malden, MA: Blackwell, 2005), pp. 101–20; and Leah Marcus, 'Shakespearean editing and why it matters', *Literature Compass*, 2 (2005), 1–5.

14   Coleridge, 'The character of Hamlet', in Hawkes (ed.), *Coleridge's Writings on Shakespeare*, p. 157.

15   R. A. Foakes, *Hamlet Versus Lear: Cultural Politics and Shakespeare's Art* (Cambridge: Cambridge University Press, 1993), p. 24.

16   Marjorie Garber, *Shakespeare After All* (New York: Anchor Books, 2004), p. 493.

17   William Shakespeare, *Hamlet*, ed. Ann Thompson and Neil Taylor (3rd Arden edn; London: Thomson Learning, 2006), p. 100.

18   Genest, *Some Account*, vol. 6, p. 211.

19   Elizabeth Reitz Mullenix, *Wearing the Breeches: Gender on the Antebellum Stage* (New York: St Martin's Press, 2000), records the popularity of Charlotte Cushman and Mary Barnes as Hamlet on British and American stages (pp. 96–122). See also Lisa Merrill, *When Romeo Was a Woman: Charlotte Cushman and Her Circle of Female Spectators* (Ann Arbor: University of Michigan Press, 1999), pp. 131–5.

20   For discussions about the Austen family private theatricals, see Byrne, *Austen and the Theatre*, pp. 3–28 and Gay, *Austen and the Theatre*, pp. 3–6 and 63–72.

21   Garber, *Shakespeare After All*, p. 494.

22   Carol Thomas Neely, *Broken Nuptials in Shakespeare's Plays* (New Haven: Yale University Press, 1985), *passim*, has observed that the test of whether a woman in Shakespeare's plays is prepared for marriage is whether she can put her future husband ahead of her father, while for a man, it is whether he can put a future wife ahead of his male friends. Ophelia fails this test.

23   Charles Lamb, 'On the tragedies of Shakspear considered with reference to

their fitness for stage representation', in Joan Coldwell (ed.), *Charles Lamb on Shakespeare* (Gerrards Cross: Colyn Smythe, 1978), p. 29.

24 Thomas Love Peacock, 'The four ages of poetry', in H. F. B. Brett-Smith (ed.), *Peacock's 'Four Ages of Poetry', Shelley's 'Defense of Poetry', Browning's 'Essay on Shelley'* (Oxford: Basil Blackwell, 1947), pp. 12–13.

25 Jane Moody, 'Romantic Shakespeare', in Stanley Wells and Sarah Stanton (eds), *The Cambridge Companion to Shakespeare on Stage* (Cambridge: Cambridge University Press, 2002), p. 47.

26 According to Robert Miles, Catherine reads the world Gothically: 'The 1790s: the effulgence of Gothic', in Jerrold E. Hogle (ed.), *The Cambridge Companion to the Gothic* (Cambridge: Cambridge University Press, 2002), pp. 41–62. Gay adds that Austen theatricalizes the English landscape in the fashion of De Loutherbourg's Gothic stage pictures (*Austen and the Theatre*, pp. 68–9).

27 Robert F. Kiernan, *Frivolity Unbound: Six Masters of the Camp Novel: Thomas Love Peacock, Max Beerbohm, Ronald Firbank, E. F. Benson, P. G. Wodehouse, Ivy Compton-Burnett* (New York: Continuum, 1990), p. 29

28 Kalman A. Burnim, *David Garrick, Director* (Carbondale: Southern Illinois University Press, 1973), pp. 167–8.

29 Quoted in ibid., p. 168.

30 James Boaden, *Memoirs of the Life of John Philip Kemble, esq., Including a History of the Stage, from the Time of Garrick to the Present Period* (2 vols; London: Longman, Hurst, Rees, Orme, Brown and Green, 1825), vol. 2, p. 98. Alan R. Young, *Hamlet and the Visual Arts, 1709–1900* (Newark: University of Delaware Press, 2002), explains that John Bell's illustrated editions of Shakespeare (1773–4) were actually based on prompt books from Drury Lane and Covent Garden, resulting in textual evidence of what audiences might have seen and heard onstage (p. 63). See also E. J. Clery's discussion of Garrick in the ghost scenes from *Hamlet* in *The Rise of Supernatural Fiction, 1762–1800* (New York: Cambridge University Press, 1995), pp. 40–9.

31 Thomas H. Schmid, *Humor and Transgression in Peacock, Shelley and Byron: A Cold Carnival* (Lewiston, NY: Edwin Mellen, 1992), p. 118.

32 Diane Long Hoeveler, *Gothic Feminism: The Professionalization of Gender from Charlotte Smith to the Brontës* (University Park: Pennsylvania State University Press, 1998), p. 143; Michael Gamer, *Romanticism and the Gothic: Genre, Reception and Canon Formation* (Cambridge: Cambridge University Press, 2000), p. 140. For Peter Know-Shaw, *Jane Austen and the Enlightenment* (Cambridge: Cambridge University Press, 2004), *Northanger Abbey* as Gothic romance or as liberal history is equally validated for its popularity and for the education of young women (Brown, *The Gothic Text*, pp. 117–18). Our reading suggests that Austen's Gothic novel demonstrates far more complexity and nuanced meanings than Brown's characterization of Gothic writing as apprentice writing (pp. 162–3).

33 For a discussion of this impact, see R. A. Foakes, 'Tragedy at the children's

---

theatres after 1600: a challenge to the adult stage', in David Galloway (ed.), *The Elizabethan Theatre, II* (Toronto: Archon Books, 1970), pp. 37–59.

34 Jacqueline Pearson, *Women's Reading in Britain, 1750–1835: A Dangerous Recreation* (Cambridge: Cambridge University Press, 1999), pp. 145–6.

35 Bharat Tandon, *Jane Austen and the Morality of Conversation* (London: Anthem Press, 2003), pp. 67–8.

5

Fatherly and Daughterly Pursuits: Mary Shelley's Matilda and Shakespeare's King Lear

CAROLYN A. WEBER

Better thou hadst not been born than not t' have pleas'd me better.

William Shakespeare, *King Lear*

On 2 April 1819, only a few months before beginning *Matilda*, Mary Shelley records her careful rereading of *King Lear*.[1] Written, revised and copied between 4 August and 9 November 1819, this novella, which Shelley referred to directly as her 'journal of sorrow', is a text of mourning.[2] Not only had she just lost a beloved child named for her father, William Godwin, but she had also been living in 'exile' from father and fatherland. Godwin responded to his grandson's death with an icy aloofness. In her depression, Shelley's creative work ceased, and she entered into sexual as well as emotional isolation from her husband, who had also failed to empathize fully with her grief. All of Shelley's previous constructions of herself – as mother, daughter, lover, author – seemed to be thrown into question. But she finished her new work. When the manuscript was complete, she sent it to her father. Godwin found *Matilda*'s subject 'disgusting and detestable' and withheld the manuscript from his daughter, despite her repeated attempts to retrieve it. As a result, the text was not published until 1959.[3]

The novella consists of the letter the heroine Mathilda writes on her deathbed. It is directed to Woodville, a lovelorn poet whom she had befriended after exiling herself from the only home she had ever known. She tells the tale of her suffering in order to explain her heartbroken will to die. Mathilda had spent a solitary childhood with a spinster aunt, who cared for her after her mother had died giving birth to her. Mathilda's father, inconsolable with grief, had then abandoned her. When the father suddenly returns, he begins to shower her with the affection she has never known and always craved. Increasingly, he confuses Mathilda with her dead mother Diana, and to the daughter's horror but also joy, Mathilda begins to discover her own attraction to her father. One day, he confesses his passion. Mathilda faints and awakes to find him gone. She pursues him to the edge of the sea, only to find a lifeless corpse. She feigns her own death and departs to live alone. Content to be publicly seen as mad, Mathilda privately identifies herself as an actress with a part to play in a tragedy whose ultimate hope lies with death, so that she may be eternally reconciled with her father in a blissful afterlife.

Shelley's scandalous plot – and her allusion to Alfieri's *Myrrha* – have inevitably attracted critics to the story's theme of incest.[4] I want to argue, however, that Mary's study of *King Lear*, in close proximity to the rebirth of her narrative gifts, reflects not only a reworking of this canonical father–daughter paradigm replete with Gothic qualities such as pathos, fear and suspense, but also an engagement with Shakespeare. *King Lear* offered Shelley a paradigm through which to explore the 'silence' of a daughter's 'nothingness', whether imposed or chosen. She casts herself as a 'speaking' or 'writing' daughter trying to please an 'irrational', unpredictable and even emotionally (if not worse) abusive patriarchy – doomed to discover its folly too late, a system in which the destruction of the daughter is essential to the ironic redemption of the father. Even the publication history surrounding Shelley's story echoes the plot of *King Lear*, in which a proud father renouncing his kingdom withholds property, and thus power and influence, from his beloved but 'transgressing' daughter.

Like the Romantics in general and Gothic writers in particular, Shelley no doubt appropriates Shakespeare as a means of claiming authority and literary respectability.[5] Harold Bloom, after all, calls Lear '*the* image of the father, the metaphor of paternal authority'.[6] As a literary daughter, however, Shelley may also illustrate Lucy Newlyn's rejoinder to Bloom, that as a solitary woman writing amidst an expatriot coterie of literary men, she experiences an 'anxiety of reception'.[7] These tensions surface in *Matilda* as the daughter becomes 'omnipotent', in both constructive and destructive terms: that is, all sources and acts of desire in the text – whether they are for creation, passion, retribution, death, redemption, reunion or posterity – are ultimately traceable to the daughter. Aimee Boutin's argument for the way in which Shakespeare shaped 'the gendered aesthetics of French Romanticism' illuminates Shelley's attraction to Cordelia. For Boutin, women writers' 'interest in Shakespeare's heroines may have been influenced by prevailing judgements about the superior characterization of women in his plays … Interest in Shakespeare's heroines focussed not merely on their variety but on the alternative model of gender that they brought with them.'[8] 'What am I writing?' Mathilda asks herself in the beginning of the text (p. 5).[9] We soon learn that she writes for herself – for the generation of her own thoughts and ideas, and for future generations. I suggest that the novella expresses a yearning for personal as well as professional acceptance and fulfilment within gender-distinct modes of production.

My examination of Shelley's appropriation, as a female Gothicist, of Shakespeare follows three tracks. First, Mathilda suggests Cordelia as the prototype of the 'good daughter' who suffers at the hand of an irrational patriarch; 'good daughtership', however, becomes problematized when we recognize that Cordelia's character is complex, even contradictory. She is not simply a sacrificial daughter. Secondly, the affinities between Shakespeare's and Shelley's fathers and daughters question the role of forgiveness in such conflicts. Finally, in *Matilda* Shelley conflates traits from both Cordelia and Lear to illustrate the interrelations between, and necessary interdependence, of victims and aggressors in power politics.[10]

Negotiating 'Nothing': property, propriety and power

King Lear's opening scene establishes the theme that dominates *Matilda*, and, by extension, much of Mary Shelley's work: the problem of 'progeny' in all of its variant symbolic ramifications. Upon the arrival of his daughters and their suitors, Lear announces:

> Meantime we shall express our darker purpose.
> Give me the map there. Know that we have divided
> In three our kingdom; and 'tis our fast intent
> To shake all cares and business from our age,
> Conferring them on younger strengths, while we
> Unburthen'd crawl toward death.
>
> (1.1.36–41)[11]

King Lear is concerned with parents and children, or, more specifically, with the legacy 'of cares and business' that the old impart to the young. The play greets us with a father's plans made in the face of impending death; we have the proposition of Lear's 'will', in both of its senses. *Matilda*, too, begins in this way, with a narrator close to death creating a literary testament while also asserting her resolve, or will, to tell her story. The anxiety over who shall receive property upon the protagonist's death – whether kingdoms political or publishable – pervades, and already begins to erode, the establishment of that protagonist as a self-professed figurehead. *Matilda* begins with the end, so to speak; at the story's opening, Mathilda has assumed the patriarchal seat, having usurped her father's place as ruler over her passions, her life story, her audience and even her will to die. Only as she begins to retrace her story do we see her return to a Cordelia-like figure, before she morphs once again, through madness (although she states that 'I never was mad'), into a character more reminiscent of the powerful and yet pitiful Lear (p. 43).

In this first scene, Lear continues with his 'ultimatum':

> Tell me, my daughters
> (Since now we will divest us both of rule,

> Interest of territory, cares of state),
> Which of you shall we say doth love us most,
> That we our largest bounty may extend
> Where nature doth with merit challenge?
>
> (1.1.48–53)

One of the main issues at stake is the division of power through the inheritance of property and therefore the related issue of dominion. Lear's words also establish the play's central concern with old and new orders. Lear tries to manipulate the 'natural' order of things by imposing conditions that ironically disadvantage those who ethically deserve the inheritance of power. Shakespeare makes his patriarch self-professedly omnipotent, even godlike, in his use of the royal 'we' pronoun. Later, after his physical and symbolic stripping, Lear switches to the more personal and relatively less self-important 'I'. But, for now, the stage has been set for Cordelia to enter into a political, not a personal, discourse with her father.

It is not surprising, then, that as the truths of Lear and Cordelia clash, so do their modes of expressing these truths. The patriarch speaks with a public and plural voice representative of his platform of power, while the daughter sidesteps participating in the father's discourse by opting for silence, then an ironic reiteration of the word 'nothing'. Following the 'affection inquisition' of her sisters, Lear turns to Cordelia, his youngest and most favoured daughter, and asks for testimony of her love. A symbolic exchange, ironically pinned on 'nothing', ensues. To Lear's command to 'Speak', Cordelia replies, 'Nothing, my lord' (1.1.86–7). The exchange continues:

> *Lear.* Nothing?
> *Cordelia*: Nothing.
> *Lear.* Nothing will come of nothing, speak again.
> *Cordelia*: Unhappy that I am, I cannot heave
> My heart into my mouth. I love your Majesty
> According to my bond, no more nor less.
> *Lear.* How, how, Cordelia? Mend your speech a little,
> Lest you may mar your fortunes.
>
> (ll. 87–94)

Words are bound to clash with silence when one discourse oppresses the other. Mathilda's father and Lear (and, incidentally, Godwin) require that their daughters 'mend their speech'. In doing so, they impose a patriarchal, or masculine, mode of expression upon the feminine, thus denying them their daughtership, as defined by their own 'voices' or truth. By decreeing that Cordelia must 'name' her love for him, Lear forces his daughter into an 'Adamic' mode of being. Cordelia, however, subverts such an imposition by choosing 'nothingness', which she then qualifies with her own definition of love and duty as divided between two 'types' of lovers: her father and her husband. Mathilda practises her own form of subversion by forcing her father to speak the unspeakable. Those forced to speak thus seal their fate, destroying themselves by the truth that their love ironically prevents them from speaking.[12] 'What shall Cordelia speak? Love, and be silent' (1.1.62). Daughters placed in such precarious positions by their fathers choose silence out of despair, or out of futility; they refuse to play a game at which they cannot win.

Does anyone, in the end, 'win' at such a game? The Romantics, a suspicious lot, were well on their way to identifying something more complex within Shakespeare's heroine than her existence as a simple abstraction of 'pure' redemptive femininity, or 'good' daughterliness. Such astute theatre critics as Hazlitt, Barbauld and Coleridge recognized in *King Lear* an interdependence between father and daughter resulting from their multifarious pursuits of each other. As they noted, Cordelia was not simply a type, or a foil, or a 'good daughter' who can be easily dismissed. Of Cordelia's response to Lear, Coleridge writes:

> There is something of disgust at the ruthless hypocrisy of her sisters, and some little faulty admixture of pride and sullenness in Cordelia's 'Nothing'; and her tone is well contrived, indeed, to lessen the glaring absurdity of Lear's conduct, but answers the yet more important purpose of forcing away the attention from the nursery-tale, the moment it has served its end, that of supplying the canvass for the picture.[13]

In another instance, Hazlitt draws attention to the way in which the 'indiscreet simplicity' of Cordelia's love 'to be sure, has a little of her father's obstinacy in it'.[14] As Stephen Booth asserts, 'Cordelia does not *sound* like a victim'. Booth raises a discomfort that the audience gradually faces with 'the favoured daughter' and echoes Hazlitt in his alignment of Cordelia, ultimately, with her father:

> When Cordelia's turn comes to bid in Lear's auction, she voices our contempt for the oily speeches of Goneril and Regan and for the premises behind the whole charade. We are relieved to hear the bubbles pricked, but Cordelia's premises do not present a clear antithesis to the faults in Lear's. Her ideas are only a variation on Lear's: she too thinks of affection as a quantitative, portionable medium of exchange for goods and services (1.1.95–104). Moreover, she sounds priggish. When she parries Lear's 'So young, and so untender?' with 'so young, my lord, and true', we share her triumph and her righteousness. We exult with her, but we may well be put off by the cold competence of our Cinderella. We agree with Kent when he says that she thinks justly and has 'most rightly said' (1.1.83), but we are probably much more comfortable with his passionate speeches on her behalf than we were with her own crisp ones ... Cordelia is justified in all that she says, but not lovable. [15]

When it comes to her relationship to her father and her construction of herself within her own story, Mathilda admits to having a 'dove's look and fox's heart: for indeed I felt only the degradation of falsehood, and not any sacred sentiment of conscious innocence that might redeem. I who had before clothed myself in the bright garb of sincerity must borrow one of divers colours' (p. 41). Her reference to the fox, an animal traditionally associated with craftiness, becomes loaded in light of Lear's comment to Cordelia later in the play when they are reconciled: 'He that parts us shall bring a brand from heaven, / And fire us hence like foxes' (5.3.22–3). Do daughters in fact learn how to 'act' from their fathers? Do they own, ultimately, the same desires, manipulations, powers and weaknesses? Father and daughter may, in fact, not be as dissimilar as initial appearances would lead us to believe.

Heading the advent of criticism on *Matilda*, Anne K. Mellor reads the story as one of biographical and fantastical subversion on behalf of its author: 'In her fantasy, Mary reverses the power dynamic of her relationship with Godwin. Now it is the father, not the daughter, who loves with an overwhelming and self-destructive passion.'[16] This fugue, or shifting of pursuits/obsessions, characterizes the texts of both *King Lear* and *Matilda* (and of *Frankenstein*, for that matter). In *King Lear*, the father demands the love of his daughters, all but one of whom speak on cue. This last daughter believes it more 'loving' not to speak, and certainly not to enter into the verbal game of deceit and mockery played by her two sisters. At the play's opening, the aged and inse-cure patriarch pursues love on a superficial level; he abuses his power to evoke this love, he equates it with verbosity and he rewards it with property. The 'good daughter' seeks her father's approval, too, but through her own appeal to truth and through a realism that betrays just how torn she feels between her bonds as a child (to her father) and her responsibilities as a sexual being (to her husband) and, ultimately, as a parent herself:

> Happily, when I shall wed,
> That lord whose hand must take my plight shall carry
> Half my love with him, half my care and duty.
> Sure I shall never marry like my sisters,
> To love my father all.
>
> (1.1.100–4)

It is Cordelia's love for another that would detract from her full devotion to her father or, put another way, the father's loss of his daughter that sends Lear into a crazed rage. He curses her and disclaims all 'paternal care', relegating her to the status of a 'some-time daughter' (ll.113, 120). Thus, the relationship between Lear and Cordelia can be read as one of fatherly obsession with the favoured daughter, perhaps (in revisionist readings) even implying incestuous desire.

Lear's irrational anger, like that of Mathilda's father, surfaces uncontrollably when he faces the possibility of his daughter's having a suitor, another man who will 'infringe' on her love for him, which is his paternal right. Reminiscent of *Frankenstein's* plot, Mathilda's father admits how Mathilda's 'disloyalty' awoke the 'fiend' in him:

But when I saw you become the object of another's love; when I imagined that you might be loved otherwise than as a sacred type and image of loveliness and excellence; or that you might love another with a more ardent affection than that which you bore to me, then the fiend awoke within me; I dismissed your lover; and from that moment I have known no peace.

(p. 34)

In both texts, the father is a Gothic villain: a dark, unknowable figure obsessed with complete ownership, even to the point of annihilation, of the motherless, passionately pursued daughter who occupies both a submissive and subversive role in the family politic.

Godwin required that his daughter attend Samuel Taylor Coleridge's lectures on Shakespeare.[17] At the time, Mary Godwin would have been an impressionable adolescent, about the same age as Mathilda when she begins to construct herself as the innocent, exiled and tragic Cordelia. Like Cordelia, Mathilda represents all of the elements of the Gothic female victim: she is the favoured daughter, the cursed daughter, the wronged daughter, the pursued daughter, the ethereal daughter and, ultimately, the daughter who must be sacrificed for the redemption of the initially haughty but eventually broken father. Like Cordelia, but perhaps even more so, Mathilda also cuts an ambiguous figure that cannot be dismissed as completely powerless, guileless or 'victimesque'. Diane Hoeveler identifies just such a fissure that is relevant to Shelley's characterization of Mathilda:

The female Gothic constitutes what I would call a rival female-created fantasy – Gothic feminism – a version of 'victim feminism', an ideology of female power through pretended and staged weakness. Such an ideology positions women as innocent victims who deserve to be rewarded with the ancestral estate because they were unjustly persecuted by the corrupt patriarch. If the heroines manage, inadvertently of course, to cause the deaths of these patriarchs, so much the better ... The Gothic feminist always manages to dispose of her enemies without dirtying her dainty little hands. The position that Radcliffe and her followers advocated throughout the female Gothic was one of 'wise passiveness' or what we might more accurately recognize as a form of passive-aggression.[18]

In her discussion of Godwin's influence on *Matilda*, Pamela Clemit traces the ambiguous construction of Mathilda's character back to the role of the father in Mary Shelley's own life:

> Like other self-justifying Godwinian protagonists, Mathilda presents herself as the victim of a 'hideous necessity', presided over by 'malignant fate' ... Just as Godwin's use of the flawed narrator invites the reader to play an active interpretative role, so too the ambiguities and contradictions of Mathilda's narrative assign to the reader the task of evaluating her guilt or innocence.[19]

Our impressions of Mathilda are forced to fluctuate along with her narrative. In the tradition of the Gothic, the audience is made uncomfortable, and the ability to make judgements rationally and objectively is thrown into question. The female Gothic takes this one step further, as Hoeveler's and Clemit's arguments elucidate. From the perspective of the author-daughter, Godwin's claim to represent 'things as they are' becomes 'things may not be as they appear to be'.[20]

An example of the ambiguous construction of such 'victimized' daughters surfaces in the descriptions of how both heroines, Cordelia and Mathilda, respond to their fathers. When, for instance, Kent asks a gentleman for a report on Cordelia's reaction to her father's letters indicating his suffering, the gentleman replies:

> Ay, sir, she took them, read them in my presence,
> And now and then an ample tear trill'd down
> Her delicate cheek. It seem'd she was a queen
> Over her passion, who, most rebel-like,
> Sought to be king o'er her.

(4.3.12–16)

The gentleman's choice of images here is telling. Cordelia, the political queen, seeks to rule over her passion, cast here as a masculine force, or king. The fact that her husband and father are also kings makes this image even more revealing. The gentleman continues to describe Cordelia in contradictory terms, as 'sunshine and rain at once', a chameleon that both laughs and cries, with 'ripe lips' and diamonds for eyes that drop pearl tears (4.3.18, 22). From one angle, the gentleman's words can be seen as sincerely flattering: Cordelia, the loving daughter, has a warm and generous heart that has been touched by her father's situation, and her grief only makes her more beautiful. Yet Cordelia wears her sorrow as a jewel; the gentleman's words openly sexualize and commodify her. His depiction therefore suggests the incongruous state of Cordelia's emotional being. While we must remember that this is the gentleman's construction of her as he speaks to another man, the description does raise the question of whether Cordelia is casting herself as a dramatic, tragic actress and as a daughter in paradoxical pursuit to and from the father.

Mathilda's character betrays this same ambiguity. Upon hearing her father's confession, for instance, she claims that 'at one moment in pity for his sufferings I would have clasped my father in my arms; and then starting back with horror, I spurned him with my foot' (p. 28). Mathilda is both moved and repulsed by the father's final admission of love for her. As a result, throughout the rest of the text she oscillates between despair and elation. While grieving for her father, Mathilda's words call forth Cordelia's response of 'nothing': 'I was in no state of mind which I would not willingly have exchanged for nothingness' (p. 45). Yet this state was self-imposed; arguably, when her father pushed, she, in her own way, pushed back, all the while under the guise of being a passive, seemingly submissive and devoted daughter. Shakespeare uses many of his female characters to express how women manipulated power, given the patriarchal dictates and social circumstances under which they were forced to operate. As a female Gothicist, Shelley appeals to Shakespeare's method to convey the plight and subversive power options of women authors and heroines, and of women authors *as* heroines. Her strategy also indicates the intricacies of quintessentially Romantic tensions involving the attraction and repulsion felt towards the imagination, creativity and legacy, especially for the female author.

Although Cordelia's response is 'truthful', she, like Mathilda, also knows how to provoke her father into revealing his 'truth'. Again, the issue at hand involves power, as the daughter desires her father's love and acceptance and yet defies his construction of her, challenging them both to the point of destruction. At first in *Matilda*, the father seems more to blame. His character undergoes a growing despair and melancholy that leaves the daughter, who desperately craves his company after years of abandonment, confused and blaming herself long before his confession. Shelley also implicates the daughter, however, by having her mercilessly pressure the father to confess. Mathilda finally throws herself at her father's feet, and taking his hand, begs of him: 'Yes, speak, and we shall be happy; there will no longer be doubt, no dreadful uncertainty; trust me, my affection will soothe your sorrow; speak that word and all danger will be past and we shall love each other as before, and for ever' (p. 27). Her words recall the underlying psychological neediness of Lear, his 'unnatural' and desperate desire for daughter and father to be all in all to each other.

Like Cordelia, the motherless Mathilda seems at once naive and innocent, manipulative and guilty. Both women play the role of the unjustly treated daughter whose truthfulness leads to her downfall; yet a deliberate cruelty or destructive provocation could arguably be said to exist in their words to their fathers. In both cases, these daughters, unwittingly or not, seduce their fathers into madness. They own the ability to pique their fathers' irrational passions, leading them to destroy their daughters and themselves. In *King Lear's* opening fateful scene, while Cordelia's reasoning speaks of good intentions, these reasons for her 'truths' are spoken as 'asides'. They are not given legitimate space in the discourse of the action. In one sense, as theories of *l'écriture féminine* would posit, any daughter's utterances are necessarily marginalized or devalued – laid 'aside' – as though what the daughter truly says and means could not possibly be valued or understood within patriarchal decrees. But, in another sense, Shakespeare makes Cordelia's asides strangely double edged. They seem 'truer' for their covertness, as evidenced by Cordelia's refusal to play her sisters' game, and yet they are suspicious for the same reason, allowing for the possibility that Cordelia may in fact be conducting her own counter-game with her father, who has already shown an inclination towards such power games.

The refrain 'like father, like daughter' therefore seems appropriate to both *King Lear* and *Matilda*. Mary Shelley imitates and enlarges the complex politics of power struggles between the real and symbolic father and daughter, as posited in *King Lear*, by having her heroine also assume many of the famous patriarch's qualities or situations. Probably the most important instance occurs when, reminiscent of Lear's behaviour towards his daughters, Mathilda curses her father and sends him into exile:

> To this life, miserable father, I devote thee! – Go! – Be thy days passed with savages, and thy nights under the cope of heaven! Be thy limbs and thy heart chilled, and all youth be dead within thee! Let thy hairs be as snow; thy walk trembling and thy voice have lost its mellow tones! Let the liquid lustre of thine eyes be quenched; and then return to me, return to thy Mathilda, thy child, who may then be clasped in thy loved arms, while thy heart beats with sinless emotion. Go, Devoted One, and return thus! – This is my curse, a daughter's curse; go, and return pure to thy child, who will never love aught but thee.
>
> (p. 30)

The 'daughter's curse', however, implicates the subject as well as its object. Its element of self-damnation speaks of a kind of sympathy. In the same breath with which she sends her father away, Mathilda also beckons him back. Implicit in her curse is the promise of reconciliation, albeit on a purer level, and a devastating devotion of the daughter to the father at the cost of all else. While Lear's curse upon Cordelia appears so relatively unfounded and merciless that it startles his audience, Mathilda's upon her father carries the caveat that purification can reinstate all things. One curse results from the perceived understatement of affection, the other from its unnatural excess. Yet Mathilda admits to her obsession with her father, declaring herself a daughter 'who will never love aught but thee'. Like Lear's, but with more immediacy, her curse leads to an ironic revelation that leads to self-knowledge, but a self-knowledge that is ultimately left open ended as to its efficacy or quality. Unlike the patriarch, however, the daughter embraces her contradictory states, thereby creating an alternative, if not more sympathetic, truth. It is a daughter's curse, not a father's, as she clearly establishes. The curse, which marks the climax, epitomizes the daughter's ambiguity, for as it condemns, it also absolves and forgives.

Redeeming 'Nothing'

Both *King Lear* and *Matilda* show that the father's salvation is bound up with the daughter's forgiveness; yet both stories disturbingly portray an 'unnaturalness' in the construct of those daughters by their fathers and the daughters' ambiguous response to these constructs. The redemptive expectation placed on their daughters is conveyed by the fathers' other-wordly description of them. When Cordelia asks Lear, 'Sir, do you know me?' after he wakes from a heavy, deathlike sleep following his fall into madness, Lear replies, 'You are a spirit, I know. When did you die?' (4.7.47–8). Likewise, Mathilda tells how 'my father has often told me that I looked more like a spirit than a human maid' (p. 15). Such spiritual or mystical attributions deify the same daughter who is cursed. As Shakespeare's tragedy unfolds, the father's growing enlightenment as a result of his suffering leads him to pursue the daughter and the emblem of unconditional love and redemption that she represents. In the meantime, the banished Cordelia is never fully free of her father – she remains haunted by his situation and seeks to help him and, arguably, to remain needed by him. Mathilda lives her story equally haunted by her father, defined by a relationship of mutual desire and dependency.

What then, are Mathilda's 'transgressive' desires, those tensions that women writers, according to Mary Poovey, felt in navigating between propriety and productivity?[21] Mary Shelley, with her own proto-feminist mother and politically famous father, surely felt pressured, paradoxically, to satisfy both gendered intellectual expectations. Her heroine's forbidden desire for her father's love becomes a loaded allegory for the conflicted position of the author-daughter in relation to her heritage, her text and her posterity. Shall she forfeit the socially accepted realm of the decorous lady writer and subvert the father's literary 'property', or shall she 'betray' the Diotimas, the Psyches, the Wollstonecrafts and even the Gothic heroines by admitting a deep need to be affirmed by a centre that excludes her?

Perhaps the answer lies in the way in which Shelley ultimately evokes *King Lear* in *Matilda*, only to invert the power play of its most central relationship. While her father initially occupies the ruling force of the familial dynamic, Mathilda eventually assumes this position. *Matilda* as 'textual object' assumes its own life, becomes its own, paradoxically posthumous subject. This takes us back to an earlier, important point: Mathilda assumes the power of not only 'willing' or controlling her own death but of simultaneously generating her own story and thereby assuring her posthumous reception. As Audra Dibert Himes suggests, Mathilda handles 'her emotional and physical desire by turning life into art – into discourse'.[22] This is her answer to 'nothing', to the demands of the father; her voice seeks the balance of remaining privatized within a journal but publicized within an imagined larger reception.

The Gothic setting of *Matilda* further supports its reading as a type of inverted *King Lear* story. By situating most of her story on the 'heath', Shelley draws upon a symbolic locus that immediately calls to mind one of the most powerful places of tragic transformation in literature: the lone, dire space of Lear's complete breakdown. At the story's climax, Mathilda, all the while braving a terrible storm, pursues her suicidal father toward the cliffs in a landscape reminiscent of *King Lear*'s final reconciliation scene at the British camp near Dover: 'When my father had arrived the storm had already begun, but he had refused to stop, and leaving his horse there, he walked on – *towards the sea*. Alas! it was double cruelty in him to have chosen the sea for his fatal resolve; it was adding madness to my despair' (p. 39; italics in original). Now it is Mathilda, not Lear, who faces dissolution of self at the death of her object of desire: 'Yet until I find him I must force reason to keep her seat, and I pressed my forehead hard with my hands – Oh do not leave me; or I shall forget what I am about' (p. 37). The dismantling of her prior self is necessary before Mathilda can take on her father's 'identity'.

In Shakespeare's tale, Edmund orders Cordelia to be hanged and her death reported as a suicide. Mathilda's father, by comparison, actually commits suicide. Viewing her father's lifeless body – 'Dreadful as the time was when I pursued my father towards the ocean, & found there only his lifeless corpse' (p. 67) – nevertheless becomes the turning point of Mathilda's narrative. As Robert Ready writes, '[f]ollowing his suicide, Mathilda mourns her lost father, and in doing so mourns her lost daughterhood'.[23] Trauma highlights the ambiguity of such constructions. Mathilda's hope for a true 'mental union' with her father grows steadily after his death, reaching its peak upon her own deathbed. In this sense, the memory of her father becomes Mathilda's salvation: she pins her hopes on being reconciled eternally with him and thinks of him as 'alive' in another form. Mathilda undergoes a self-professed 'death' – a death of her Cordelia-like construction – to then assume a 'new life' as a Lear-like recluse. Her desperation to seek reconciliation, even redemption, from her father's death recalls Lear's frantic reasoning that if Cordelia still lived, her presence would redeem all his sorrows (5.3.266–8). In *King Lear*, it would seem that Cordelia must die in order for Lear to obtain the brief, but tragic, insight that atones for his past foolishness, so poignantly conveyed in his loaded line, '[M]y poor fool is hang'd' (5.3.306). Is it the similarity between daughters and fathers, rather than their differences, that leads to a necessary negation?

Perhaps the Gothic's 'trickster' daughter understands the need for her death in the redemption of the father and so feigns death, as well. We have already discussed how Mathilda does this, but as Shakespearean critic Harold C. Goddard questions, can we be absolutely certain that Cordelia is dead?[24] After all, as Goddard points out, Lear's judgement has never been sound, but certainly by the play's conclusion Lear is an elderly, broken and mad old man. We have no proof beyond his faltering observations of Cordelia's body that she actually has died. Even Lear himself seems uncertain. Of course, traditional readings, and the tragic genre itself, mandate this assumption. But, if we approach *King Lear* as a source for the female Gothic, the ambiguity of Cordelia's death becomes significant. Booth argues that the entire structure of Shakespeare's tragedy is ambiguous; the play both 'is and is not an identity'; its elements 'turn into or fuse into other things' to 'duplicate the simultaneously fixed and unfixed quality of the whole of *King Lear*'.[25] Such tensions would have furthered Shelley's attraction to the play. Similar to that of the monster in *Frankenstein* and of the heroine Euthanasia of *Valperga*, Cordelia's death – like Mathilda's, as well – hangs in a nebulous space, exists in 'nothing'. Throughout *Matilda*, the writer keeps telling us that she is about to die, but we never know for certain that she does, since we are still reading her story. She creates the same ambiguous fate for herself in death that the daughter who opts for 'nothingness' within patriarchy achieves in life.

Lear has been deemed the most 'preternaturally eloquent' of all of Shakespeare's characters; 'Lear matters', Bloom claims, 'because his language is uniquely strong, and because we are persuaded that this splendour is wholly appropriate to him'.[26] For Mathilda, whose father has, in her eyes, a similarly godlike status, the act of becoming like the father intimates the great creative power of '*logos*'. By writing her own story and feigning her own identity, she can 'will' another life into being by simply speaking (or writing) it. Mathilda thereby plays with, and overturns, the initial and morbid 'will' set forth by the father. Yet, ironically, she achieves this triumph by in fact becoming the father, so that she can take on his position of influence, eternality and authority – as well as his vulnerability. Thus, upon her father's death, Mathilda assumes, or perhaps more fittingly, sublimates the father as an ambiguous symbol of patriarchal power and powerlessness.

It could be said, then, that one obsession replaces the other; Mathilda chooses the desire for power through literary production as a replacement for, and even a reconfiguration of, the desire for power represented by her father. But, to obtain this end, she must first cast herself as a Lear-like character who is arguably 'mad', and having been exposed to the elements on the heath, finally is dressed in the 'redemptive' clothing of a 'whimsical nun-like habit'. Mathilda assumes these Lear-like qualities because the daughter, no matter how 'rebellious', still feels compelled to draw authority from the same source that she ironically seeks to subvert. Caught between two desires in the generation of her own text – to be desiring subject *and* desired object – Mathilda enacts the dynamics of attraction and repulsion by her assumption of victimhood and its various modes of both empowerment and disempowerment. The story also reveals how male and female constructions are afflicted by 'victimhood'. Mathilda's father, like Lear, is also a victim, 'to the point of incipient madness, of his arrogance, his anger, his vanity and his pride'.[27] *Matilda* thereby displays the multifaceted roles of 'good/sacrificial/subversive daughter' and 'tyrannical/humbled/redeemed father' through the exultation and dissolution of each set of roles. Neither father nor daughter can be liberated from gendered constructions because of their affiliation with one another other through mutual desire and dependency.

In writing her story while living as a recluse, Mathilda chooses a medium as indefinite as her character that also indicates her quest for subversion and power. She is mute, in that she refuses to speak publicly her story, and yet she writes it fervently for future generations to read and perpetuate. She claims to write her story for one reader only, her pseudo-lover or 'fool', the poet Woodville, but in the same breath argues for it to be rendered objectively for the sake of a wider audience. The thought of strangers experiencing her story actually gives Mathilda a 'thrill':

> What am I writing? – I must collect my thoughts. I do not know that any will peruse these pages except you, my friend, who will receive them at my death. I do not address them to you alone because it will give me pleasure to dwell upon our friendship in a way that would be needless if you alone read what I shall write. I shall relate my tale therefore as if I wrote for strangers.
>
> (pp. 5–6)

In an irrational, impossible and yet effective Gothic gesture, Mathilda writes her memoirs from 'beyond the grave'. The technique transforms the reader into an 'artful voyeur' – transfixed by transgression, an innocent bystander who is made an accomplice through the act of reading. This is one of the effects that the Gothic does best: making its reader 'satanic', or much like Milton's Satan and Lear's fool, illegitimately apart from and yet also a part of the action. On the stage, Shakespeare perfects this effect through his use of dramatic irony. In the female Gothic, however, the motif of the 'transgressing daughter' assumes the connotations of the 'monstrous' female author. By implicating her audience in her own guilt, Mathilda creates a sympathetic identi-fication with her rendering of a complex daughter – a daughter who seeks and yet rebels against her father's approval, a daughter who in fact seems purposely to pique patriarchal power in order to become its self-vindicating balm. Furthermore, by writing from beyond the grave, from a maternal space of tomb/womb or of 'nothingness', Mathilda sets up a 'legitimate' alternative discourse by subverting the very discourse that excludes her.

The most tragic outcome in the stories of both Cordelia and Mathilda, however, lies in how communication suffers as a result of the vying for power between two subjects who do truly care for one another. 'The weight of this sad time we must obey, / Speak what we feel, not what we ought to say' (5.3.324–5): Edgar's advice at the conclusion of *King Lear* represents the curse of destructive miscommunication whenever one discourse, in this case the patriarchal, attempts to appropriate another, that of the daughter.[28] In Shakespeare's ethos, the authentic should win out over the façade. But, as a female Romantic writer, Mary Shelley shows that speaking emotively comes with its own risks. Indeed, because Mathilda's father speaks 'what he feels', he causes the demise of both subject and object. 'What we ought to say' is set against what Mathilda begins to write, as a daughter/author caught between her desires to be both redeemer and redeemed. Her story betrays the hypocritical, and yet necessary, need for propriety as a mask for desires too dangerous to be told. As a result, in the two texts at hand, *both* sets of father–daughter char-acters become victims in the power struggle required by the oppression of individuality and expression in gendered social constructs. Within the father's need to control the daughter lies his desire to be affirmed and needed by her, while the daughter desires her father's love and acceptance and yet defies his construction of her. It is the tension between these desires that challenges both father and daughter to the point of a destruction in which they are still, and forever, intertwined.

As Marianne Novy points out, Lear's need for forgiveness emphasizes *King Lear*'s implicit criticism of the prerogatives of the father and an exploration of behaviour that patriarchy fosters in men and women. The apparently mutual dependence of Lear and his older daughters, following conventional patterns of male and female behaviour, is deceptive: 'What the characters need are bonds of forgiveness and sympathy based on a deeper and less categorized sense of human connection.'[29] Mathilda's desire to give and receive forgiveness, to seek and supply sympathy, forces her to create a new 'afterlife' for herself. Yet her yearning for relationship in the reconciliation between father and daughter, who are bonded in part by their similar vying for power, can be actualized only within the solitary imagination. This makes Mathilda the most tragic kind of Gothic heroine, a 'living-dead' figure doomed to wander in imaginative search of the father:

> I dared not die, but I might feign death, and thus escape from my comforters: they will believe me united to my father, and so indeed I shall be. For alone, when no voice can disturb my dream, and no cold eye meet mine to check its fire, then I may commune with his spirit; on a lone heath, at noon or at midnight, still I should be near him.
>
> (p. 41)

Like *King Lear*, *Matilda* is predicated upon a complex portrayal of a psychosexual familial relationship whose primary concern lies with sublimated constructions of power in terms of social identity, inheritance, property and production. Examining *Matilda* as a text haunted by *King Lear* points to the way in which Mary Shelley's eerie evocation and at times ironic inversion of Shakespeare's play inform her own appropriation of a father–daughter tragedy. *Matilda*'s echoing of *King Lear* illustrates a distinctly female Gothic interest in the intertwinement of, and thus, similarities between, those who hold power and those who desire it.

Notes

[1] *The Journals of Mary Shelley: 1814–1844*, ed. Paula Feldman and Diana Scott-Kilvert (Baltimore and London: Johns Hopkins University Press, 1995), p. 673.

2   Elizabeth Nitchie traces the dates of *Matilda*'s composition and their significance in 'Mary Shelley's *Mathilda*: an unpublished story and its biographical
significance', *Studies in Philology*, 40 (1943), 447–62.

3   For Godwin's reaction, see Peter Marshall, *William Godwin* (New Haven and
London: Yale University Press, 1984), p. 331. Composed in 1819, *Matilda*
was not published until 1959 by Elizabeth Nitchie (Chapel Hill: University
of North Carolina Press, 1959). Terence Harpold explores the symbolism
behind Godwin's act of suppression in '"Did you get Mathilda from Papa?":
seduction fantasy and the circulation of Mary Shelley's *Mathilda*', *Studies in
Romanticism*, 28, 1 (1989), 49–67.

4   See Judith Barbour, '"The meaning of the tree": the tale of Mirra in Mary
Shelley's *Mathilda*', in Syndy M. Conger, Frederick S. Frank and Gregory
O'Dea (eds), *Iconoclastic Departures: Mary Shelley after* Frankenstein (Madison,
NJ: Fairleigh Dickinson University Press, 1997), pp. 98–114; and Ranita
Chatterjee, '*Mathilda*: Mary Shelley, William Godwin and the ideologies of
incest', in Conger, Frank and O'Dea, *Iconoclastic Departures*, pp. 130–49. See
also Margaret Davenport Garrett, 'Writing and re-writing incest in Mary
Shelley's *Mathilda*', *Keats-Shelley Journal*, 45 (1996), 44–60.

5   On Shakespeare and the Romantics, see Jonathan Bate, *Shakespeare and the
English Romantic Imagination* (Oxford: Clarendon Press, 1986); and Frederick
Burwick, 'Shakespeare and the Romantics', in Duncan Wu (ed.), *A
Companion to Romanticism* (London: Blackwell, 1998), pp. 512–19.

6   Harold Bloom, 'Introduction' to *William Shakespeare's* King Lear (New York
and Philadelphia: Chelsea House, 1987), p. 3; italics in original.

7   Lucy Newlyn, *Reading, Writing and Romanticism: The Anxiety of Reception*
(Oxford: Oxford University Press, 2000).

8   Aimee Boutin, 'Shakespeare, women and French Romanticism', *Modern
Language Quarterly*, 65, 4 (December 2004), 511.

9   All references to *Matilda* are from Pamela Clemit's edition in vol. 2 of *The
Novels and Selected Works of Mary Shelley*, ed. Nora Crook and Pamela Clemit
(gen. eds) and Betty Bennett (consulting ed.) (8 vols; London: Pickering and
Chatto, 1992), pp. 5–67. Mary Shelley spelled the title of her story '*Matilda*'
but referred to the character as 'Mathilda'; I will remain true to this distinction in my discussion.

10 I am indebted to my colleague Professor Bill Taylor for so patiently and
generously sharing his immense knowledge of *King Lear* and his own
profound insights into this complex play.

11 All references to *King Lear* are from *The Riverside Shakespeare*, ed.
G. Blakemore Evans et al. (2nd edn; Boston: Houghton Mifflin, 1997).

12 Interestingly, Percy Bysshe Shelley would portray this same paradox,
although for different purposes, in his drama *The Cenci*, composed during
Mary's work on *Matilda*, when his heroine Beatrice refuses to speak of her
father's crime.

13 Samuel Taylor Coleridge, *Remains*, in Jonathan Bate (ed.), *The Romantics on
Shakespeare* (London and New York: Penguin, 1992), p. 389.

[14] William Hazlitt, *Characters of Shakespear's Plays*, in Bate (ed.), *The Romantics on Shakespeare*, p. 395.

[15] Stephen Booth, *King Lear, Macbeth, Indefinition and Tragedy* (New Haven: Yale University Press, 1983), p. 67; italics in original.

[16] Anne K. Mellor, *Mary Shelley: Her Life, Her Fiction, Her Monsters* (New York: Routledge, 1988), pp. 194–5.

[17] Miranda Seymour, *Mary Shelley* (New York: Grove, 2000), p. 64.

[18] Diane Long Hoeveler, *Gothic Feminism: The Professionalization of Gender from Charlotte Smith to the Brontës* (University Park: Pennsylvania State University Press, 1998), p. 7.

[19] Pamela Clemit, '*Frankenstein, Matilda* and the legacies of Godwin and Wollstonecraft', in Esther Schor (ed.), *The Cambridge Companion to Mary Shelley* (Cambridge: Cambridge University Press, 2003), p. 38.

[20] I have in mind here Godwin's subtitle to *Caleb Williams*.

[21] Mary Poovey, *The Proper Lady and the Woman Writer: Ideology as Style in the Works of Mary Wollstonecraft, Mary Shelley and Jane Austen* (Chicago: University of Chicago Press, 1984).

[22] Audra Dibert Himes, '"Knew shame, and knew desire": ambivalence as structure in Mary Shelley's *Mathilda*', in Conger, Frank and O'Dea, *Iconoclastic Departures*, p. 121.

[23] Robert Ready, 'Dominion of Demeter: Mary Shelley's *Mathilda*', *Keats-Shelley Journal*, 52 (2003), 100.

[24] Harold C. Goddard, 'King Lear', in Harold Bloom (ed.), *William Shakespeare's* King Lear (New York and Philadelphia: Chelsea House, 1987), p. 35.

[25] Booth, *Indefinition and Tragedy*, p. 57.

[26] Harold Bloom, 'Introduction' to *William Shakespeare's* King Lear, p. 3.

[27] Goddard, 'King Lear', p. 19.

[28] Edgar speaks these lines in the folio version of Shakespeare's *King Lear*; in Q1 and Q2, the lines are spoken by the 'Duke' – that is, by Albany.

[29] Marianne Novy, *Love's Argument: Gender Relations in Shakespeare* (Chapel Hill and London: University of North Carolina Press, 1984), p. 150.

Figure 1
Ellen Terry as Ophelia in *Hamlet*, by William Henry Grove. Reproduced
by kind permission of the National Portrait Gallery, London.

Figure 2
Ellen Terry as Lady Macbeth in *Macbeth*, by William Henry Grove. Reproduced
by kind permission of the National Portrait Gallery, London.

Figure 3
Charles Kean as Leontes and Ellen Terry as Mamillius in *The Winter's Tale*.
Reproduced by kind permission of the National Portrait Gallery, London.

Figure 4
Set from the 1984 Royal Shakespeare Company production of *Hamlet*, directed
by Ron Daniels. Joe Cocks Studio Collection, reproduced by kind permission
of the Shakespeare Birthplace Trust.

Figure 5
Hamlet and the Ghost, from the 1992 Royal Shakespeare Company production
of *Hamlet*, directed by Adrian Noble. Malcolm Davies Collection, reproduced
by kind permission of the Shakespeare Birthplace Trust.

Figure 6
Boydell Shakespeare Gallery, 2:44, Henry Fuseli, 'Hamlet, Horatio, Marcellus and the Ghost' (Hamlet, 1.4). Engraved by Robert Thew (29 September 1796).

Figure 7
Boydell Shakespeare Gallery, 1:37, Henry Fuseli, 'A Heath – Macbeth, Banquo and Three Witches' (*Macbeth*, 1.3). Engraved by James Caldwell (23 April 1798).

Figure 8
Boydell Shakespeare Gallery, 1:39, Sir Joshua Reynolds, 'A Dark Cave. Three Witches, Macbeth, Hecate' (*Macbeth*, 4.1). Engraved by Robert Thew (1 December 1802).

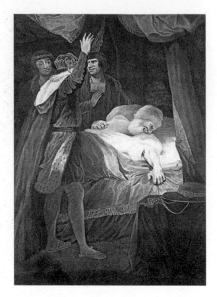

Figure 9

Boydell Shakespeare Gallery, 2:17, Sir Joshua Reynolds, 'The Death of Cardinal Beaufort' (*2 Henry VI*, 3.3). Engraved by Caroline Watson (1 August 1792).

Figure 10

Boydell Shakespeare Gallery, 2:17, John Opie, 'Mother Jourdain, Hume, Southwell, Bolingbroke, Eleanor' (*2 Henry VI*, 1.4). Engraved by Charles Gautheir Playter and Robert Thew (1 December 1796).

6

Into the Madman's Dream: the Gothic Abduction of Romeo and Juliet

YAEL SHAPIRA

ঙ

Shards of William Shakespeare's *Romeo and Juliet* are scattered throughout Matthew Lewis's Gothic novel *The Monk* (1796). The most obvious moment of intersection occurs towards the end of the book, when Ambrosio, Lewis's villain-hero, descends secretly to a burial vault containing the body of a beautiful girl. Antonia lies in her grave in a state of unnatural slumber, caused by 'a juice extracted from certain herbs known but to few, which brings on the Person who drinks it the exact image of Death'. After swallowing the drug, Antonia's 'blood … gradually cease[d] to flow, and heart to beat; A mortal paleness … spread itself over her features, and She … appear[ed] a Corse to every eye'.[1] Lying in the vault, however, she seems a picture of blooming life:

> By the side of three putrid half-corrupted Bodies lay the sleeping Beauty. A lively red, the fore-runner of returning animation, had already spread itself over her cheek; and as wrapped in her shroud She reclined upon her funeral Bier, She seemed to smile at the Images of Death around her.
>
> (p. 379)

Lewis's 'soporific medicine' (p. 377) evokes Shakespeare's more famous 'distilling liquor' that sends through the drinker's veins 'a cold and drowsy humour', so that 'Each part depriv'd of supple government, / Shall stiff and stark and cold appear, like death' (*Romeo and Juliet*, 4.1.94, 102–3).[2] Romeo's 'mattock' and 'wrenching iron' (5.3.22) find their parallel in Ambrosio's 'iron crow' and 'pick-axe' (p. 378). And, like Ambrosio, Romeo faces the spectacle of an unconscious girl whose 'beauty makes / This vault a feasting presence, full of light' (5.3.85–6) and whose tellingly pink complexion prompts him to declare that 'Thou art not conquer'd. Beauty's ensign yet / Is crimson in thy lips and in thy cheeks' (5.3.94–5).

Small fragments of the tragedy also appear in *The Monk*'s subplot of Raymond and Agnes, young lovers whose union is repeatedly thwarted by the pressures of family obligation and monastic authority. To escape from the clutches of her relatives and marry Raymond, Agnes poses as a bloodstained ghost; in a fascinating revision of Romeo's plight, Raymond finds himself accidentally 'wedded' to the dead woman Agnes has impersonated, an 'animated Corse' (p. 160) who regards him as the object of her undying love. Agnes then enters a convent, the same fate that the Friar suggests for Juliet when her clandestine marriage ends in disaster ('Come, I'll dispose of thee / Among a sisterhood of holy nuns' (5.3.156–7)). After a secret tryst with Raymond in the convent garden, Agnes, pregnant and disgraced, is forced by the abbess to choose between two ways of dying: a dagger or a drink of poison (pp. 354–5). The latter, as Agnes discovers when (to her surprise) she wakes up, is yet another incarnation of the Friar's death-mimicking drug. Juliet's fearful fantasy – 'O, if I wake, shall I not be distraught, / Environed with all these hideous fears, / […] / And, in this rage, with some great kinsman's bone, / As with a club dash out my desperate brains?' (4.3.49–50, 53–4) – finds a near-literal fulfilment in Agnes's ordeal. Awakening to 'a noisome suffocating smell', she sees 'skulls, shoulder-blades, thigh-bones and other leavings of Mortality … scattered upon the dewy ground' and contemplates her own desperate measures: 'Often was I on the point of striking my temple against the sharp corner of some Monument, dashing out my brains, and thus terminating my woes at once' (pp. 403–4, 405).

The focus of this essay, however, is Ambrosio's story, where the dialogue with *Romeo and Juliet* forms a persistent and intriguing subtext. I begin by examining how Lewis constructs his villain's tale as a 'perversion' of the Shakespearean love story; in Ambrosio's erotic exploits, the tragedy's ideal of romantic mutuality becomes a violent obsession, and theatrical role-playing itself is turned into a form of sexual assault. The second part of the essay seeks to place this radical difference in historical context by considering it in relation to the late eighteenth century's polarized view of Shakespeare and the Gothic as representing, respectively, the top and bottom of the modern literary hierarchy. *The Monk* endorses the superiority of *Romeo and Juliet* by making it a normative, even ideal, backdrop to Gothic violence and depravity. At the same time, the Gothic reworking of Shakespeare underscores the tragedy's 'Gothic' components and asserts the authority of the popular novel to subject canonical stories to judgement and revision.

A madness most discreet: Juliet in the Gothic vault

Like other Gothic novelists (and Shakespeare before them), Lewis drew openly on a wide range of literary sources. Cited as the legitimizing precedent for the revolt against neoclassical standards,[3] Shakespeare provided the Gothic with both a literary pedigree and an abundant repertoire of relevant materials. Just as Horace Walpole's tale of usurpation and its ghostly consequences, *The Castle of Otranto* (1764), clearly shows the influence of *Hamlet*,[4] Lewis's interest in dark eroticism made *Romeo and Juliet* an obvious target for pillaging.[5] The tragedy, moreover, had gained considerable prominence in the decades preceding the novel's publication. By some estimates, it was the most popular of all Shakespearean plays appearing on the London stage in the latter half of the century.[6] Its fame reached an apex in 1750, when rival performances ran for nearly two weeks at Drury Lane and Covent Garden, drawing crowds and excited commentary. Like most Shakespearean media events in the eighteenth century, this one bore the fingerprints of David Garrick, whose version of *Romeo and Juliet* would dominate the stage for almost a century. Garrick directed Spranger Barry as Romeo in the 1748 debut of his adaptation, and two years later, during the Shakespearean showdown between the two theatres, he starred in the Drury Lane production opposite Barry's Covent Garden Romeo, arousing a flurry of comparisons and criticism.[7]

Clearly, Lewis was working with well-known Shakespearean materials that bore a strong thematic kinship to his own narrative. What interests me, however, is the way in which *The Monk* deliberately sets itself up as an *antithesis* to Shakespeare's celebrated love story. The Shakespearean subtext of Ambrosio's tale is a chain of allusions mired in profound difference: the famous lovers are reborn as rapist and victim. To name but a few evident contrasts, Antonia does not toss back the sleeping potion with a heady cry of 'Romeo, Romeo, Romeo … I drink to thee!' (4.3.58); rather, she unknowingly ingests it when it is slipped into her evening medicine, the late eighteenth-century equivalent of a date-rape drug. Ambrosio, descending into the vault, is fully aware that Antonia is not dead, since it was he who orchestrated her abduction in the first place. The rape and murder that follow are a logical, if horrific, extension of the metamorphosis that turned Romeo into a stalker and Juliet into a passive receptacle, Shakespeare's passionate heroine reimagined as Gothic puppet.

When the novel is reread from the vantage point of the rape scene, where the Shakespearean influence is most palpable, a string of subtle connections emerges, and these initially align Ambrosio's erotic biography with that of Western culture's quintessential boy-lover. The analogy is steeped in irony: Ambrosio is not a boy but a thirty-year-old man experiencing a belated sexual awakening. Because of his repressive monastic upbringing, he

> never saw, much less conversed with, the other sex: He was ignorant of the pleasures in Woman's power to bestow … But no sooner did opportunity present itself, no sooner did He catch a glimpse of joys to which He was still a Stranger, than Religion's barriers were too feeble to resist the overwhelming torrent of his desires.
>
> (p. 238)

This biographical sketch appears midway through the novel, after Ambrosio has already become sexually involved with Matilda. However, the novel here follows the example of *Romeo and Juliet* by privileging a desire that, in fact, comes second. Although it is quickly forgotten after meeting Juliet, Romeo's initial infatuation with Rosaline is essential to understanding his union with Juliet. Lewis's hero also advances from a one-sided erotic fascination to a reciprocated sexual relationship. However, the transition proves short-lived, and Ambrosio's increasingly violent quest for 'perfect' sexual fulfilment marks the divergence of the novel from the Shakespearean beaten path towards its own darker terrain.

Constructed of Petrarchan convention and classical allusion, linked both to the virginal Diana and, by way of negation, to the ineffectively secluded Danaë (1.1.206–14), Shakespeare's Rosaline represents the inaccessibility of the female icon enshrined not only in sexual purity but also in pure textuality. 'Always a word rather than a presence', as Gayle Whittier puts it, Rosaline 'bears a name that might entitle a sonnet cycle and that resonates with the love tradition … Like the rose in her name, she will be nominal and brief'.[8] What causes the shift in Romeo's romantic interest is precisely the prospect of mutuality: in his own well-known words to the Friar, 'her I love now / Doth grace for grace and love for love allow. / The other did not so' (2.3.81–3).[9] As Marianne Novy has argued, while the word mutuality 'does not necessarily imply equality or inequality, it implies sharing and companionship, recognition of the activity and subjectivity of both partners'.[10] Set against the strictly textual presence of Rosaline, Juliet's passionate subjectivity is a vital component in the tragedy's preferred economy of desire, labelled 'natural' through juxtaposition with the overt artificiality of Petrarchan courtship.[11]

Like Romeo, Ambrosio arrives at his encounter with Matilda already primed by a previous, unsatisfied longing, focused in his case on two objects – a picture of the Madonna that hangs in his room and a young novice named Rosario. The two objects of Ambrosio's initial desire both parallel Rosaline, the idealized object of Petrarchan fixation. Etymology signals the unlikely kinship between Rosario and Rosaline: as Clara D. McLean comments, Rosario, surrounded by roses and rosaries and 'seeming to unfold one dark secret after another', is 'exactly the flower necessary to lure the upright Ambrosio into sin'.[12] Although Rosario, unlike Rosaline, is a character who speaks for himself, he too is shrouded in inaccessibility, more an abstract question than an embodied presence:

> A sort of mystery enveloped this Youth, which rendered him at once an object of interest and curiosity ... He seemed fearful of being recognized, and no one had ever seen his face. His head was continually muffled up in his Cowl; Yet such of his features as accident discovered, appeared the most beautiful and noble.
>
> (p. 42)

Like Romeo, Ambrosio is bound to his 'rose' by the aesthetics and erotics of deferral; the monk 'could not help sometimes indulging a desire secretly to see the face of his Pupil; But his rule of self-denial extended even to curiosity, and prevented him from communicating his wishes to the Youth' (p. 43).[13]

The other 'half' of Ambrosio's first sexual stimulant is the portrait of the Virgin, which for two years 'had been the Object of his increasing wonder and adoration'. The language Ambrosio uses to express his awe is heavily imbued with Petrarchan lyricism:

> How softly her cheek reclines upon her hand! Can the Rose vie with the blush of that cheek? Can the Lily rival the whiteness of that hand? ... Were I permitted to twine round my fingers those golden ringlets, and press with my lips the treasures of that snowy bosom!
>
> (pp. 40–1)

While the passage obviously parodies Catholicism (and maybe Petrarchism as well),[14] iconicity also concerns Lewis in the broader thematic context of erotic preference; through the parallel allure of Rosario and the Virgin, he stresses the hero's early fixation on what cannot be obtained. The novel links the supposed transcendence of the religious icon, the stylized remoteness of the Petrarchan lady and, finally, Rosario's masculinity, part of *The Monk*'s palpably homoerotic undercurrent.[15] With the Gothic's trademark excess, *The Monk* joins the love that *Romeo and Juliet* rejects for its pure textuality to the love that dare not speak its name and, compounding both with the inner contradictions of Mariolatry,[16] reinvents Rosaline as a triply inaccessible object of desire.

At first, Lewis seems to march his hero through a Romeo-like initiation, in which the icon makes way for a forbidden but satisfying consummation. The twin rose-like objects of Ambrosio's awakening desire converge into one figure, Matilda. 'Father, I am a Woman!' announces 'the feigned Rosario' (pp. 58–9); later she removes her cowl to reveal the familiar features of the Madonna painting, for which she claims to have posed. The distant object of longing emerges in the novel as an artificial façade, which is (alarmingly, but blissfully) discarded to reveal the 'real thing', a flesh-and-blood woman eager to reciprocate Ambrosio's passion.

The multiple textual strings tying Matilda to Juliet include the allusive resonance of the seduction scene in the abbey garden, where 'the full Moon ranging through a blue and cloudless sky, shed upon the trees a trembling lustre' and 'the Nightingale poured forth her melodious murmur' (p. 50). The iconography directly evokes Shakespeare's balcony scene, in which the name of the rose is stripped away as the lovers take a decisive step forward from the verbal abstractions of courtship towards their carnal union.[17] The decisive moment of seduction is also the twist that tightens the allusion to *Romeo and Juliet*. Matilda produces a dagger and threatens to stab herself in the chest: 'The weapon's point rested upon her left breast … The Moonbeams darting full upon it enabled the Monk to observe its dazzling whiteness. His eye dwelt with insatiable avidity upon the beauteous Orb' (p. 65). The key word here, 'orb', brings together a cluster of Shakespearean echoes. In the balcony scene, Juliet refers to 'th'inconstant moon, / That monthly changes in her circled orb' (2.2.109–10). Under the moon's revealing glow, Matilda displays her own 'orb', which threatens in turn to receive the blade and thus duplicate both Juliet's statement, 'O happy dagger, / This is thy sheath. There rust, and let me die' (5.3.168–9), and her father's lament that the dagger is 'mis-sheathed in my daughter's bosom' (5.3.204).

The success of Matilda's threat – she gains Ambrosio's permission to stay in the abbey – prefigures and facilitates the monk's complete sexual surrender a few scenes later. *The Monk* echoes the Shakespearean progression from infatuation to consummation, however, only to add a further stage of erotic development – or perhaps, in the tragedy's terms, of regression. Having evoked the two stages of Romeo's desire, Lewis introduces a third, intermediary position: an infatuation whose focus is neither a fully realized subject, nor a distant and unresponsive object, but a peculiar composite of both. It is this crucial step 'backwards' that dictates the course of Ambrosio's story and underwrites its violent culmination in the vault scene.

Fueling the monk's drawn-out sexual obsession with Antonia is the girl's combination of iconicity and volition, a blend that finds perfect expression in Lewis's magic mirror. Having learned that 'On pronouncing certain words the Person appears in it, on whom the Observer's thoughts are bent' (p. 270), Ambrosio looks into the mirror and sees Antonia:

> She threw off her last garment, and advancing to the Bath prepared for her, She put her foot into the water ... Though unconscious of being observed, an in-bred sense of modesty induced her to veil her charms; and She stood hesitating upon the brink, in the attitude of the Venus de Medicis. At this moment a tame Linnet flew towards her, nestled between her breasts, and nibbled them in wanton play. The smiling Antonia strove in vain to shake off the Bird, and at length raised her hands to drive it from its delightful harbour. Ambrosio could bear no more; His desires were worked up to a phrenzy.
>
> (p. 271)

Still figured as an art work – in this case, a statue of Venus instead of the Virgin's painting – the woman on whom Ambrosio finally settles his longing looks alive; yet the nature of the mirror's promise clearly links this image back to the fantasizing mind of the beholder. Performing a pseudo-striptease before Ambrosio, Antonia is self-propelled and yet clearly manipulated by the vision and direction of another. Shakespearean mutuality lingers only as a bare echo in Ambrosio's premeditation of the rape, which includes a wish that Antonia will actually respond to his caresses:

He resolved that should She prove obstinate, no consideration whatever should prevent him from enjoying her ... If He felt any repugnance, it arose not from a principle of shame or compassion, but from his feeling for Antonia the most sincere and ardent affection, and wishing to owe her favours to no one but herself.

(pp. 377–8)

Yet the two options – consent and rape – are really part of the same pornographic fantasy, in which the woman's on-demand performance of desire becomes even more titillating because it *is* a performance, and a coerced one at that.

Lewis's Gothic 'Romeo' does not want a truly Shakespearean Juliet, a passionate and responsive partner. What he wants is a hybrid of subject and object, a seeming agent who is in fact acting out a pre-scripted fantasy that takes from Shakespeare's Juliet little more than her status as a dramatic character. Psychosexual dynamics and theatrical reference overlap here: Juliet, we are reminded, is not a woman, but a part to be played, a textual shell awaiting incarnation, and as such she is easily appropriated into a coercive sexual fantasy.[18]

Romeo's famous wish, 'O that I were a glove upon that hand, / That I might touch that cheek' (2.2.24–5) is horribly reversed in what follows; it is Antonia who finds herself turned, against her will, into an empty sheath, and her puppet-like animation within Ambrosio's fantasy prefigures her physical violation a short while later. To Antonia's frightened cry, 'But why am I here? Who has brought me? ... Here are nothing but Graves, and Tombs, and Skeletons!' Ambrosio replies:

What matters it where you are? This Sepulchre seems to me Love's bower; This gloom is the friendly night of mystery, which He spreads over our delights! Such do I think it, and such must my Antonia. Yes, my sweet Girl! Yes! Your veins shall glow with fire, which circles in mine, and my transports shall be doubled by your sharing them!

(p. 381)

The Monk transforms the irony of Romeo and Juliet's missed encounter into the unbridgeable schism between the perspectives of attacker and victim. The scene's tragic intimacy is likewise rewritten; instead of extending, with poignant irony, the young couple's short-lived nuptial bliss, the vault becomes the symbol of a violent alienation that only masquerades as the closeness of love. In making this intimate underground space an analogue for the insularity of the assailant's obsession, *The Monk* prefigures a repeated preoccupation of Gothic storytelling in the centuries to follow, a fascination that would find memorable expression in works as diverse as Edgar Allan Poe's 'The Cask of Amontillado', John Fowles's *The Collector* and Jonathan Demme's *The Silence of the Lambs*.[19] The subterranean enclosure imprisons in more ways than one; it represents the trap posed by a violent private narrative, a narrative that includes a pre-scripted, coerced role for the victim. No longer 'love's bower', the vault instead comes to signify a hellish theatre of the mind, where sexual violence expresses itself in a travesty of dramatic performance.

Eighteenth-century Shakespeare and the Gothic: perversion and subversion

Lewis's rape scene anchors the novel's conversation with *Romeo and Juliet* and forms the crux of a concentric set of comparisons, all yielding a constant result of radical difference. The unbridgeable psychic gap between Ambrosio and Antonia extends into a homological contrast between the two 'couples' – Shakespeare's passionate lovers juxtaposed against the rapist and victim of Lewis – which in turn suggests a broader contrast between Shakespeare's tragedy and the Gothic novel. In setting up this overdetermined gulf of difference, *The Monk* reflects the late eighteenth century's newly articulated cultural divide between two even broader categories: Shakespeare and popular fiction.

The very idea of a select and distinctive 'ancient' English canon, with Shakespeare as its reigning deity, is in some ways a negative mirror image of the eighteenth century's abundant literary production and democratization of authorship, reading and criticism.[20] The latter processes, as Michael Gamer has argued, came to be embodied by the Gothic novel, which 'functioned at the turn of the nineteenth century as a synecdoche', a shorthand critical term for the commercialization of literature and its alarming consequences.[21] The Gothic invocation of Shakespeare brought together forms of writing that, within the cultural vocabulary of the time, represented the two ends of the great chain of literature. Awareness of this hierarchical thinking colours the dialogue between *Romeo and Juliet* and *The Monk* and gives it a self-reflexive dimension: the novel's engagement with the tragedy demonstrates not only what a particular Gothic text finds relevant in Shakespearean drama but also, more generally, the options available to a popular novel as it approaches the hallowed legacy of the Bard. On the one hand, *The Monk* thematizes the Gothic retelling of Shakespeare as perversion, the corruption of a hallowed ideal; at the same time, it also frames this retelling as an empowering appropriation that destabilizes notions of hierarchy by seizing the authority of the canonical text and questioning its privileged status.

From one perspective, the novel pays tribute to Shakespeare's superiority by using *Romeo and Juliet* as a measuring rod, a practice that gestures towards the Greek etymology of *canon*. The tragedy, it has been argued, contains a powerful articulation of the modern heterosexual romantic norm, which the play celebrates (though not without tension and ambiguity) by allowing it to trump same-sex bonds, family allegiances and the demands of a violent patriarchal culture.[22] In Dympna Callaghan's words, *Romeo and Juliet* 'produc[es] for posterity the lovers' desire as at once transgressive ... and as a new orthodoxy (tragically legitimated)'.[23] *The Monk* affirms this orthodoxy when the novel makes Romeo's history into a diagnostic gloss on Ambrosio's sexual awakening. Romeo is the standard, a privileged 'original', to which Ambrosio, a flawed 'reproduction', is held up and found wanting. Not only the monk's status as rapist and killer, but the doubts raised in the text about his sexual orientation underscore his divergence from Romeo's 'authoritative' example.

Lewis's 'perverted' Romeo articulates, in hyperbolic terms, an essential aspect of the mystique of Bardolatry – namely, its investment in Shakespearean writing as an ideal whose realizations are always flawed.[24] In the case of *Romeo and Juliet*, idealization is bound up in the youth and purity of the lovers, whose very embodiment on stage by adult actors struck contemporary observers as grotesque. Who, wondered Arthur Murphy in 1750, 'can help laughing to see ... a great huge tall creature about six foot high, and big in proportion, wishing "O that I were a glove upon that hand / That I might touch that cheek"'?[25] Writing about a Drury Lane production in 1796, a reviewer for *The Times* complained that:

> Mr Wroughton in *Romeo* wants youth, voice and every thing but judgement; and that he displayed in an eminent degree. He is a fat 'stripling', and to cut him out into little stars, would cost more nights than one; he is an *old* boy too, and perhaps would make a fitter husband for the *Nurse*.[26]

In Lewis's case, the discrepancy between the ideal and its flawed reiteration is deliberate; inserting echoes of Romeo into the tale of a lecherous thirty-year-old cleric adds another level of grotes-querie to Gothic transgression, and it creates as well an ironic similarity between Romeo's youthful innocence and Ambrosio's initial saintliness, which – like the ideal Romeo on stage – is corrupted by fusion with the overripe body of a grown man.

Shakespearean superiority also reverberates in the way digres-sion from the Shakespearean example is linked by *The Monk* to rape. The vault scene, in which Ambrosio's sexual and social transgressions reach their peak, is also the novel's most blatant 'perversion' of its Shakespearean precedent. The knowing readers/spectators, who recognize how this scene is *supposed* to play out, can identify its 'corruption' in Lewis's hands. The Gothic retelling of Shakespeare thus parallels the destructive actions of the hero, while the tragedy becomes analogous to Antonia – two avatars of purity and beauty that, by the novel's ending, have both been mercilessly violated. Their mangled remains mobilize the function of canonical literature as a collective touchstone, a source of communal cohesion. Evoking Shakespeare as a common basis for scandalized response, *The Monk* symbolically revives a collectivity that the solitary habits of novel reading had seemed to shatter.[27] The disapproving gaze of an imaginary audience coalesces around the double outrage done to Antonia and to Shakespeare's tragedy; the implicit blending of reader and theatrical spectator invokes an audience of many, a collective that draws on a common literary statute as it sits in judgement.

In thematizing Gothic digression from Shakespeare as individual pathology and implicitly framing it as a cultural affront, *The Monk* internalizes its own era's hierarchical assumptions and gestures towards a view of Shakespeare as the crowning glory of an evaluative system in which every text, including the transgressive popular novel, knows its proper place. In this, *The Monk* sets a precedent for later mass-produced texts that have turned to Shakespeare *as* canon – that is, as a symbol of the hierarchy in which they themselves occupy an inferior position. One example, as Susan Baker has shown, is the classic English detective novel of the twentieth century, in which Shakespearean allusions endorse the Bard's authority and identify him with social, moral and cultural superiority.[28] Intriguingly, Baker demonstrates that, while detective fiction – itself a distinct part of the mass-literature market – recognizes the financial value of Shakespearean artefacts and embeds this value in plots of larceny and greed, it sometimes also insists that '"Shakespeare" specifically and "great literature" more broadly are supposed (in both senses) to circulate independent of the marketplace ... Mysteries in this pattern require a contradictory Shakespeare, at once high-priced and outside any system of market exchange.'[29]

Implicit within this contradiction is the binary and hierarchical opposition between the Shakespearean legacy and popular tradition, an opposition to which, in this case, the popular novel itself gives voice. Paying dutiful homage to the Bard's transcendence, it makes no claim to participate in that elevated sphere where commercial forces dare not penetrate. A similar tribute to Shakespeare's privileged position can be found in *The Monk*, but it is only part of the novel's more ambiguous portrayal of Shakespeare. For all their obvious differences, the overlapping vault scenes of *Romeo and Juliet* and *The Monk* also highlight the kinship between these two texts, inviting a re-evaluation of their relationship: is it really one of contrast, or could *similarity* be the predominant quality, with difference being a matter of degree and not of kind? It is thus possible to read the Gothic reworking of *Romeo and Juliet* not as self-effacing homage, but rather as self-asserting critique – a critique that, in bringing to light disturbing elements of the tragedy, renders a binary distinction between Shakespeare and the Gothic difficult to sustain.

Shakespeare's Verona, after all, has much in common with the violent patriarchal world of *The Monk*, whose sinister orthodoxies and harsh notions of duty are instrumental in bringing about the live 'burial' of both Antonia and Agnes. Already in *Romeo and Juliet*, the vault scene represents the trap of misogynistic aggression that surrounds Shakespeare's young couple and finally infiltrates even their 'role-transcending private world of mutuality in love'.[30] Robert N. Watson and Stephen Dickey's recent discussion of the 'legacy of rape' in *Romeo and Juliet*, a reading that teases out hints of sexual violence present throughout the lovers' courtship, suggests an even more disturbing commonality between the two texts.[31] The nightingale that sings for Shakespearean lovers as well as Gothic villains evokes the incomplete silencing of Philomela; and, while *The Monk* does not take from Shakespeare the image of the pomegranate, which Watson and Dickey explicate as an allusion to the Persephone myth, the novel certainly offers its own vivid image of a young girl wrenched from her mother's protection and held captive by a male 'deity' in his underworld. A shared iconography, then, locates *both* texts in an ancient and ongoing tradition of rape and abduction narratives; the 'cluster of allusions linking [Romeo] to the most notorious rapists of classical culture'[32] also links him forward, so to speak, to his 'perverse' eighteenth-century incarnation as a Gothic killer.

The construction of Antonia as a drained and de-subjectivized Juliet likewise can be seen as the novel's canny exposure of an anxious erotic fantasy already contained within the Shakespearean tragedy. To be reunited with Romeo, Juliet must set aside her passionate subjectivity and enter a state of pseudo-death; she must allow herself to be carried, as the Friar explains, 'as the manner of our country is, / In thy best robes, uncover'd on the bier' (4.1.109–10). Such a transformation, Juliet intuits, is not easily reversed. Her magnificent speech of terror before she drinks (4.3.24–58) rightly predicts the dangers of her chosen plan:

Shall I not, then, be stifled in the vault,
To whose foul mouth no healthsome air breathes in,
And there die strangled ere my Romeo comes?

(4.3.33–5)

Juliet does not imagine the scenario that indeed transpires, the
fatal irony of bad timing; instead, she envisions a loss of self that
extends her objectification in the 'suicide' scheme, which will
undo the empowering effects of mutuality by placing her, literally,
inside the ancestral plot.[33]

Indeed, the duration of Juliet's first 'death' temporarily suspends
her active participation in the plot and opens up an interim space,
during which she becomes the object of a male fantasy – a
fantasy that, significantly, affords her, too, the status of an eroticized semi-subject. Both Romeo and her father imagine Juliet's
death as an erotic assignation: 'O son! the night before thy
wedding-day, / Hath Death lain with thy wife. There she lies, /
Flower as she was, deflowered by him' (4.5.34–6), says Capulet,
and Romeo, seeing Juliet's rosy cheeks, wonders darkly,

Ah, dear Juliet,
Why art thou yet so fair? Shall I believe
That unsubstantial Death is amorous,
And that the lean abhorred monster keeps
Thee here in dark to be his paramour?

(5.3.101–5)

The fantasy has a necrophilic tinge, of course, yet its sexual charge
is heightened by the possibility that Juliet might actually be a *partici-
pant* in the erotic bond with Death, not merely its passive recipient.
She, too, becomes the focus of a fantasy narrative that implicitly
endows the insentient woman with the capacity to reciprocate.
Viewed this way, *Romeo and Juliet* is not a foil for the Gothic but an
inspiring source for it, a source whose troubling components are
isolated and sharpened in Gothic retelling. Divergence from the
Shakespearean model is redefined in this perspective as a method
of amplification, a magnifying glass placed over the canonical text
to bring its latent qualities into focus.

Blurring the boundary between Shakespeare and the Gothic is one kind of challenge to the perception of their opposition. But the novel also has a levelling effect on literary hierarchy by questioning the distinction between the readers of Shakespeare and of the Gothic – a distinction of some importance for the eighteenth-century discourse of politeness, in which aesthetic preferences and patterns of cultural consumption functioned as indices of social identity. The same common literacy that enables the recognition of difference between the Shakespearean text and the Gothic is also proof of their shared readership. And, if the novel suggests that Gothic readers know their Shakespeare, it also points to the Gothic predilections of the audience that has gathered to see *Romeo and Juliet* over and over again.

After all, eighteenth-century stage tradition had capitalized blatantly on the visual thrill of Juliet's 'death'. In Garrick's successful adaptation of the play, the dialogue surrounding the discovery of Juliet's body was reduced, to enhance the 'focus ... on the beautiful, becalmed Juliet'.[34] Moreover, from 1750 on, productions of *Romeo and Juliet* responded to popular demand by adding an elaborate funeral scene in which Juliet's inert body, surrounded by mourners, torchbearers and musicians, made its slow way to the vault in a drawn-out procession.[35] *The Monk*, then, diagnoses a cultural, rather than an individual, 'condition'. Ambrosio's 'perverse' fascination with a dead/live woman is couched in a shared vocabulary of desire; his private obsession reflects a collective one, whose enduring appeal bears the affirming seal of the box office.

Viewed this way, *The Monk*'s free play with Shakespearean materials carries a charge of irreverence; through a 'perversion' of Shakespeare, it brings the tragedy's own 'perversities' to light. The challenge to authority, however, extends beyond the interpretive cast of the Gothic text; the very adaptation of materials from Shakespeare's tragedy aligns the Gothic act of writing with the authoritative practices of Shakespeare's own canonizers. The Bard's eighteenth-century apotheosis, after all, was achieved through a series of appropriations by editors and adapters, who took radical textual liberties with Shakespeare's plays as they went about creating what they perceived to be a 'corpus' and a

'Shakespeare' worthy of one another.[36] David Garrick is a case in point; he built his career on mastery of the delicate manoeuvre by which difference from Shakespeare became 'authentic' Shakespeare, so that adaptation became a mark of fidelity. Using his carefully cultivated public persona as Shakespeare's living embodiment, Garrick authorized himself to prune and embellish the plays and thus to render them 'truly' Shakespearean.[37]

The *Romeo and Juliet* that still resonated in the minds of readers in 1796 was itself blatantly a 'version' of the story, a version whose 'authenticity' rested entirely on the prestige and authority of the adapter. Garrick used that authority to institute considerable changes in the tragedy; among other things, he eliminated Rosaline (to make Romeo seem more consistent), raised Juliet's age to eighteen and cut many of her bawdier lines, reduced the overall amount of wordplay, added the funeral procession and, following the example of previous adapters, allowed the lovers a brief, poignant moment of joint awakening in the vault.[38] The openly fluid state of the Shakespearean corpus thus made engagement with Shakespearean materials into a bid for cultural power. To offer a Gothic retelling of Shakespeare's play – a retelling, what is more, that could be read as foregrounding the 'true' qualities of Shakespeare – was an audacious mimicry of canonization that usurped the authority on which canonicity itself rested.

The Monk's portrayal of adaptation and its consequences identifies the reworking of Shakespearean materials as a form of manipulative power. Cynically reflecting the private benefits to be gained from serving humbly at the Shakespearean altar, the novel shows adaptation to be a potent tool of coercion and self-gratification. Ambrosio's rather crude Shakespearean fantasy, whose implementation ultimately relies on brute force, pales in comparison with the machinations of Matilda. In the garden scene, discussed above, she reworks familiar images from Shakespeare's balcony scene into a virtuoso allusive performance that, significantly, achieves precisely the desired effect on her spellbound observer.

Interestingly, *The Monk* suggests that the successful manipulation of venerated stories requires a position outside the culture that regards them with awe. Agnes and Raymond's thwarted elopement is a case of failed adaptation; instead of successfully harnessing the legend of the Bleeding Nun to their own advantage, they become trapped inside it, foiled by a mystique that they cannot dispel. Matilda's figure, by contrast, ties a fluency in the language of cultural icons to a chameleon-like personal indeterminacy; neither man, woman or even human, Matilda lies outside the reach of cultural mystique and can therefore put textual manipulation to her own use. The transgressive power she deploys parallels, in the end, that of the Gothic author himself, whose refusal to succumb to the cult of Shakespeare allows him to reinvent the adapter as a demonic trickster armed with a grab-bag of Shakespearean allusions.

'Go hence, to have more talk of these sad things', the prince orders the people of Verona at the end of *Romeo and Juliet*, while the bereaved fathers promise to enshrine their children's memory: 'I will raise her statue in pure gold', pledges Montague,

> That whiles Verona by that name is known,
> There shall no figure at such rate be set
> As that of true and faithful Juliet[.]

and Capulet vows that 'As rich shall Romeo's by his lady's lie, / Poor sacrifices of our enmity' (5.3.298–303). The conclusion of *Romeo and Juliet* ties the command of reiteration to the story's transformation into a monument, a precious and unchanging object of reverence.[39] At the same time, the ending locates this potential icon in telling proximity to an excited popular chatter:

> O, the people in the street cry 'Romeo',
> Some 'Juliet', and some 'Paris', and all run
> With open outcry toward our monument[,]

reports Lady Capulet with alarm (ll. 190–2). The prince's exhortation to Montague – 'Seal up the mouth of outrage for a while / Till we can clear these ambiguities' (ll. 215–16) – is an attempt to control not only the crime scene but also the narrative situation by fixing the lovers' tragedy as a static, privileged lesson. Yet, if *Romeo and Juliet* envisions its own future as a cultural monument, it also cannily points to the function of the monument as a none-too-effective defence against popular iterations of the lovers' tale. Two centuries later, *The Monk* picks up the gauntlet. Gazing up at the statue, the novel nonetheless insists on making audible the persistent voice of the 'mouth of outrage', which has its own versions of the story to tell.

Notes

1   Matthew Lewis, *The Monk: A Romance* (1796), ed. Howard Anderson (Oxford: Oxford University Press, 1998), p. 329. Further references are incorporated into the text.

2   Quotations from *Romeo and Juliet* are taken from *The Arden Edition of the Works of William Shakespeare*, ed. Brian Gibbons (London: Methuen, 1980; reprint, 2003).

3   See E. J. Clery, 'The genesis of "Gothic" fiction', in Jerrold E. Hogle (ed.), *The Cambridge Companion to Gothic Fiction* (Cambridge: Cambridge University Press, 2002), pp. 21–39.

4   See Kristina Bedford, '"This castle hath a pleasant seat": Shakespearean allusion in *The Castle of Otranto*', *English Studies in Canada*, 14, 4 (1988), 415–35; and Michael Pincombe, 'Horace Walpole's *Hamlet*', in Marta Gibinska and Jerzy Limon (eds), *Hamlet East-West* (Gdansk: Theatrum Gedanebse Foundation, 1998), pp. 125–33.

5   *The Monk* also alludes to other Shakespeare plays, including Shakespearean epigraphs from *Measure for Measure*, *Macbeth* and *Cymbeline*. The novel also echoes *As You Like It* when the duke dismisses Lorenzo's ongoing grief over Antonia and encourages him to marry because 'He was of opinion, and not unwisely, that "Men have died, and worms have eat them; but not for Love!"' (p. 399).

6   Katherine L. Wright, *Shakespeare's* Romeo and Juliet *in Performance: Traditions and Departures* (Lewiston, NY: Edwin Mellen, 1997), p. 56.

7   See ibid., pp. 54–6; and George Winchester Stone, Jr., '*Romeo and Juliet*: the source of its modern stage career', *Shakespeare Quarterly*, 15, 2 (spring 1964), 191–206.

8   Gayle Whittier, 'The sonnet's body and the body sonnetized', *Shakespeare Quarterly*, 40, 1 (spring 1989), 29.

9   Juliet, in fact, dismantles the apparatus of her own idealization and casts Romeo as counter-idol – 'swear by thy gracious self, / Which is the god of my idolatry' (2.2.113–14). As Juliet Dusinberre comments, 'Shakespeare metamorphosed the effect of the male cult of idolatry by making it reciprocal … Mutual idolatry nourishes the intimacy which male idolatry discourages' (*Shakespeare and the Nature of Women* (3rd edn; Basingstoke, Hampshire and New York: Palgrave Macmillan, 2003), p. 156); see also

Evelyn Gajowski, *The Art of Loving: Female Subjectivity and Male Discursive Traditions in Shakespeare's Tragedies* (Newark: University of Delaware Press, 1992), pp. 26–40.

10 Marianne Novy, *Love's Argument: Gender Relations in Shakespeare* (Chapel Hill and London: University of North Carolina Press, 1984), p. 4.

11 In Rosalie Colie's words, 'Love-at-first-sight is here made to seem entirely natural, set against the artificiality and unreality of Romeo's self-made love for Rosaline' (*Shakespeare's Living Art* (Princeton: Princeton University Press, 1974), p. 145).

12 Clara D. McLean, 'Lewis's *The Monk* and the matter of reading', in Linda Lang-Peralta (ed.), *Women, Revolution and the Novels of the 1790s* (East Lansing: Michigan State University Press, 1999), p. 116.

13 As McLean writes, 'The erotic poignancy of the rose, in this system, is its deferring layers … it inflames desire because, and not in spite of, its hymeneal veils' (ibid., p. 116).

14 Steven Blakemore discusses the novel's anti-Catholic aspect in 'Matthew Lewis's black mass: sexual, religious inversion in *The Monk*', *Studies in the Novel*, 30, 4 (1998), 521–39.

15 As George E. Haggerty writes, 'The ambiguous sexuality of Rosario/Matilda provides a backdrop of homoeroticism against which the larger dramas of the plot are played out' (*Queer Gothic* (Urbana and Chicago: University of Illinois Press, 2006), p. 11). See also Haggerty, 'Literature and homosexuality in the late eighteenth century: Walpole, Beckford and Lewis,' *Studies in the Novel*, 18, 4 (1986), 341–52; Lauren Fitzgerald, 'The sexuality of authorship in *The Monk*,' in Michael O'Rourke and David Collings (eds), *Queer Romanticism, Romanticism on the Net*, 36–7 (November 2004–February 2005), *http://www.erudit.org/revue/ron/2004/v/n36–37/011138ar. html* (accessed 16 February 2007); and Clara Tuite, 'Cloistered closets: Enlightenment pornography, the confessional state, homosexual persecution and *The Monk*', in Frederick Frank (ed.), *Matthew Lewis's* The Monk, *Romanticism on the Net*, 8 (November 1997), *http://www.erudit.org/revue/ron/1997/v/n8/index.html* (accessed 16 February 2007).

16 For an overview of paradoxical elements in the figure of Mary, see Elizabeth Morgan, 'Mary and modesty', *Christianity and Literature*, 54, 2 (2005), 209–33.

17 See Whittier, 'The sonnet's body', 36–7.

18 On the significance of textuality in Antonia's portrayal, see Robert Miles's reading of the novel in *Gothic Writing, 1750–1820: A Genealogy* (London, Routledge, 1993), pp. 150–9. Also relevant here is Wendy Jones's analysis of the mirror scene as a visual icon that points back to its own textual origins; see Jones, 'Stories of desire in *The Monk*', *ELH*, 57 (1990), 29–150, especially pp. 130–2.

19 Fowles's novel is especially interesting for the present context because it, too, has a Shakespearean subtext: the kidnapped girl is named Miranda, and her abductor identifies himself to her as Ferdinand.

[20] On the concept of literary canonicity and its development in the eighteenth century, see Jonathan Brody Kramnick, *Making the English Canon: Print Capitalism and the Cultural Past, 1700–1770* (Cambridge: Cambridge University Press, 1998); and Trevor Ross, 'The emergence of "literature": making and reading the English canon in the eighteenth century,' *ELH*, 63, 2 (1996), 397–422.

[21] Michael Gamer, *Romanticism and the Gothic: Genre, Reception and Canon Formation* (Cambridge: Cambridge University Press, 2000), p. 67.

[22] Influential readings that consider the tension between the lovers' bond and other forms of attachment include Coppélia Kahn, 'Coming of age in Verona', *Modern Language Studies*, 8, 1 (1978), 5–22; and Janet Adelman, 'Male bonding in Shakespeare's comedies', in Peter Erickson and Coppélia Kahn (eds), *Shakespeare's Rough Magic: Renaissance Essays in Honour of C. L. Barber* (Newark: University of Delaware Press, 1985), pp. 73–103. Jonathan Goldberg challenges the claim that the play celebrates the heterosexual norm in '*Romeo and Juliet*'s open R's', in Jonathan Goldberg (ed.), *Queering the Renaissance* (Durham: Duke University Press, 1994), pp. 218–35.

[23] Dympna C. Callaghan, 'The ideology of romantic love: the case of *Romeo and Juliet*', in Dympna Callaghan, Lorraine Helms and Jyotsna Singh, *The Weyward Sisters: Shakespeare and Feminist Politics* (Oxford/Cambridge: Blackwell, 1994), p. 59.

[24] Stephen Orgel suggests this perspective in his discussion of Shakespearean editing over the centuries: 'The assumption is that behind the obscure and imperfect text lies a clear and perfect one, and the editor's task is to reveal it. The play is conceived here as a platonic idea, only imperfectly represented by its text' ('The authentic Shakespeare', in *The Authentic Shakespeare and Other Problems of the Early Modern Stage* (New York: Routledge, 2002), p. 244).

[25] Arthur Murphy, 'Free remarks on the tragedy of *Romeo and Juliet*' (1750), in Brian Vickers (ed.), *Shakespeare: The Critical Heritage* (6 vols; London and Boston: Routledge and K. Paul, 1974–1990), vol. 3, p. 375.

[26] *The Times*, 29 April 1796, issue 3572, page 3, column D; italics in original.

[27] On the inverse relationship between novel-reading and theatregoing, see J. Paul Hunter, 'The world as stage and closet', in Shirley Strum Kenny (ed.), *British Theatre and Other Arts, 1660–1800* (Washington, DC and London: Folger Shakespeare Library and Associated University Presses, 1983), pp. 271–87.

[28] According to Baker, familiarity with Shakespeare's work functions in the detective novel as both a class marker and an empowering resource; the initiated possess a privileged knowledge that, in some cases, enables them to solve crimes. Moreover, the Bard's hallowed status is affirmed in certain plots, which make the misuse or destruction of Shakespearean artefacts a motive for murder. 'Within the logic of a classic detective story', Baker comments, 'this is a clear case of justifiable homicide, an act of cultural self-defense' (p. 432). See Susan Baker, 'Shakespearean authority in the classic detective story', *Shakespeare Quarterly*, 46, 4 (1995), 428–48.

29 Baker, 'Shakespearean authority', 431.
30 Novy, *Love's Argument*, p. 100.
31 Robert N. Watson and Stephen Dickey, 'Wherefore art thou Tereu? Juliet and the legacy of rape', *Renaissance Quarterly,* 58 (2005), 127–56.
32 Ibid., 127.
33 Kahn notes that 'Juliet's moving soliloquy on her fears of waking alone in the family monument amplifies its fitness as a symbol of the power of the family, inheritance and tradition over her and Romeo' (Kahn, 'Coming of age', 18). Juliet's metamorphosis fits a broader pattern that Valerie Traub traces in 'Jewels, statues and corpses: containment of female erotic power in Shakespeare's plays', *Shakespeare Studies,* 20 (1987), 215–38.
34 Wright, Romeo and Juliet *in Performance*, p. 103.
35 Wright, Romeo and Juliet *in Performance*, pp. 102–8.
36 Michael Dobson describes this process as characterized by the 'coexistence of full-scale canonization with wholesale adaptation, of the urge to enshrine Shakespeare's texts as national treasures with the urge to alter their content' (*The Making of the National Poet: Shakespeare, Adaptation and Authorship, 1660–1769* (Oxford: Clarendon, 1992), pp. 4–5). See also Gary Taylor, *Reinventing Shakespeare: A Cultural History, from the Restoration to the Present* (Oxford: Clarendon, 1993).
37 Dobson, *The Making of the National Poet*, pp. 164–84.
38 This convention was introduced by Thomas Otway in *The History and Fall of Caius Marius* (first performed 1679, published 1780), which transferred the lovers' story to ancient Rome, and then repeated in Theophilus Cibber's 1744 revival of the Shakespeare play. On Garrick's version and its enduring influence, see Stone, *Romeo and Juliet*; George C. Branam, 'The Genesis of David Garrick's *Romeo and Juliet*', *Shakespeare Quarterly*, 35, 2 (1984), 170–9; Nancy Copeland, 'The sentimentality of Garrick's *Romeo and Juliet*', *Restoration and Eighteenth-Century Theatre Research*, 4, 2 (1989), 1–13; and Wright, Romeo and Juliet *in Performance*, pp. 54–64.
39 Dympna Callaghan argues that the golden statues erected at the end of *Romeo and Juliet* epitomize the tragedy's impulse to perpetuate the romantic model at its centre; constituting 'a means of monumentalizing … and thereby reproducing *ad infinitum* … the ideological imperatives of the lovers' most poignant erotic moments' ('The ideology of romantic love', p. 61).

7

Gothic Cordelias: the Afterlife of King Lear and the Construction of Femininity

DIANE LONG HOEVELER

Opie's The Father and Daughter

During 1801, a novella entitled *The Father and Daughter, A Tale in Prose*, written by Amelia Opie, went through twelve editions, selling close to ten thousand copies. Within eight years, Ferdinando Paër had adapted the novella into an opera he entitled *Agnese di Fitz-Henry*, while two British dramatists adapted the tale for two different productions, Mary Thérèse Kemble's *Smiles and Tears* (1815) and William Thomas Moncrieff's *The Lear of Private Life* (performed in 1820). These facts alone tell us that Opie's didactic piece spoke powerfully to the fears, sentiments and prejudices of its culture. Opie was so famous during her heyday that Thomas Love Peacock felt the need to satirize her as 'Miss Philomela Poppyseed, the sleep-inducing lady novelist' in his *Headlong Hall* (1815). Walter Scott confessed that he cried over *The Father and Daughter* 'more than I ever cried over such things', and Mr Prince Hoare, editor of the journal *The Artist*, reported that he 'could not sleep all night' after reading it.[1] Tears and pathos were exactly the reactions intended by Opie, and we may go further to claim that, by depicting hyperbolic passions and unbearable grief in her male characters, she was actually attempting to elicit emotional excesses and pity from her male readers rather than simply her presumed female audience. The fact is that Opie's tale brings together a number of important strains not simply in the Gothic construction of gender but also in the modern understanding of how subjectivity has evolved. The issues here are not simply sentimentality, agency, intention or bourgeois control of the emotions, although all of these are important aspects of the Gothic's construction of passion. Rather, the question that this essay will explore is how and why a number of largely forgotten literary and musical texts based on Shakespeare's *King Lear* intersected to create what we now understand as the modern, female national subject. In appropriating the cultural capital of Shakespearean narratives and domesticating them for an emerging middle-class reader, women writers such as Opie actually positioned women as the dominant purveyors of personal morality and civic virtue.

Deidre Lynch has recently observed that from the mid-eighteenth century through the Romantic period, readers developed a growing sense of personal investment in their own fictional reading, acquiring the sense that they could interpret fictional characters as they needed or wanted to because they had come to identify with those characters as if they were real. In particular, analysing Shakespeare's characters became one way of talking about the emerging national 'British' culture, its aesthetic values, its construction of the emotions and its conflicted political and domestic rearrangements.[2] Seizing on to and appropriating Shakespeare's characters, particularly his female characters, became a sort of cultural shorthand for depicting options available to women as either innocent victims (Cordelias) or vicious victimizers (Lady Macbeths) in the new and secularized Britain.

Anatomizing the emotions

The development of the bourgeois novel occurred in tandem with the growing science of psychology. What we now call psychoanalysis began when the behaviour, motivations and emotions of characters in literature were open to scrutiny and analysis by literary critics. By looking at literary characters as if they were actual case studies of how the human mind and emotions operate during periods of stress, literary critics provided the first models for psychologists, as in Freud's essays on Sophocles or E. T. A. Hoffmann's tales as blatant, but later, examples of this tendency. The earliest modern professional male literary critics – Samuel Johnson, Coleridge, Lamb and Hazlitt – spent a considerable amount of their writing careers analysing characters in drama and, more specifically, in Shakespearean works. As these critics developed analyses of Shakespeare's major characters and their use of language, they were at the same time constructing a paradigm of what it meant to be human – a fully functioning and empathetic member of both a family and of the state. But, clearly, the emphasis began to shift from the public to the private sphere in all of the popular adaptations of Shakespeare's dramas, so that finally what we have of Shakespeare during the heyday of the Gothic period is a series of dysfunctional family portraits. Adam Smith's *The Theory of Moral Sentiments* (1759) defined what, for his age, was the ideal display of moral sentiment: a male aristocratic sufferer whose intense attempts at self-control in the face of great suffering cause tears in his immediate community. What Julie Ellison has called the 'early cultural prestige of masculine tender-heartedness' can be understood if we recognize that the culture at large was seeking to define what it meant to be not simply human but also British.[3]

There have been many recent studies of the emotions during this period in addition to Ellison's, and another influential position has been put forth by Adela Pinch, who argues that emotions are not located exclusively within the self but rather are 'vagrant' or 'traveling', located 'among rather than within people'. Selfhood and emotions meet in 'the social performative', the domain of 'rituals by which subjects are formed and reformulated'.[4] Bourgeois women writers intended to civilize the general population through their works. Specifically, I would claim that a writer such as Opie intended, in her fictions, to teach her growing middle-class audience to control their emotions and display those feelings properly by attending theatrical performances, reading popular literature and then making themselves the heroes and heroines of their own familial melodramas. Shakespeare just happened to be the patron saint of this emotional and national transformation, with his dramas providing the master narratives for what it meant to be an authentic British citizen (or, in Harold Bloom's recent formulation, simply to be 'human').[5]

How does the Gothic construction of emotion, then, intersect with the theatre and opera and, specifically, with Shakespearean adaptations during the early Gothic period? When David Garrick worked out his technique for portraying emotion on the stage, he used Charles Le Brun's *Méthode pour apprendre à dessiner les passions* (1702), a treatise consistently quoted by both artists and actors during the eighteenth century that was predicated on an essential connection between expressions on the face and the emotions within. According to Le Brun, there were only a certain number of emotions, and to illustrate their expression was also to provide a 'kind of descriptive inventory of the soul'. Le Brun may have been the first to generalize about the emotions as if they consti- tuted a field of scientific inquiry, but he was followed quickly by Charles Macklin, who thought that actors should have 'philo- sophical knowledge of the passions' by knowing their 'genus, species and characteristics as a botanist might those of plants'.[6] Macklin was followed by Aaron Hill, whose 1746 tract on acting was more like a taxonomy and claimed that there were 'only ten dramatic passions', all of which had to be expressed in exactly ten stylized expressions.

In an analogous manner, literary critics established criteria for judging character and motivation based on generalized assump- tions about the consistency of personality or a sort of universal 'humanity' that all people shared. Acting and criticism overlapped to the extent that the age was obsessed with defining, performing and thereby controlling the emotions. Both efforts were at the same time working out a psychological and emotional inventory that ran parallel with – and in some ways, was complementary to – the scientific advancements and developments that were being made by such people as Erasmus Darwin and Charles Bell, who believed that the emotions arise from an organic brain-body unit in predictable, species-specific ways.[7] And *King Lear*, with its use of violent storms, an isolated and threatening heath, the cliff, blind- ness, madness and emotional excess, became the very embodiment of the literary sublime for the Enlightenment reading public. The sublime, however, becomes domesticated as pathos in the novels of the early Gothic period, and tears become the coin of the realm for powerful men and fallen women. The various performances and the sustained critical and creative reading of Shakespeare's characters shaped not only British literary culture but also its emotional and national identity. British citizens learned as a culture to understand and model acceptable private and public behaviour – appropriate emotional responses and civic responsibilities – by studying the fates of Shakespeare's characters.

Finally, it is necessary to connect the variety of emotional displays in drama and opera to the growing nationalistic movement that sought to define true British character. It is helpful here to observe, as Gerald Newman does, that during the mid-eighteenth century, Britain sought to depict itself and its citizens in national and secular, rather than in religious or tribal terms. This shift was made possible, according to Newman, because of cultural rather than political activity, with one of the central figures being the 'artist-intellectual', an individual who 'both creates and organizes nationalist ideology'.[8] The figure of 'Shakespeare' begins to emerge here: the adaptation and use of his work functions as a sort of hallowed presence hovering as a protector over the domesticated landscape of Gothic discourse. Cato, in other words, is replaced by Cordelia as the cultural standard bearer, and it is her tears, not his, that signify in the new Gothic economy of emotions.

In his *Sermons to Young Women* (1766), for instance, James Fordyce writes: 'The world, I know not how, overlooks in our sex a thousand irregularities which it never forgives in yours; so that the honour and peace of a family are, in this view, much more dependent on the conduct of daughters than of sons.'[9] Jean Marsden observes that 'the family acts as a type of the state, the dutiful daughter becomes the pattern of national honour: family drama becomes national drama, and the daughters of England stand responsible for the honour and peace of the nation'. What is interesting about the Romantic period, however, is that the fiction consistently shows the bond between father and daughter to be the 'necessary pillar of patriarchy': 'Not only do these daughters uphold the familial power structure, but they also reject or subordinate romantic love in favor of their filial piety.'[10]

Romanticizing the Lear *narrative*

In order to understand the proliferation of *Lear* narratives during this period, we need to appreciate the cultural anxiety that must have circulated in a powerful country that knew it was ruled by a king who periodically suffered from insanity. Consider that the 'family' of England felt vulnerable to external assaults from its enemy, France, and besieged internally by the rebellion and defection of its most prestigious holding, the American colonies. I would claim that this charged and anxious political situation was replayed allegorically in sentimental novels and melodramas as the seduction and insanity narrative. In fact, the private or closeted qualities of these stories are actually belied by their sheer prevalence. But why would a culture need to retell compulsively the same story, and why would these revivals occur during the height of the king's madness and attempts to impose a regency? The dominant ideology replayed for public consumption positions the vulnerable daughter as the emblem of embattled nationhood. Crucial to this construction of the new English national identity were the qualities of generosity and sincerity, exactly those traits that dutiful daughters were expected to display toward their families and communities. The good daughter is the loyal Briton, willing to endure any slight for the pleasure of sitting in blissful obedience and deference at the mad father's feet. To be a Briton meant to assume a supine position, a tolerant, indeed even a grovelling posture before absolute, unquestioned – and irrational – power. The ideological formula stated that domestic discord leads to political upheaval; the hierarchy of the state was duplicated in the hierarchy of the family, with the father as moral arbiter and final authority, no matter what his flaws. Father becomes quite literally fatherland, while the daughter – like Britain's beleaguered citizens – could only smile gamely through her tears.

However, the *Lear* the eighteenth-century and early nineteenth-century British theatre-going audience would have known was

Nahum Tate's anti-Whig version, not Shakespeare's. In 1681, Tate decided to rewrite Shakespeare's *Lear*, a play he considered to be a confused 'Heap of Jewels, unstrung, and unpolish'd'.[11] In addition to adding references to the popish plot, he eliminated the role of the fool, inserted a love affair between Cordelia and Edgar and excluded the king of France altogether. Tate's most infamous transformation, however, was the addition of a happy ending, in which Lear retires in order to hand his kingdom over to Cordelia, happily married to Edgar. In Tate's version, Cordelia's cold comments to her father in the opening scene are motivated by her love for Edgar and her desire to avoid a dynastic marriage. Cordelia becomes, in other words, a pre-Gothic heroine whose virtuous love transforms the character of Edgar, so that instead of a political drama, the audience has a good deal of familial and personal distress and pathos to savour. Tate's Cordelia does not lead an army to rescue her father, as she does in Shakespeare's drama. Instead, she alternately cries and waits for Edgar to rescue her from her would-be rapist, Edmund.[12]

Tate thought that he was improving on his source material when he increased in prominence Edmund's role, which included his thwarted plan to rape Cordelia during the storm. Cordelia's rescue by Edgar concludes with a speech in which she lauds private love and virtue over Edgar's lowly public status and his lack of royalty. And so, in spite of his Tory sympathies, Tate's version of *King Lear* concludes by anticipating the bourgeois shift that would occur during the next century. For Tate, Cordelia is transformed into an almost-seduced maiden who is only too willing to forsake the corrupt aristocracy to marry a superior bourgeois British citizen, while Lear becomes a simple father who just needs to see his favourite daughter settled in a successful marriage so that he can retire and hand over the (e)state to them. An article published in 1783 went so far as to see Cordelia as the 'patron saint of the private sphere' because of her 'propriety', 'fine sensibility' and 'softness of female character', qualities that were all praised as the marks of appropriate British bourgeois females.[13]

David Garrick is the actor most closely associated with the portrayal of Lear throughout the eighteenth century, and, indeed, he played the role over a thirty-four-year period, from 1742 to

1776. His revision of the *Lear* story downplayed the portrait of a pathetic Cordelia in favour of an appeal for sympathy for the confused father and his devoted daughter. Garrick's stated intention was to draw 'amiable tears' from his audience rather than to make them miserable or titillate them with a threatened rape scene. And, although Garrick made a number of attempts to restore some of Shakespeare's original language and plot to his 1756–76 versions of *King Lear*, Tate's revision was actually kept alive on the British stage because of the increasing madness of King George III. His insanity made for more than a few awkward social and political moments, and so *Lear* was finally banned altogether from the London stage from 1811 to 1820. Indeed, the only caricature we have of George as Lear was drawn by George Cruikshank in January 1811, just as the Regency Bill was being debated. Titled 'King Lear and his Daughter', it depicts George with arms upraised in horror at the sight of a prone woman, meant to represent Cordelia, dead at his feet. The actual subject of the caricature is the death of George's youngest and favourite daughter Amelia in November 1810, an event that was believed to have sent the king into his final and irreversible insanity.[14] What is most interesting about this caricature – besides its sheer cruelty – is that it positions the king within his personal domestic space, as a father first and a monarch second. It also asserts pictorially that the reasons for George's insanity were not his political failures, but his disappointments and tragedies as a parent.

Samuel Johnson also played a crucial role in finally institutionalizing Shakespeare as a cultural icon when, in 1765, he published his eight-volume edition of the plays. As Michael Dobson observes, Johnson's actual agenda was to nationalize and standardize Shakespeare's language by using his words as illustrations throughout his *Dictionary*.[15] Most tellingly, however, Johnson could not abide the conclusion of Shakespeare's *Lear*, feeling it to be unbearably tragic and finally admitting that he preferred the happy conclusion provided by Tate. For him, it was unnatural that evil should triumph while good is destroyed. But Johnson actually was late in entering this contested Shakespearean turf, for earlier attempts to canonize Shakespeare as the premier British Bard had been made by Charles Gildon's *Remarks on the Plays of Shakespear*

(1710), John Upton's *Critical Observations on Shakespeare* (1746), William Dodd's *The Beauties of Shakespeare* (1752), William Richardson's *Philosophical Analysis and Illustration of Some of Shakespeare's Remarkable Characters* (1774), Alexander Gerard's *Essay on Genius* (1774) and Thomas Whately's *Remarks on some of the Characters of Shakespeare* (1785). In 1753, Charlotte Lennox published *Shakespear Illustrated,* and in 1769 Elizabeth Montagu published *An Essay on the Writings and Genius of Shakespear,* while Elizabeth Griffith composed a book of sermons entitled *The Morality of Shakespeare's Drama Illustrated* (1775). In short, Shakespeare was contested ground, and female literary critics were as quick as male authors to appropriate his dramas for their own purposes. Male critics, however, tended to grapple with aesthetic or textual questions in Shakespeare, while female critics were wont to see moral and ethical lessons – and actually to produce sermons, as Griffith did – from the actions of the dramas. This female tendency to domesticate and moralize about Shakespeare's characters comes to perhaps its most extreme (and some might say, absurd) conclusion in Mary Cowden Clarke's three-volume set, *The Girlhood of Shakespeare's Heroines* (1850–2).

William Hazlitt, perhaps the premier Shakespearean of the Romantic age, found Shakespeare's greatness to lie in his presentation of empathy. For Hazlitt as well as Coleridge, Shakespeare's greatness was located in his ability to feel a perfect sympathy for all of his characters, while at the same time displaying a standard of 'disinterest'. It is not far, of course, to move from this notion to Keats's negative capability and, indeed, Keats's definition itself is suffused with illustrations from Shakespeare's characters, revealing how thoroughly a reading of the plays had infiltrated his understanding of aesthetic and psychological principles. Keats would, of course, have heard Hazlitt's lecture on Shakespeare and the English poets (published by Hazlitt later as 'On Shakespeare and Milton').[16] Finally, in his *Characters of Shakespear's Plays,* Hazlitt observes:

> It has been said that tragedy purifies the affections by terror and pity. That is, it substitutes imaginary sympathy for mere selfishness. It gives us a high and permanent interest, beyond ourselves, in

humanity as such … It makes man a partaker with his kind. It subdues and softens the stubbornness of his will. It teaches him that there are and have been others like himself, by showing him as in a glass what they have felt, thought and done. It opens the chambers of the human heart … It is the refiner of the species; a discipline of humanity.[17]

For male closet-drama theorists, human emotions were to be elicited and experienced in the privacy of one's own reading chamber because the staged version could never match the imaginative drama that occurred in the 'mental theatre'. In his 1811 essay, Charles Lamb stated the reasons for his preference for Shakespeare in the closet: 'While we read it, we see not Lear, but we are Lear'; 'do we not feel spell-bound as Macbeth was?'[18] But the 'we' that is referenced in these comments does not include the female reader.

For women writers, the theatre was largely out of bounds. Shakespeare was most frequently read at home in bowdlerized versions, while women were discouraged from attending the public theatre because of concerns for both the content of the plays and the composition of the audience.[19] As Susan Wolfson has noted, Shakespeare's works were 'already, and indelibly, established as the excellence of English literature embodied. The challenge was to refashion him for female company.'[20] I would claim that it was in the woman's novel that Shakespearean tropes, themes and concerns could be addressed and safely domesticated. The emotional excesses of women's novels, particularly Gothic novels, can be understood as enactments of the love, guilt, betrayal, repentance and revenge that characterized Shakespeare's works (forbidden territory to women, and all the more seductive for being out of bounds).

If Romantic male critics and poets identified with Lear, it is fair to say that Romantic women writers identified with Cordelia – that is, with the problem of female disinheritance and its attendant consequences, sexual vulnerability and victimization. In her *Memoirs*, Mary Robinson informs us that as a schoolgirl the first dramatic performance she ever saw was *King Lear*, performed in 1763 at a boarding school she attended, one run by Hannah

More's sisters. In a *Memoir* in which Robinson depicts herself as a betrayed wife as well as a disillusioned mistress of a personage no less important than the Prince Regent, what we remember most vividly is the extended description of her anger and sorrow at paternal desertion and betrayal. Keeping this vignette in mind will allow us to see how the *Lear* story resonated not simply in Robinson's life, but in the lives of late eighteenth-century and early Gothic bourgeois women writers. The Shakespeare who was adapted by Gothic women writers is the dramatist who was able to capture the terror, desperation, humiliation and tragic sacrifices of powerless women. The very public dynastic downfall and personal tragedy of an early British king becomes, for a series of Gothic and sentimental women writers, rewritten as what we might call closet epic tragedy – that is, a large trunk whose misery gets unpacked and then is stuffed again into the small space of a novella.

Handel / Opie / Paër

Moving Shakespeare's royal characters out of the palace and into the domestic hearth and home was actually the major strategy of Amelia Opie (1769–1853) when she rewrote the *Lear* story. We are told by her biographer that when she was not attending murder trials, Opie was visiting insane asylums in Norwich and London.[21] An astute student of human passions in extreme situations, she traces, in her sentimental novella, the history of motherless Agnes and her devoted father. Adored by her successful father and worshipped by the community, Agnes falls prey to Clifford, a seducer, who persuades her to elope with him. Thinking that they are on their way to be married in London, Agnes is pregnant before she knows it, and her lover has disappeared in order to marry – at the request of his corrupt aristocrat father – a woman with a larger estate. Destitute and humiliated, Agnes and her infant son return to her native village, only to encounter a madman wrapped in chains on the forested outskirts, raving about his dead daughter. Unlike Lear on the heath, this father has been driven to madness through no fault of his own.

He is blameless, while the Cordelia of this piece – Agnes – has brought this calamity on him and her community through her own act of sexual licentiousness and pride, for she

> thought herself endowed with great power to read the characters of those with whom she associated, when she had even not discrimination enough to understand her own: and while she imagined that it was not in the power of others to deceive her, she was constantly in the habit of deceiving herself.[22]

The climactic recognition scene between father and daughter occurs after Agnes returns with her son Edward to her birthplace and encounters a chained madman roving around in the woods, claiming that he is there to visit his daughter's grave:

> At the name of 'father', the poor maniac started, and gazed on her earnestly, with savage wildness, while his whole frame became convulsed; and rudely disengaging himself from her embrace, he ran from her a few paces, and then dashed himself on the ground in all the violence of frenzy. He raved, he tore his hair; he screamed and uttered the most dreadful execrations; and with his teeth shut and his hands clenched, he repeated the word father, and said the name was mockery to him.[23]

The recognition scene, such a standard device that it had become a literary cliché fifty years earlier, reminds us that the emotional freight of this piece can be found in the meaning of the troubled father–daughter dyad.[24] And it is no coincidence that it was this scene that was consistently emphasized in all of the later dramatic and operatic adaptations of Opie's novella. The hyperbole here, the frenzy, the gnashing of teeth and violence of display, all of these actions code emotional excess as dangerous, insane and unacceptable behaviours in the new bourgeois British citizen. To cause such extravagance of feeling in another person – particularly one's father – is an unforgivable sin in the new, middle-class emotional economy. Agnes must pay for her error, and she does so promptly: as her father gazes on her with 'inquiring and mournful looks', Agnes begins to cry: 'Tears once more found their way, and relieved her bursting brain, while, seizing her father's hand, she pressed it with frantic emotion to her lips' (p. 94). In this scene, it is the daughter who sheds tears for the blameless father, the daughter as citizen who has failed her insane ruler.

However, Agnes is a victim as well as the victimizer of her father's hopes and trust. Seduced by a wealthy aristocratic man, Agnes is powerless against his family, reminding us of Ellison's observation that 'as sensibility's social base becomes broader, its subject paradoxically becomes social inequality. Sensibility increasingly is defined by the consciousness of a power difference between the agent and the object of sympathy.'[25] Class inequities provoke our sympathy for Agnes, but it is her father's humiliation that stirred the strongest emotions in Opie's readers. It is the loss of his daughter's virginity, as a piece of valuable property that the father himself possessed, that most incensed the contemporary male readers of this text. As Susan Staves has noted, Opie's novella needs to be read in light of the Marriage Act of 1753, which caused 'an expression of anxiety about the weakening of older restraints on the independent behaviour of children'.[26]

Agnes leads her father to shelter in an insane asylum that he himself had built in his prosperous days, before the ruination of his business brought about by depression over his daughter's disastrous elopement. Here, Agnes patiently serves as her father's attendant, while he spends his days sketching charcoal drawings of her tomb on his wall. His madness consists in telling Agnes that his daughter – who is standing in front of him – is dead. After seven years of such penance, Agnes is rewarded finally with her father's recognition of her, quickly followed by the father's death and then by that of Agnes. They are ultimately (and ironically) buried together in the same grave that the father had sketched so carefully and lovingly on his madhouse wall. It is no coincidence, I think, to see the sudden profusion of sentimental prints of Cordelia and Lear published at this time as a response to the popularity of Opie's work. John Thurston's engraving, *King Lear: O My Dear Father* (1805) depicts a very maternal Cordelia comforting and cradling her father in her arms, while Henry Corbould's engraving *King Lear: His Sleep is Sound* (1817) also features Cordelia watching anxiously over her insane father, who now is safely sleeping.

The climactic pathetic scene, in which father and daughter both recognize each other for the first time since her fall and the last time before both of their deaths, is dramatically framed by the use of an aria, adapted from Handel's oratorio *Deborah* and transformed into a popular parlour song, which father and daughter sing to each other and which concerns paternal love and hope, *Tears, such as tender fathers shed*. The use of the aria at this particular point in Opie's novella is telling, for it suggests that at points of high emotional intensity, we turn to staged recitals of our feelings: hence, the distancing effect of the Handel piece at the precise moment when the emotional intensity overwhelms both father and daughter. The very specific use of the Handel piece within Opie's narrative also suggests the melodramatic, hyperbolic quality of a text that was just a short step away from being operatic in its excesses. In fact, the adaptation of Gothic and sentimental novels as source material for the theatre and opera was becoming a common convention, suggesting the growth of a literate society that demanded a form of visual entertainment that repeated and replayed the tropes of popular novels.

Given its currency, we should not be surprised that within eight years of its publication Ferdinando Paër adapted Opie's novella into an opera entitled *Agnese di Fitz-Henry*. Paër's 1809 opera follows in almost exact detail his source in Opie, although the action is set in Italy and the opera has a happy ending, with Agnese marrying her lover Ernesto and moving in with her suddenly recovered father. In his *Life of Rossini*, Stendhal recorded his disgusted reaction to seeing a performance of *Agnese*:

> Even the remarkable popularity of the opera cannot shake my conviction that it is profoundly wrong for art to deal with purely horrifying subjects. The madness of Shakespeare's Lear is made tolerable by the most touching devotion of his daughter Cordelia; but I personally feel that there is nothing to redeem the ghastly and pitiable condition of the heroine's father in *Agnese* ... [which] has always remained with me as a thoroughly disagreeable memory.[27]

Paër (1771–1839), an Italian who spent most of his productive life in Germany and France, is remembered today as one of the major practitioners of *opera semiseria*, a style that combined the comic and the horrible, using both aristocratic and lower-class characters. We may go so far as to observe that the genre of *opera semiseria* is the musical equivalent of the literary genre of melodrama, while rescue operas are the literary equivalent of the Gothic. Well suited to the sentimentality of the period, *opera semiseria* specialized in juxtaposing the pathetic with the appalling without having to carry through the action to a tragic conclusion – as evidenced in the mad scenes in *Agnese*.[28] Before he composed *Agnese* in 1809, Paër's most famous opera was *Camilla, ossia Il sotterraneo* (*Camilla; or, the Tunnel*, 1799), one of the rescue operas – largely based on the plot lines and conventions of Gothic novels – about the French Revolution.[29] *Agnese*, however, is an almost literal adaptation of the Opie novel, with Luigi Buonavoglia writing the libretto and adding for comic relief the character of the director of the insane asylum, who treats its inmates as laughable and easily cured if they would just stop indulging their extreme emotional responses to a variety of life's typical events. *Agnese* was the first opera to take its audience literally into a lunatic asylum and to depict, in almost clinical detail, the behaviour of a madman. Was its blatant depiction of insanity a cheap attempt to exploit the sensibility of the era? Certainly, visits to observe the inmates of Bedlam had become a sort of sport for people like Opie, not to mention the general bourgeois population.

Paër, however, transforms Opie's use of the Handel aria, *Tears, such as tender fathers shed*, and instead has Agnese play the harp and sing a favourite song so that her father will finally recognize her through her singing voice. Instead of using the Handel piece, taken as it was from a gruesome Old Testament story, Paër has Agnese sing a decidedly New Testament lament that figures the daughter as her namesake, St Agnes (or *agnus*, meaning lamb), the patron saint of virginity and rape victims; Agnese is thus a lost lamb seeking for her father, the good shepherd:

> If the lost lamb
> Finds her good shepherd once more,
> Grief quickly

169

Changes to joy;
With her harmonious bleating
She sets the hill ringing;
Nor from her face could you tell
How dismayed she has been
So to her father
Return Agnese.[30]

The change in imagery is significant, in that the Old Testament patriarch is replaced in Paër by the father as a forgiving Christ-figure – a shepherd seeking his lost lambs, not a vengeful deity.

Although composed in 1809, *Agnese* was not performed in London until 1817 and, unfortunately, competed directly with *Don Giovanni* during that particular season. Despite a fine production and enthusiastic reviews, the opera had only five performances before it was suspended 'on account of some similitude which was thought to exist between the situation of Hubert [the insane father] and that of his majesty George III'.[31] But what is most striking about the use of Handel in Opie, and later in the popular melodramas written by Mary Thérèse Kemble in 1815 (*Smiles and Tears*) and Thomas Moncrieff in 1820 (*The Lear of Private Life! or, Father and Daughter*), is that the music is used in all of these pieces at what we would recognize in the text as the 'moment of desire'. Specifically, the aria is used to frame what can be identified as the Oedipal crisis of the narrative: the moment at which the father struggles to recognize his daughter as a sexual woman, an individual who has defied him and allowed herself to enter into an illicit passion with a seducer who has no intention of making her his wife. This recognition is so painful to the father that he distances it by performing his pain in a stylized, almost ritualized manner, couching it in distinctly Old Testament biblical imagery. Such a move emphasizes Opie's emotional pathos in order to suggest that the sexual disgrace of the daughter is equivalent to the warfare between rival Old Testament tribes. To lose one's virginity is tantamount to losing national honour and one's standing as a member of God's chosen people.

One is reminded here of Slavoj Žižek's answer to the question, why do we listen to music? His reply:

[I]n order to avoid the horror of the encounter of the voice qua object. What Rilke said for beauty goes also for music: it is a lure, a screen, the last curtain, which protects us from directly confronting the horror of the (vocal) object ... Voice does not simply persist at a different level with regard to what we see, it rather points toward a gap in the field of the visible, toward the dimension of what eludes our gaze. In other words, their relationship is mediated by an impossibility: *ultimately, we hear things because we cannot see everything.*[32]

What the music screens from view is the father's fantasized vision of his daughter in the sexual act. The music blocks, in other words, a reversed primal scene so that what cannot be imagined or viewed by the culture at large is the daughter's seduction, the daughter's uncontrolled sexuality. It is interesting to note that the three most recent adaptations of the *Lear* narrative written by women, Jane Smiley's *A Thousand Acres* (a 1992 Pulitzer Prize winner), Elaine Feinstein and the Women's Theatre Group's *Lear's Daughters* (1987) and Margaret Atwood's novel *Cat's Eye* (1988) all reveal patriarchal incest and physical abuse to be the dark secrets hidden in the father–daughter relationship.[33] For Freud, *Lear* was another narrative about the acceptance of the intermingling of *eros* with *thanatos*, but for contemporary women writers the Lear story has to be focused on the father's corruption of the virgin daughter as a metaphor for his rape of land, resources and innocence.[34]

Another romantic serio-comedy based on Opie's novella, Kemble's *Smiles and Tears*, combines the low comedy of a confusion of identities with the pathos of a disastrous seduction. Performed in 1815, the play is given a happy ending. The father does suffer from insanity, but he recovers when Agnes and her seducer are finally able to marry. Hazlitt was in the audience on opening night, and he gave the play a very negative review indeed.[35] Finally, the popular melodrama by Thomas Moncrieff, *The Lear of Private Life*, sums up the shift we have charted from public concerns with the state to private issues of domestic harmony and marital fidelity. Performed in 1820, the play also rewrites Opie, giving the father his sanity back after Agnes and the seducer marry. As in the case of Tate so many years earlier, audiences were simply unable to accept the bleak, pessimistic, deeply moralistic ending that both Shakespeare and Opie had provided to their readers. The middle-class British audience that attended the theatre wanted piety, melodrama and pathos, but in moderation. They wanted just enough suffering; they could not abide a tragic ending, which they could see only as nihilism.

As we have seen, the narrative of *Lear* was domesticated so that the national and dynastic issues that Shakespeare explored could be transformed into popular novels, dramas and operas that moved the action from the public to the private realm. The shift that we see in the secularization and domestication of high cultural artifacts to popular ones says a good deal about the construction of the national as well as the Gothic ethos in this period. 'I think, therefore I am' seems to have been transformed into 'I cry, therefore I am', or 'I suffer, therefore I am', or 'I am guilty and in pain, therefore I am'. Provoking intense suffering and displaying that suffering in a stylized, almost ritualized manner became the dominant mode for this culture to define universalized humanity. Citizens of Britain were able to recognize their shared humanity – their shared 'Britishness' – only when they could see demonstrated intense guilt about failed filial duty, extreme shame about sexual licence and hyperbolic grief about causing madness in one's family members.

As late as 1837, *Blackwood's Edinburgh Magazine* stated that the fame of Opie's *The Father and Daughter* would endure 'till pity's self be dead'.[36] Opie herself wrote that her aim in writing was to

> excite profitable sympathies in many kind and good hearts and ...
> in small degree enlarge our feelings of reverence for our species,
> and our knowledge of human nature, by shewing that our best
> qualities are possessed by men whom we are too apt to consider,
> not with reference to the points in which they resemble us, but to
> those in which they manifestly differ from us.[37]

Very similar, if more direct, sentiments were expressed in 1847 by George Gilfillan, who observed in *Tait's Edinburgh Magazine* that 'the finest compliment that it is possible to pay to woman, as a moral being, is to compare her to "one of Shakespeare's women"'.[38] We return, then, to the need to universalize about an intrinsic 'human nature' that all people share because it is rooted in 'feelings', emotions that we can all enact because we have learned the scripts, seen them performed on stage and – by extension – now in films and on television. One could also note that in the Chinese alphabet the figure for 'to feel' and 'to think' is the same and that such a union of faculties would appear to be the goal of much Gothic and Western speculation on the nature of the mind. To become a composite self who thinks and feels in a unified, coherent manner would appear to be the ideal of an age that sought to replace a theocentric conception of the world with one in which humans were believed to be potentially godlike, at least if a unification of their faculties could occur.

Conclusion

In conclusion, it is perhaps instructive to cite an observation made by Iris Murdoch:

> [O]ur present situation is analogous to an eighteenth-century one. We retain a rationalistic optimism about the beneficent results of education, or rather technology. We combine this with a Romantic conception of 'the human condition', a picture of the individual as stripped and solitary. The eighteenth century was [like the twenty-first] an era of rationalistic allegories and moral tales.[39]

Murdoch appears to be suggesting here that what we now recognize as the ideology of 'affective individualism' began during a period that idealized isolated individuals who were alone with their feelings, attempting to seek meaning for life in understanding the moral significance of the emotions that buffeted them. But standing alone, stripped and bare like Lear on the heath, was precisely what was too painful for the Romantic or Gothic sensibility to bear. The moral of the Lear tale, as rewritten by the Gothic ethos, was that no one finally stood alone. All of us – even the insane and the disgraced – are loved by the members of our families and our communities. If we master the scripts and perform the emotional excesses required from us, we can all enact indefinitely the drama of denying our solitary selfhood, denying that we are isolated and alone in an alien or indifferent universe.

Shakespeare and the Bible have provided the master narratives on which Western civilization has been constructed. These texts have taught us what to feel, how to feel and how to enact those feelings in ways that preserve the patriarchal family and position all of us in one subservient role after another. When a tender father sheds tears for a disgraced daughter, we have constructed the most benign face of the patriarchy we can imagine. But it is Cordelia's silence that I remember – her frustration, her futility – and, finally, it is her tears that I think I feel.

Notes

1 Margaret E. Macgregor, *Amelia Opie, Wordling and Friend* (Northampton, MA: Smith College Studies in Modern Languages, 1933), p. 32.
2 Deidre Shaun Lynch, *The Economy of Character: Novels, Market Culture and the Business of Inner Meaning* (Chicago: University of Chicago Press, 1998).
3 Julie Ellison, *Cato's Tears and the Making of Anglo-American Emotion* (Chicago: University of Chicago Press, 1999), p. 9.
4 Adela Pinch, *Strange Fits of Passion: Epistemologies of Emotion, Hume to Austen* (Stanford: Stanford University Press, 1996), pp. 16, 167 and 10.
5 For the most extensive and provocative discussion of the racist, sexist and anti-semitic issues involved in Harold Bloom's construction of Shakespeare, see Christy Desmet and Robert Sawyer (eds), *Harold Bloom's Shakespeare* (New York: Palgrave, 2002). This collection contains Caroline Cakebread's very perceptive analysis of the contemporary construction of the Cordelia figure in the fiction of Margaret Atwood, Jane Smiley and Gloria Naylor ('Shakespeare in transit', pp. 199–211).
6 Desmond Shawe-Taylor, 'Performance portraits', *Shakespeare Survey*, 51 (1998), 112.
7 See Alan Richardson, *British Romanticism and the Science of the Mind* (Cambridge: Cambridge University Press, 2001); Edward Reed, *From Soul to Mind: The Emergence of Psychology from Erasmus Darwin to William James* (New Haven: Yale University Press, 1997); and Graham Richards, *Mental Machinery: The Origins and Consequences of Psychological Ideas, Part I: 1600–1850* (Baltimore: Johns Hopkins University Press, 1992).
8 Gerald Newman, *The Rise of English Nationalism: A Cultural History, 1740–1830* (London: Weidenfield and Nicholson, 1987), p. 56.
9 James Fordyce, *Sermons to Young Women* (London: Printed for A. Millar and T. Cadell, 1766); quoted in Jean I. Marsden, 'Daddy's girls: Shakespearean

daughters and eighteenth-century ideology', *Shakespeare Survey*, 51 (1998), 21.

[10] Marsden, 'Daddy's girls', 17, 26 and 22.

[11] 'Epistle dedicatory' to Nahum Tate, *The History of King Lear*, in Montague Summers (ed.), *Shakespeare Adaptations* (New York: Benjamin Blom, 1922), p. 177.

[12] Jean I. Marsden, *The Re-Imagined Text: Shakespeare, Adaptation and Eighteenth-Century Literary Theory* (Lexington: University Press of Kentucky, 1995), p. 36.

[13] Michael Dobson, *The Making of the National Poet: Shakespeare, Adaptation and Authorship, 1660–1769* (Oxford: Clarendon, 1992), p. 93.

[14] Jonathan Bate, *Shakespearean Constitutions: Politics, Theatre, Criticism, 1730–1830* (Oxford: Clarendon Press, 1989), pp. 85–6.

[15] Dobson, *The Making of the National Poet*, p. 214.

[16] William Hazlitt, 'On Shakespeare and Milton', in Jonathan Bates (ed.), *The Romantics on Shakespeare* (London: Penguin, 1992), pp. 180–8. Keats was keenly interested in *Lear*, as both his 1818 poem 'Sitting down to read *King Lear* once again' and this letter to George and Thomas Keats, 21 December 1817, attest:

> I spent Friday evening with Wells & went the next morning to see West's *Death on the Pale horse*. It is a wonderful picture, when West's age is considered; but there is nothing to be intense upon; no woman one feels mad to kiss; no face swelling into reality. The excellence of every Art is its intensity, capable of making all disagreeables evaporate, from their being in close relationship with Beauty & Truth – Examine *King Lear* & you will find this exemplified throughout; but in this picture we have unpleasantness without any momentous depth of speculation excited, in which to bury its repulsiveness.

> *The Letters of John Keats, 1814–1821*, ed. Edward Rollins Hyder (2 vols; Cambridge, MA: Harvard University Press, 1958), p. 192.

[17] William Hazlitt, *Characters of Shakespear's Plays* (2nd edn; London: Taylor and Hessey, 1818), p. 42.

[18] Charles Lamb, 'On the tragedies of Shakspear, considered with reference to their fitness for stage representation', in Joan Coldwell (ed.), *Charles Lamb on Shakespeare* (Gerrards Cross: Colyn Smythe, 1978), pp. 37 and 39.

[19] Susan Wolfson, 'Shakespeare and the Romantic girl reader', *Nineteenth-Century Contexts*, 21, 2 (1999), 204.

[20] Ibid., 210.

[21] Macgregor, *Amelia Opie*, p. 5; Cecilia Lucy Brightwell, *Memorials of the Life of Amelia Opie, Selected and Arranged from Her Letters* (London: Longman, Brown, 1854), pp. 12–17.

[22] Amelia Opie, *The Father and Daughter, with Dangers of Coquetry*, ed. Shelley King and John B. Pierce (Peterborough, Ont.: Broadview Press, 2003), p. 93.

[23] Ibid.

[24] On the recognition scene, see Ruth Perry, *Novel Relations: The Transformation*

of Kinship in English Literature and Culture, 1748–1818 (Cambridge: Cambridge University Press, 2004).

25 Ellison, *Cato's Tears*, p. 18.

26 Susan Staves, 'British seduced maidens', *Eighteenth-Century Studies*, 14, 2, (1980), p. 133.

27 Quoted in Jeffrey Commons, *100 Years of Italian Opera* (London: Opera Rara, 1982).

28 David Kimball, *Italian Opera* (Cambridge: Cambridge University Press, 1991), p. 244.

29 For a full discussion of 'rescue' operas as adaptations of Gothic novels in both Britain and France, see Diane Long Hoeveler and Sarah Davies Cordova, 'Gothic opera as romantic discourse in Britain and France: a cross-cultural dialogue', in Larry H. Peer and Diane Long Hoeveler (eds), *Romanticism: Comparative Discourses* (Aldershot: Ashgate, 2006), pp. 11–34.

30 Ferdinando Paër, *www.ferdinandopaer.ch/index.php?p=home* (accessed 25 February 2009).

31 Theodore Fenner, *Opera in London: Views of the Press, 1785–1830* (Carbondale: Southern Illinois University Press, 1994), p. 31.

32 Slavoj Žižek, 'I hear you with my eyes; or, the invisible master', in Renata Seleci and Slavoj Žižek (eds), *Gaze and Voice as Love Objects* (Durham: Duke University Press,), p. 93; italics in original.

33 In her own comments on the writing of *A Thousand Acres*, Jane Smiley observed:

> I imagined Shakespeare wrestling with the *Lear* story and coming away a little dissatisfied, a little defeated, but hugely stimulated, just as I was. As I imagined that, I felt that I received a gift, an image of literary history, two mirrors facing each other in the present moment, reflecting infinitely backward into the past and infinitely forward into the future.

'Shakespeare in Iceland', in Marianne Novy (ed.), *Transforming Shakespeare: Contemporary Women's Re-Visions in Literature and Performance* (New York: St Martin's, 1998), p. 173.

34 Freud, in 'The theme of the three caskets' (1913), writes:

> Lear is not only an old man: he is a dying man ... But the doomed man is not willing to renounce the love of women; he insists on hearing how much he is loved. Let us now recall the moving final scene, one of the culminating points of tragedy in modern drama. Lear carries Cordelia's dead body on to the stage. Cordelia is Death. If we reverse the situation, it becomes intelligible and familiar to us. She is the Death-goddess who, like the Valkyrie in German mythology, carries away the dead hero from the battlefield. Eternal wisdom, clothed in the primaeval myth, bids the old man renounce love, choose death and make friends with the necessity of dying.

Sigmund Freud, 'The theme of the three caskets', in *The Standard Edition of* the Complete Psychological Works, ed. James Strachey et al. (24 vols; London: Hogarth Press, 1953–74), vol. 12, p. 301.

[35] Ann Jones, *Ideas and Innovations: Best Sellers of Jane Austen's Age* (New York: AMS, 1986), p. 290.

[36] Quoted in ibid., p. 52.

[37] Quoted in Eleanor Ty, *Empowering the Feminine: The Narratives of Mary Robinson, Jane West and Amelia Opie* (Toronto: University of Toronto Press, 1998), p. 58.

[38] George Gilfillan, 'Female authors. no. 1 – Mrs Hemans', *Tait's Edinburgh Magazine*, n.s., 14 (1847), 360.

[39] Quoted in Catherine M. S. Alexander, 'Shakespeare and the eighteenth century: criticism and research', *Shakespeare Survey*, 51 (1998), 1.

PART III

Shakespeare as Gothic Writer

8

'We are not safe': History, Fear and the Gothic in Richard III

JESSICA WALKER

Scholars commonly date the genesis of 'the Gothic' from the fateful night when Horace Walpole dreamed of 'a gigantic hand in armour', which led to his Gothic novel *The Castle of Otranto* (1764).[1] But the conventions we associate with Gothic literature surfaced long before Walpole, in the drama of the Renaissance. By exploring one characteristic of the Gothic – its role as a tool for exploring a nation's relationship with its own history – I will argue for the 'Gothic' nature of Shakespeare's *Richard III* as it relates to Walpole's own use of the Gothic in *The Castle of Otranto*.

Scholars have noted similarities between the conventions of Renaissance drama and the Gothic novel, and there are specific echoes of *Richard III*'s themes in Walpole's *The Castle of Otranto*, such as ghosts set on avenging past wrongs and a rightful heir claiming the bride whom he has rescued from an incestuous marriage to a usurping villain. But is it enough simply to list the play's Gothic conventions – ghosts, monsters, curses, nightmares, prisons, secrets, evil uncles and murdered children? I would argue that not only the presence of these conventions, but also the purpose they serve in addressing the Tudor period's relationship with its medieval past, make *Richard III* a Gothic work. The haunted house here is the House of York; its ghosts and bleeding corpses are the spectres of the past, and the 'damsel in distress' is

England herself. Audiences unfamiliar with the events of the *Henry VI* plays nevertheless see in *Richard III* the Wars of the Roses reassembled like Frankenstein's creature, pieced together from bits of dead memories and revived as a monster that stalks the stage. In the figure of Richard, Shakespeare has created a spectre of medieval monstrosity, a metaphor for a past that constantly invades and usurps the present, and such forces cannot be put down as easily as is Richard himself.

As Mark Madoff argues in 'The useful myth of Gothic ancestry', the eighteenth century's fascination with a 'Gothic' or pseudo-medieval past, evident in the 'Gothic revival' in architecture and fiction, first served as 'a way to revis[e] the features of the past in order to satisfy the imaginative needs of the present. It flourished in response to current anxieties and desires.'[2] The Gothic creates a new vision of history for the purposes of understanding contemporary issues and the nation's relationship with its own past, a national myth 'invented to serve specific political and emotional purposes'.[3] As Longueil argues, the word 'Gothic', which primarily suggested barbarity when it came into use in the sixteenth century, gradually took on an additional connotation of 'medieval'.[4] Both definitions imply a contrast, referring to behaviours and eras distinct from the eighteenth century, when the term came into vogue. As England began to establish itself as an imperial nation, the Gothic helped the English to establish a sense of self both within and against a 'Gothic' past.[5] This sense of distance emerges in the remote settings of Gothic fictions, often medieval, Catholic Italy or Spain. Yet there was a certain proximity as well to the Gothic: in the eighteenth century, Gothic architecture was praised as an 'indigenous aesthetic, defined in opposition to a rule-based Neo-classicism'.[6] The Gothic, considered to be innately 'English', 'consistently drew strength from a generally patriotic attitude to the past'.[7]

Hence, the Gothic setting, simultaneously familiar and foreign, uses distance to address concerns about national identity, troubling the notion of a clear division between past and present. As 'the ideologies of nation both invented and performed social and historical difference', the Gothic endeavoured both to define eighteenth-century England against the 'otherness' of foreign times and places and to take lessons from them.[8] Such nostalgia for, but also anxiety about, the medieval period did not originate with the eighteenth century, as we see from the surge of interest in the study of history during the early modern period and the popularity of drama dealing with events of the Middle Ages. Madoff's characterization of the relationship between history and the Gothic recalls the nature of historiography and historical fiction in the Elizabethan period. Just as the eighteenth century used the 'Gothic' medieval past to navigate national identity, Shakespeare and his contemporaries attempted a similar 'Gothic' enterprise in their dealings with their own medieval history.

As the providential view of history that was common in the Middle Ages gave way to a humanistic interest in how people cause events, the Renaissance increasingly viewed history as a way of using lessons from the past to uncover how the present came to be. Historical writing – be it the work of historical scholars or poets tackling historical matters – provided 'good examples and cautionary tales' and helped people to understand the events leading up to major historical occurrences.[9] In a time of great social change such as the Renaissance, therefore, the study of the past could be used as a key to understanding the shaping of the Tudor state.[10]

The history play, a relatively new and unexplored genre when Shakespeare began to develop it in the late sixteenth century, played a prominent role in such study. Shakespeare's inquiry into civil disorder in *Richard III* is characteristic of both this early modern way of looking at history and the 'myth of Gothic ancestry' associated with the eighteenth century. *Richard III* is not 'Goth'-ic per se – its events go back only a century – but the play does take place in a medieval world characterized by brutality, feudalism and civil war. Certainly, the attitude towards a relatively recent medieval past found in the Renaissance differs from the eighteenth century's view of the period; but the propaganda surrounding the 'Golden Age' of Elizabeth nevertheless puts the Tudor state in opposition to the medieval Catholic world of the Plantagenets, making the days of the Wars of the Roses near in national memory (Richard III is, after all, Elizabeth's great-great-uncle) and yet ideologically distant.

The uncertain placement of *Richard III* in English history leads to potentially oppositional readings of the play. Is the Tudor victory at the play's close really a 'happy ending' that represents a clear division between the war-torn Middle Ages and the tranquillity of the Tudor Age? Or does the civil strife visible in *Richard III* persist even after Richmond takes the throne, and well on into the sixteenth century? The Wars of the Roses have special significance for the shaping of the Elizabethan state because the Tudor dynasty sprang from the victory of Elizabeth's grandfather against Richard III in the final battle of the civil wars at Bosworth. By inquiring into 'the absolute nadir of the English past',[11] Shakespeare is able to question how the Tudor state was shaped through 'the devious paths by which the crown descended to Elizabeth', as well as to consider whether the 'Golden Age' is really so different from the medieval period.[12] While earlier in the twentieth century, *Richard III* was taken as an example of Tudor propaganda – the story of Elizabeth's heroic grandfather, Richmond, overcoming the usurper Richard III and uniting both sides of the civil conflict through marriage to Edward IV's daughter – in recent decades literary historians have become aware of the 'probability that some of the Elizabethans themselves saw through the ruses of the dominant ideology … the impressive displays of highly theatrical myths of order and greatness [and] the everyday failures of the nation to function as the monarch pretended it did'.[13] By inquiring into the Plantagenet past, Shakespeare simultaneously shapes and troubles the national myth of the security of Elizabeth's dynasty and the post-Armada nationalism of the late sixteenth century. To trouble Tudor propaganda, *Richard III* draws parallels between the civil war that threatened the Yorkist court and the civil anxiety that surrounded Elizabeth. These parallels between past and present address an overarching theme: that despite propaganda advertising a new age, whether Elizabeth I's or Edward IV's, the nation's relationship with its own history and with the restless ghosts of its violent past cannot be dismissed easily.

The 'Gothic' elements at work in *Richard III* highlight the uneasy relationship between the Tudor nation and its history. The 'chief characteristic of the Gothic', as Susan Rowland notes, 'is to trouble boundaries'.[14] Such troubling frequently emerges in the form of the Gothic monster, a creature who falls outside the normal limits of human physiognomy and resists categorization, qualities that were disturbing during the Renaissance as much as they were in the eighteenth century:

> Throughout the period, a fresh interest in instrumentation and technology, a new enthusiasm for classificatory systems and a growing reliance on observation and experiment compete and merge with established systems of belief and older notions of 'truth' ... At a time when a spirit of rationalism was shaping the cultural *mentalité*, the discourses of 'monstrosity' found a metaphorical utility considerably beyond their immediate frames of reference.[15]

Inhabiting a liminal space somewhere between king and beast – at once loathsome monster and attractive seducer, stage Machiavel, morality Vice and tragic hero – Richard defies boundaries of characterization and genre, becoming a Proteus who changes shape at will.[16] But monstrosity had particularly political resonances for Renaissance audiences who, familiar with the notion of the king's two bodies (private and public, earthly and royal), would understand Richard's twisted body as representative of the civil disorder that still haunts Edward's court. Early modern writing frequently links monstrosity to historical trauma and civil strife, and the play 'finds in the shape of Richard's "monstrous" proportions a commentary on England's uncertain political fortunes'.[17] More than simply a figure of moral corruption, he is a symbol of political decay, the festering body of the state, 'the physical representation not only of a monster but of a deformed body politic'.[18]

With the elderly, unmarried queen well beyond childbearing years, yet still refusing to name an heir, the nation was consumed with anxiety at the prospect of civil war after her death. Political tracts use bodily metaphors of 'mutilated or separated bodies' to assess the health of the commonwealth, and 'these configurations ... bear a striking resemblance to comparable linguistic clusters in *Richard III*'.[19] The play speaks to anxiety about civil strife not only through the monstrous imagery associated with such discord but also by confronting the issue of civil conflicts that refuse to stay buried; the violence of the *Henry VI* plays haunts *Richard III*, just as the Elizabethans feared that the succession issues that had led to the Wars of the Roses would again result in war at Elizabeth's death.

Family strife serves as a metaphor for the state torn apart by civil war, and Gothic images of family turmoil plague *Richard III*: fratricide, murdered children, evil guardians, family secrets, incest and anxiety about the maternal body. The Wars of the Roses, after all, were not a quarrel between two families but a quarrel *within* a family – the line of Edward III. Earlier in the tetralogy, when Edward, Clarence and Richard slaughter Henry VI's son, '[c]onjunct assassination represents the high watermark of union and mutuality among the three royal brothers', a violent sort of family bonding.[20] But, when the wars end, the conflict moves from the battlefield to inside the house – that is, to within the house of York. As Richard himself declares, 'I have no brother, I am like no brother' (*3 Henry VI*, 5.6.80).[21]

Richard, as a bad father-figure and, consequently, a bad king, is responsible for most of this familial violence. The events of the *Henry VI* plays remind us that Richard is no lone sociopath; his betrayal of kin, murder of children and disruption of the succession echo the war crimes of Yorkists and Lancastrians alike. Yet, in the tetralogy's final play, he bears the weight of these crimes as a quasi-supernatural figure, a monstrous embodiment of civil dispute and the horrifying spectre of a violent past, a 'villain who has absorbed and come to embody all the evils plaguing England'.[22] These echoes of violence demonstrate that despite the 'glorious summer' advertised by Edward's propaganda, the wars have not really ended (*Richard III*, 1.1.2).

Richard's own particular brand of Gothic monstrosity embodies this repetition. He is born with teeth, an image that suggests advanced development – of being ahead of himself, ambitious, impatient to 'bite the world', running 'before his horse to market' (*3 Henry VI*, 5.6.54; *Richard III*, 1.1.160). But, if Richard 'came into the world with [his] legs forward' so that he might 'make haste' in destroying his enemies, he is also the 'tardy cripple' whose delay in sending Clarence's pardon causes his brother's death; like the civil war that will not conclude until his demise, Richard is 'unfinished' (*3 Henry VI*, 5.6.70–2; *Richard III*, 2.3.90). Born prematurely, impatient to enter the world and yet underdeveloped, he is characterized as both running ahead of himself and lagging behind.

If the monster in a Gothic work 'evoke[s] a wider monstrosity that disrupt[s] systems of classification and value',[23] Richard's monstrosity disrupts the very notion of linear time: his 'unbalanced and twisted body and his disposition, which make him incapable of having any natural rhythm in his life … mak[e] him akin to a nonliving creature, or as someone living in the realm of the undead'.[24] His time is out of joint: a manifestation of unfinished history in an unfinished body, he forces history to repeat itself. Vampires, ghosts, hauntings, Frankenstein's monster – what makes a Gothic monster, if not a troubling of the boundaries between the present and a past that will not die? Rowland cites 'rapid social changes' as a cause of 'Gothic anxiety', arguing that 'Gothic spectres haunt the fringes of the rapid transitions that mark out modernity'.[25] Here, Richard's monstrosity places him in the liminal space between wartime and peacetime and, for the Renaissance audience, between the medieval and the early modern.

Richard III's very first lines place the play within a comparative moment in time, contrasting 'now', the glorious post-war summer, with an implied 'then' (*Richard III*, 1.1.1). But the joyful court that Richard describes in his opening soliloquy bears little resemblance to the hostility and paranoia that are seen throughout the rest of the play. Rather, his machinations cause the post-war world to revert to the same atmosphere of fear and violence that had characterized the 'bad old days', enabling Richard's rise to power. If he is 'determined to prove a villain', he does so in direct opposition to the process of historical change, to 'hate the idle pleasures of these days' (1.1.30, 31). While those around him struggle to move in a linear fashion from the turmoil of war to an age of post-war peace, Richard's very existence embodies an interruption of that movement; his reminders of what has been and ambition for what is to come remove the play from its own theatrical 'present', constantly relocating it to the violent past of collective memory and the violent future of Richard's vision.

The threat that Richard poses to linear time surfaces in the play's supernatural occurrences: 'It is not surprising that a coffin figures early in the play, and ghosts make their cameo appearances toward its end, for the drama ... is concerned with the presence of those who are not present and the absence of those who should be.' [26] The corpse of the violent past, the '[p]ale ashes of the house of Lancaster', is represented onstage by the coffin of Henry VI, whose body, awaiting burial, remains present throughout Richard's wooing of Anne, the widow of Edward, Henry VI's son (*Richard III*, 1.2.6). A dead body should cease to bleed, be buried, decay, crumble to dust and be forgotten by succeeding generations, not bleed freely as if the violence perpetuated upon it had occurred only that day; yet Richard's presence causes Henry's wounds to '[o]pen their congeal'd mouths and bleed afresh' (l. 56). Anne claims that Richard's 'deeds inhuman and unnatural / Provokes this deluge most unnatural', but more than the sin of murder is at stake here (ll. 60–1). The image of Henry's bleeding corpse disturbs us not simply because it is violent but because it is *untimely*. The corpse that had stopped bleeding 'bleeds afresh', repeats itself and reverts to past violence; Richard's presence therefore disrupts the natural order of things.

Margaret, widow of Henry VI, serves a similar function as a spectre of the past, playing the ghost to Richard's monster. Her anachronistic appearance in the last play of Shakespeare's tetralogy – she was dead by the time represented in *Richard III* – 'gives the sense that she is a figure out of time, or an embodiment of time ... whose memories, the longest and bitterest ones, make the spectators stand back from the present and see history as a tragic cycle'.[27] Like Anne, Margaret reminds Richard of his crimes against her family. But, unlike Anne, she is not eager to escape her past; rather, she wishes to raise old ghosts. The old queen's accusations expose Richard's true nature, and, if he had seen Margaret as a threat, he could have disposed of her as he does the others. But, paradoxically, she serves Richard's purpose: for all his posturing as a reformed sinner, his true security lies in ensuring that those around him remember 'what I have been, and what I am' (*Richard*

III, 1.3.132). The ghosts that Richard and Margaret raise produce a palpable atmosphere of fear among the play's characters, and this serves Richard's purpose.

Unlike most Gothics, *Richard III* rarely frightens its audiences; other plays of the period certainly offer us more gruesome violence and more harrowing supernatural elements. But fear of the past is the driving force behind the events of *Richard III*, for Richard uses this fear as a weapon. Given his talent for deception, his victims may not be aware of the full extent of his villainy, but they are perfectly aware, as Queen Elizabeth says, that he 'loves not me, nor none of you' (*Richard III*, 1.3.13). Richard succeeds not because he lies, but because he tells the truth: that, despite their pledges of reconciliation, opposing factions still threaten to break out into civil strife. His lies about Queen Elizabeth, for instance, would not be believed if hostility did not already exist: 'Though he may exaggerate or twist the truth, Richard does not have to use deceit to convince others of the venality of the Queen's faction.'[28] By implying that Elizabeth is responsible for Clarence's imprisonment, Richard accomplishes something more valuable than simply deflecting the blame from himself: he creates paranoia and hostility between the Yorkist and Lancastrian factions at court, spreading anxiety through constant reminders that the queen's family was once 'factious for the house of Lancaster' (1.3.127). Fear of opposing forces on the battlefield is transferred to a dread of the machinations of various hostile factions within the royal family and, under these conditions, Richard is able to divide and conquer: the warning Richard gives his brother – 'We are not safe, Clarence, we are not safe' – ironically turns out to be true (1.1.70). A sense of paranoia envelops the characters as the drama unfolds:

> The hearts of men are full of fear.
> You cannot reason (almost) with a man
> That looks not heavily and full of dread.
>
> (2.3.38–40)

Images of imprisonment further emphasize the Gothic power of past events. All good Gothics need a haunted house, one 'marked, haunted by "history" – the events of its own development':

The ghosts – whether real or imaginary – derive from the past passions, past deeds, past crimes of the family identified with this structure. The psychic as well as the physical space of the castle bears its marks ... That the house embodies the family history reminds us that the word 'house' has two meanings relevant to Gothic fictions – it refers both to the building itself and to the family line.[29]

Ghosts of war haunt the house of York, and characters who cannot escape their pasts find themselves imprisoned in the Tower of London. Hastings's attempt to drive history forward by crowning Edward V results in his arrest and execution. The young princes, whose arrival heralded the end of 'sour annoy' at the conclusion of *3 Henry VI*, are locked up and made to die for the sins of their fathers (*3 Henry VI*, 5.6.45). Although Clarence can flee the Tower in his sleep, he cannot escape his family history, and his dream is marked by Gothic imagery that underscores the persistence of past violence – memories of 'a thousand heavy times, / During the wars of York and Lancaster' (*Richard III*, 1.4.14–15); the fratricidal image of Richard's knocking Clarence overboard; the 'dead men's skulls' at the bottom of the ocean and, finally, in the 'kingdom of perpetual night', the terrible spectres of his father-in-law Warwick, whom he betrayed, and Prince Edward, whom he murdered (ll. 29, 47).

Clarence's dream in which Richard drowns him may be prophetic, but the scene is more concerned with Clarence's 'dismal terror' when faced with the ghosts of the past (1.4.7). Such is the nature of omens, prophecies and portents – so characteristic of the Gothic – that are found in *Richard III*. Anne, Buckingham and Hastings curse themselves, Richard recalls his father's curse on Margaret, and Margaret herself curses nearly everyone with whom she comes into contact. But, although curses typically look to the future, these are concerned with the past, underscoring its tenuous relationship with the present. They are prophecies of revenge that see the future only as a time in which the past may be repeated, and hope only that the sins of the past will be avenged. These ever present curses *create*, rather than *foresee*, an atmosphere of violence: Richard can easily destroy

Clarence because Edward 'hearkens after prophecies and dreams' (1.1.54), and Margaret's pronouncements fill the listeners with terror, as Buckingham attests: 'My hair doth stand on end to hear her curses' (1.3.303).

These ghosts of history finally appear, on the night before the battle at Bosworth Field, as literal ghosts who claim Richard as their final victim. 'Despair and die!', they bid him, and he obeys: 'I shall despair' (5.3.125, 200). The monstrous creature that Richard had created to terrify others finally turns on him: 'Cold fearful drops stand on my trembling flesh. / What do I fear? Myself? There's none else by' (ll. 182–3). These ghosts prove a greater challenge to Richard than does Richmond's army:

> Shadows to-night
> Have strook more terror to the soul of Richard
> Than can the substance of ten thousand soldiers.
>
> (ll. 216–18)

Rather than being defeated by divine providence in the form of the Tudor hero Richmond, I would argue that Richard is ultimately overcome by the same fear he has inspired in others – his 'coward conscience', the horror of realizing that his own past has caught up with him (l. 179).

The play's conclusion looks to a glorious future of Tudor rule in which 'peace lives again' (*Richard III*, 5.5.40), but 'enough had happened in the 1580s to evidence the fragility of the Tudor myth and cracks in its ideology'.[30] Rather than comforting Renaissance audiences with the assurance that such turmoil was safely behind them, it may only have served as a reminder that the past is always present and also as a direct comment on the nation's succession crisis:

> Nowhere in the two tetralogies does the past come closer to the present than here, where Shakespeare stages the origins of the Tudor dynasty for his own monarch. And nowhere, perhaps, is the conjunction between past and present more unsettling. For however central the story of Richmond's triumph at Bosworth field was to the Tudor's own legitimating myth of history, to retell

that story at the close of the century is to offer a perplexing tribute to the last Tudor monarch, the Virgin Queen who had no hope of continuing Richmond's line.[31]

Although the play's closing lines express the hope that civil war is over for good, 'the drama looks backwards to contemplate the treatment England might receive at the hands of history', and anxiety over the succession betrays the populace's fear that history is bound to repeat itself – that the sins of the nation will be visited upon its children.[32]

This sounds, of course, like *The Castle of Otranto*. Walpole, as W. S. Lewis argues, was well aware of the power of writing to reshape the meaning of history, an awareness that is particularly apparent in his own memoirs: 'The *Memoirs* gave him a sense of power. He could not make history, but he could write it. Posterity would learn from him the events of his time and how they came about.'[33] Through his Gothic fictions, Walpole sought to reshape the Gothic past to support his political viewpoints. He 'favoured the weaker side and was against authority'; deeply opposed to authority and those who abused it, frequently 'on the side of the rebellious' (such as the American colonists), he laboured passionately to promote his causes.[34] Examination of the political climate surrounding Walpole during the period leading up to the composition of *Otranto* suggests that, like Shakespeare, he used a removed, medieval setting to comment on a current political crisis. The year preceding *Otranto* saw controversy over a subject's right to criticize the king, rioting over the issue of free speech and the dismissal of Walpole's friend and cousin, Henry Conway, from his civil and military positions.[35] Walpole's 'hatred of tyranny or the undue exercise of power' surfaces in his criticism of the tyrannical Manfred from *The Castle of Otranto*.[36] Betsy Perteit Harfst suggests that '[t]his manifest content shows traces of the current political problems of 1764':

> By making just a few identifications, these surface incidents can be viewed as an expression of Walpole's current ambition to attain his father's power and to protect Conway. The governmental opposition can be represented by the tyrant, Manfred. Walpole can be

identified with Theodore, who overcomes all dangers and protects the virtuous maiden, Isabella or Conway, and who finally achieves the position held by his father.[37]

Walpole's use of the Gothic in *Otranto* reminds the reader that the tyranny associated with medieval times threatens to resurface in the Age of Reason, and the 'uncanny eruption of the past' in the novel frequently reminds us of *Richard III*.[38] The ghosts of war, violence and usurpation haunt the royal houses of both works, and it is only a matter of time before they rise to reclaim what they are owed.

Parallels between *The Castle of Otranto* and *Richard III* highlight the Gothic's uneasy relationship with the past. Both Richard and Manfred attempt simultaneously to retain the privileges of and to silence the voices of their family pasts: Richard has come to power by prolonging the violence of the civil wars begun by his father, and Manfred by holding on to the title usurped by his grandfather. Yet with those nefariously gained past triumphs come the voices of the wronged, crying out for justice. Both tyrants are haunted by prophecies made long ago: Richard by predictions that Richmond will destroy him and become king; and Manfred by the prophecy that '*the castle and lordship of Otranto should pass from the present family, whenever the real owner should be grown too large to inhabit it*'.[39] The material ghosts of historical violence confront both characters. As events unravel, these villains become increasingly anxious, distracted and out of control; afraid of losing their wrongfully gained power, both resort to immoral, incestuous and murderous means to retain it, seeking inappropriate marriages with Elizabeth of York and Isabella (the Italian form, conveniently enough, of 'Elizabeth') in order to prolong their usurping lines of inheritance. Both marriages are inappropriate because they follow swiftly on the heels of a death of a family member, for which our villain is in some way responsible: Richard tries to seduce Elizabeth of York through her mother shortly after he has had her brothers put to death; Manfred proposes to Isabella soon after her betrothed has fallen victim to a ghost angered by the continued usurpation of his rights. Manfred fails in his endeavours because of past events: Isabella is disgusted at the proposal because she was betrothed to Manfred's son, and Manfred is frightened during their exchange by the sudden appearance of the 'fatal helmet' and the grandfather's sighing portrait.[40] Likewise, Richard is unsuccessful in winning Elizabeth's hand because Queen Elizabeth is unwilling to forget the past, and he falls in battle because the ghosts who comforted his enemy have destroyed his confidence. Ultimately, each tyrant's crowning act of villainy is the murder of children meant to be in his care: destruction of the family acts as a metaphor for civil discord.

We find such parallels not only in the villains' methods, but in their adversaries. The ghosts of the saintly rulers whose crowns were usurped by the villains' forebears (Henry VI and Alfonso the Good) haunt both tyrants. Richmond and Theodore, the dashing young heroes who defeat the tyrants and are heirs of the rightful rulers, are both marked as special from youth – Richmond by Henry VI's prophecy that he will rule, Theodore by his resemblance to Alfonso. Both heroes are raised in obscurity – Richmond in exile, Theodore as a slave and peasant – for only an outsider, someone 'not acquainted with your castle' who has not been involved in the war and strife that causes these problems, can become the hero to save the nation.[41] Rescuing damsels from haunted houses, Theodore helps Isabella escape 'this fatal castle' just as Elizabeth escapes the house of York and the threat of marriage to Richard by marrying the Tudor hero.[42] As rightful heirs, both receive supernatural aid from their forefathers, figures whose positive familial support contrasts with the infighting found in the tyrants' families: dreams of Richard's victims rejuvenate Richmond as they destroy Richard, while Theodore refers to Alfonso's giant helmet as his 'accomplice'.[43] Ultimately, the 'house' – be it the house of York or the castle of Otranto – is knocked to the ground, destroyed by the violence within, and the villain 'pay[s] the price of usurpation for all'.[44]

While Walpole will doubtless continue to be considered the father of the Gothic, we cannot ignore the spectral presence of that old ghost, Shakespeare, whispering in his ear; though born from Walpole's dream, the genre has its own literary forefathers with which to come to terms. Both Shakespeare studies and Gothic studies will surely benefit from such an inquiry. An under-

standing of how the Renaissance conceived of history and historical fiction as a way to address the issues of the present while
coming to terms with the past deepens our understanding of the
Gothic enterprise; similarly, an understanding of Gothic imagery
highlights the significance of the Gothic elements in *Richard III*
and helps us understand what is at stake when Shakespeare
attempts to raise the ghosts of his own medieval past.

Notes

[1] Horace Walpole, *The Yale Edition of Horace Walpole's Correspondence*, ed. W. S.
     Lewis et al. (48 vols; New Haven: Yale University Press, 1937–83), vol. 1,
     p. 88.
[2] Mark Madoff, 'The useful myth of Gothic ancestry', *Studies in Eighteenth-
     Century Culture*, 8 (1979), 337.
[3] Ibid.
[4] Alfred E. Longueil, 'The word "Gothic" in eighteenth-century criticism',
     Modern Language Notes, 38, 8 (December 1923), 456.
[5] Kathleen Wilson, *The Island Race: Englishness, Empire and Gender in the
     Eighteenth Century* (London: Routledge, 2003), p. 5.
[6] James Watt, 'Gothic', in Thomas Keymer and Jon Mee (eds), *The Cambridge
     Companion to English Literature, 1740–1830* (Cambridge: Cambridge
     University Press, 2004), pp. 119–20.
[7] Simon Bradley, 'The Englishness of Gothic: theories and interpretations
     from William Gilpin to J. H. Parker', *Architectural History*, 45 (2002), 325.
     Both S. Lang, 'The principles of Gothic revival in England', *The Journal of the
     Society of Architectural Historians*, 25, 4 (December 1966), 240–67, and
     Wilmarth Sheldon Lewis, *Horace Walpole*, A. W. Mellon Lectures in the Fine
     Arts (London: Rupert Hart Davis, 1961) argue that Walpole's interest in the
     Gothic was driven, in part, by a patriotic attitude towards what was consid-
     ered to be a uniquely 'English' form of architecture.
[8] Wilson, *The Island Race*, p. 4.
[9] Janis Lull, 'Plantagenets, Lancastrians, Yorkists and Tudors: *1–3 Henry VI,
     Richard III, Edward III*', in Michael Hattaway (ed.), *The Cambridge Companion
     to Shakespeare's History Plays* (Cambridge: Cambridge University Press,
     2002), p. 89.
[10] This use of lessons from history is evident in the *de casibus* tradition of histo-
     riography, particularly the Renaissance work *A Mirror for Magistrates*. This
     tradition employed a great deal of Gothic imagery, often with the actual
     ghosts of historical figures coming forward to tell their stories. See Paul
     Budra, *A Mirror for Magistrates and the De Casibus Tradition* (Toronto:
     University of Toronto Press, 2000).

11   Donald G. Watson, *Shakespeare's Early History Plays: Politics at Play on the Elizabethan Stage* (Athens: University of Georgia Press, 1990), p. 80.

12   Michael Hattaway, 'The Shakespearean History Play', in Michael Hattaway (ed.), *The Cambridge Companion to Shakespeare's History Plays* (Cambridge: Cambridge University Press, 2002), p. 9.

13   Watson, *Shakespeare's Early History Plays*, p. 13.

14   Susan Rowland, 'Margery Allingham's Gothic: genre as cultural criticism', *Clues: A Journal of Detection*, 23, 1 (fall 2004), 27.

15   Mark Thornton Burnett, *Constructing 'Monsters' in Shakespearean Drama and Early Modern Culture* (New York: Palgrave Macmillan, 2002), pp. 4 and 7.

16   Richard's ability to shape-shift further evokes political anxieties; anti-theatrical discourse characterized actors as 'monsters', and Elizabeth, who constantly reinvented her image to gain power, was the consummate actress. See Phyllis Rackin, *Stages of History: Shakespeare's English Chronicles* (Ithaca: Cornell University Press, 1990), p. 73; Burnett, *Constructing 'Monsters'*, p. 9; and Nina S. Levine, *Women's Matters: Politics, Gender and Nation in Shakespeare's Early History Plays* (Newark: University of Delaware Press, 1998), p. 22.

17   Burnett, *Constructing 'Monsters'*, p. 6.

18   Marie-Hélène Besnault and Michel Bitot, 'Historical legacy and fiction: the poetical reinvention of King Richard III', in Michael Hattaway (ed.), *The Cambridge Companion to Shakespeare's History Plays* (Cambridge: Cambridge University Press, 2002), p. 110.

19   Burnett, *Constructing 'Monsters'*, p. 70.

20   E. Pearlman, 'The invention of Richard of Gloucester', *Shakespeare Quarterly*, 43, 4 (1992), 426.

21   All references to Shakespeare's plays are to *The Riverside Shakespeare*, ed. G. Blakemore Evans, et al. (2nd edn; Boston: Houghton Mifflin Company, 1997). Further references will be incorporated into the body of the text.

22   Watson, *Shakespeare's Early History Plays*, p. 121.

23   Fred Botting, 'Monstrosity', in Marie Mulvey-Roberts (ed.), *The Handbook of Gothic Literature* (New York: New York University Press, 1998), p. 163.

24   Richard Marienstras, 'Of a monstrous body', in Jean-Marie Maguin and Michèle Willems (eds), *French Essays on Shakespeare and His Contemporaries: 'What Would France with Us?'* (London: Associated University Presses, 1995), p. 167.

25   Rowland, 'Margery Allingham's Gothic', 27.

26   Heather Dubrow, 'The infant of your care: guardianship in Shakespeare's *Richard III* and early modern England', in Kari Boyd McBride (ed.), *Domestic Arrangements in Early Modern England* (Pittsburgh: Duquesne University Press, 2002), p. 161.

27   Besnault and Bitot, 'Historical legacy and fiction', p. 119.

28   Watson, *Shakespeare's Early History Plays*, p. 113.

29   Anne Williams, *Art of Darkness: A Poetics of Gothic* (Chicago: University of Chicago Press, 1995), p. 45.

30   Watson, *Shakespeare's Early History Plays*, p. 22.

31   Levine, *Women's Matters*, pp. 99–100.

32   Burnett, *Constructing 'Monsters'*, p. 92.

33   Lewis, *Horace Walpole*, p. 91.

34   Lewis, *Horace Walpole*, pp. 65 and 78.

35   Timothy Mowl, *Horace Walpole: The Great Outsider* (London: John Murray, 1996), pp. 171–2; E. J. Clery, 'Introduction' to Horace Walpole, *The Castle of Otranto: A Gothic Story*, ed. W. S. Lewis (Oxford: Oxford University Press, 1996), p. xxviii; Betsy Perteit Harfst, *Horace Walpole and the Unconscious: An Experiment in Freudian Analysis* (New York: Arno Press, 1980), pp. 25–6.

36   John Brooke, 'Horace Walpole and the politics of the early years of the reign of George III', in Warren Hunting Smith (ed.), *Horace Walpole: Writer, Politician and Connoisseur: Essays on the 250th Anniversary of Walpole's Birth* (New Haven: Yale University Press, 1967), p. 7.

37   Harfst, *Horace Walpole and the Unconscious*, p. 71.

38   Watt, 'Gothic', p. 122. A preoccupation with the abuse of authority was not unique to Walpole in this period; productions of *Richard III* were frequent in the years leading up to the composition of *The Castle of Otranto*, and the popularity of this and other history plays may stem from 'a contemporary preoccupation with leadership, usurpation and the qualifications of the ideal ruler, developed in turn by Walpole in his Gothic romance' (Kristina Bedford, '"This castle hath a pleasant seat": Shakespearean allusion in *The Castle of Otranto*', *English Studies in Canada*, 14, 4 (December 1988), 416).

39   Horace Walpole, *The Castle of Otranto*, p. 17; italics in original.

40   Ibid., pp. 25 and 26.

41   Ibid., p. 45.

42   Ibid., p. 29.

43   Ibid., p. 31.

44   Ibid., p. 113.

9

Remembering Ophelia: Ellen Terry and the Shakespearizing of Dracula

CHRISTY DESMET

∾

In chapter 3 of *Dracula*, the count warns Jonathan Harker to be careful where he sleeps in the castle, 'for it is old, and has many memories, and there are bad dreams for those who sleep unwisely'.[1] This warning sounds uncannily familiar, but its reference does not finally 'click' into place until later that same night, as Jonathan writes in his diary in an effort to stave off panic:

> Up to now I never quite knew what Shakespeare meant when he made Hamlet say –
>
> > My tablets! Quick, my tablets!
> > 'Tis meet that I put it down, etc.
>
> > > (*Dracula*, p. 41)[2]

In this context, Dracula's warning about falling asleep in 'unwise' places points towards Hamlet's 'To be or not to be' soliloquy, in which he acknowledges that he fears 'what dreams may come' to him in death's long sleep (*Hamlet*, 3.1.65), and perhaps towards Macbeth's anticipation of the 'terrible dreams' that will plague the regicide who has murdered sleep (*Macbeth*, 3.2.18). Harker's dawning recognition that Castle Dracula, like Denmark, is a prison (*Dracula*, p. 32; *Hamlet*, 2.2.243) and that the count, like

Claudius in Shakespeare's play, can 'smile, and smile' but still 'be a villain' (1.5.108) pushes him to make his escape from both. Jonathan, however, is not alone in his knowledge and deployment of Shakespearean sayings. Citing, quoting, misquoting and alluding to Shakespeare is commonplace in *Dracula*, but the novel's kinship with the Bard fades in and out of focus as the references are more or less marked as Shakespearean and are more or less appropriate to the situation in which they appear. Shakespearean quotations do not so much populate as haunt the text of *Dracula*.

Shakespearean citation is part of both the Gothic novel's heritage and Bram Stoker's day job as the manager of Henry Irving's Lyceum Theatre. Douglas Lanier suggests that citation – turning Shakespearean passages into 'freely applicable cultural truisms' – becomes a malleable mechanism for bridging the gap between high and low culture.[3] Perhaps Stoker, as Gothic novelist, incorporated Shakespearean references both to boost the status of the genre and, more playfully, to invite readers into a game of 'identify that allusion'. For Stoker in his role as the Lyceum director under Henry Irving, the Shakespeare text also possessed a particular kind of cultural capital. Both he and Ellen Terry, as the Lyceum's leading lady, were particular about the acting text and its delivery; Irving revised the play text of *Hamlet*, for instance, no fewer than four times,[4] and he and Terry individually marked up prompt books and printed texts with commentary on topics ranging from characterization to enunciation.

Between the director and his star actress and between Irving and his audience, the Shakespearean text could also be contested territory. In *Much Ado About Nothing*, Irving followed Beatrice's shocking request that Benedick 'kill Claudio' with a gallant tag line, 'As sure as I'm alive, I will', in order to lighten the play's mood and keep it firmly within a comic ethos. Stoker says: 'Against this Ellen Terry protested. Almost to tears. She thought that every word of Shakespeare was sacred; to add to them was wrong.'[5] In her memoir, Terry casts the disagreement less in terms of Bardolatry than of theatrical decorum – she objected to the broad comedy as much as to the desecration of Shakespeare – but her account and Stoker's both note, with surprise, that for once the audience did not comment unfavourably on Irving's 'monkeying' with Shakespeare's text, as Stoker puts it.[6] As both theatrical and novelistic property, then, Shakespeare's plays provide Stoker and his characters with thematic touchstones for rooting out Dracula's, and *Dracula's*, mystery.

Bits of Shakespeare in the body of Dracula

Shakespeare appears in bits and pieces throughout *Dracula*. While some of the references are produced self-consciously by the novel's characters as they attempt to sort out their situations, in many cases the citations are unmarked and achieve an ominous significance only by virtue of accumulation. Not surprisingly, the lion's share are drawn from *Hamlet* and *Macbeth*. More surprisingly, perhaps, a nexus of references to *King Lear* structures the subplot involving Dracula, Dr Seward and the madman Renfield. Finally, a cloud of allusions to Shakespearean heroines surrounds the doomed Lucy and her more fortunate friend Mina Harker.

Hamlet, that favourite of Gothic novelists, permeates the first half of *Dracula*. In the novel, this play seems to be the property of western European men in positions of power and authority – specifically, Jonathan Harker and Dr Seward – who rely on the familiar Shakespearean text to cope with unfamiliar and unsettling situations. (Neither Dracula nor Van Helsing, as outsiders to England and its culture, has *Hamlet* at his fingertips, and neither has perfect English.) There is, perhaps, a preliminary connection between Dracula and the Ghost established in chapter 1 (if Dracula is, indeed, the coachman who brings Jonathan to the castle) when Jonathan sees the driver, confronting one of the blue flames that bar their passage along the road, through an odd optical illusion: 'When he stood between me and the flame he did not obstruct it, for I could see its ghostly figure all the same' (p. 19). The figure surrounded by a blue aura, although reflecting generally the Romantics' interest in such optical effects, may evoke Henri Fuseli's by then canonical image of Hamlet confronting the ghost; more locally, Tom Mead, the Lyceum ghost in both Irving's 1874 and 1878 productions, had been bathed in a moonlight created by combining green footlights with blue lights overhead.[7] In a subtle way, the Shakespearean stage has already been set.

Daily life at Castle Dracula follows the nocturnal pattern established by *Hamlet*'s Ghost; Jonathan recognizes, if unconsciously, the similarity when he remarks that with Count Dracula, 'everything has to break off at cock-crow' (p. 35). In this metaphysical no-man's-land, Dracula (again like the ghost) is at once himself – recognizable through his bearing, facial characteristics and even his expression – but also a dehumanized 'thing' (1.1.21) that inspires in Harker the horror that stage Hamlets had felt at least since David Garrick employed a hydraulic wig to enact the Ghost's suggestion that his tale would make 'each particular hair' on Hamlet's head stand on end (1.5.19). In her analysis of *Hamlet*'s Ghost, Marjorie Garber argues that in Shakespeare's play the Ghost, as a figure of patriarchy, functions as Lacan's 'the Name of the Father', the Law whose ultimate signifier, the phallus, is marked by absence rather than presence: 'To put the matter in a slightly different way: the Name of the Father is the dead father. *This* father – the Ghost – isn't dead enough.'[8] The ghost of Hamlet's father, it seems, is an early modern member of the undead.

Although linked primarily with the Ghost, Dracula also has a smack of Hamlet in him (to appropriate Coleridge's self-dramatizing phrase). Dressed in black, imprisoned in his ancestral country and even his home, he lives every day surrounded by the funereal smell of decaying earth. Dracula, we may say, encounters repeatedly the sights and sounds that Hamlet experiences as a special epiphany during his colloquy with Yorick's skull in the graveyard scene. By way of their shared kinship with Hamlet, Dracula therefore reflects back to Jonathan Harker not difference, but a dangerous sameness. The line between living and dead, Alexander and the beggar through whose guts he passes, and virtue and vice becomes as porous in *Dracula* as it is in *Hamlet*.

When Dracula arrives in England, *Hamlet*'s allusive power wanes, while that of *Macbeth* grows, shifting the novel's ethos from metaphysical angst to supernatural melodrama. From the novel's beginning, Dracula and his female vampires are linked consistently with *Macbeth*'s feminine evil. After his first encounter with them at Castle Dracula, Jonathan equates the three lady vampires, themselves *infanti-phagi*, with Shakespeare's 'weird sisters' and their gory brew, which includes 'finger of birth-strangled babe' (p. 51; see *Macbeth*, 4.1.30). As infanticides, the vampires are also linked to Lady Macbeth. So, too, are Dracula and Lucy, who both adopt, apparently without consciousness, her salient mannerisms. While instructing Jonathan, for instance, Dracula 'motioned with his hands as if he were washing them' (p. 38); and Lucy begins her characteristic sleepwalking even before Dracula's ghost-ship has landed on English shores (p. 78). During the voyage, members of the *Demeter*'s unfortunate crew find themselves in Macbeth's own predicament. The first mate's experience of having his knife slice through the apparition of Dracula recalls, and inverts, the insubstantial dagger that leads Macbeth to the commission of his first material crime, and therefore to his doom (p. 83). The mate's condition, in which according to the captain, his 'stronger nature seems to have worked inwardly against himself' (p. 82), also recalls that of Macbeth, whose 'seated heart' knocks against his ribs at the very suggestion of murder (*Macbeth,* 1.4.134–7).

Finally, Dracula's arrival at Whitby climaxes with a storm whose Shakespearean resonances are both overdetermined and completely unmarked. The *Dailygraph* correspondent records how 'the roar of the tempest, and the crash of the thunder and the booming of the mighty billows came through the damp oblivion even louder than before' (p. 77). Most commentators, if they see Shakespeare at all in this extended scene painting, identify the atmospheric source as either *Macbeth* or *Othello*; because of the particular complex of words, however, *Lear*, the *Tempest* and even *Hamlet* are possible touchstones. One other possible, if deeply buried, source for the transitional device of Dracula's arrival by sea occurs, significantly, after the insubstantial dagger appears to Macbeth, leading him to the murder of Duncan:

> Nature seems dead, and wicked dreams abuse
> The curtain'd sleep; witchcraft celebrates
> Pale Hecate's off'rings, and wither'd Murther,
> Alarum'd by his sentinel, the wolf,
> Whose howl's his watch, thus with his stealthy pace,

With Tarquin's ravishing [strides], towards his design
Moves like a ghost. (*Macbeth*, 2.1.50–6)

Dracula leaves the boat in the shape of a wolf–dog; Lucy will be
abused by wicked dreams, and Murther will follow the wolf
through London in search of prey for Dracula who, like a ghostly
Tarquin, strides (or flies, when in the shape of a bat) unerringly
toward Lucy Westenra.[9]

After *Dracula* has completed his pilgrimage from continental
Europe to England, *Hamlet* and *Macbeth* continue to inform the
novel's plot. Hamlet's acquiescence to the Ghost's command,
'Remember me', becomes a collective imperative for the vampire
hunters as they piece together the chronological record that will
allow them finally to defeat Dracula. The 'weird' atmosphere of
Macbeth also becomes ubiquitous, as bats, wolves and rats run
rampant through London and as the group struggles against the
rugged terrain of Dracula's home country. While *Hamlet* and
Macbeth make a natural pair in framing the horror of *Dracula*'s
main plot, the infusion of *King Lear* into the subplot involving
Dracula, the madman Renfield and Dr Seward is more unusual.
The play was not popular on stage during the nineteenth century,
in the early part because of perceived connections between Lear's
madness and that of George III and generally because of the
Romantic revulsion against what Charles Lamb, most famously,
identified as the creaky mechanics of a realistic stage that reduced
the patriarch himself to a 'tottering' old man.[10]

Dr Seward, as a rational European, sees the prize inmate of his
asylum as a mad parody of the nineteenth century's overly intel-
lectualized Hamlet. 'There is method in his madness', the doctor
feels (p. 69). Seward calls Renfield a 'zoophagous' or 'life eating
maniac' who tries 'to absorb as many lives' as he can in a 'cumula-
tive' manner (p. 71). Renfield collects flies, which he then feeds to
spiders, which are sacrificed to his birds, which Renfield himself
then eats and vomits. His compulsive food cycle, of course, parodies that of Dracula, who devours in order to replicate his tribe of
the undead. Significantly, however, the madman himself views his
behaviour through the lens not of *Hamlet*, but of *Lear*. Renfield
has been worrying the question of how he might consume the

life of other beings without stealing their souls. With the intention of being 'cruel only to be kind' – Hamlet's professed intention toward his mother in the closet scene (*Hamlet*, 3.4.178) – Seward pushes the issue. Renfield replies that he does not want the souls of flies and spiders 'buzzing around' him and concludes: 'I don't take any stock at all in such matters. "Rats and mice and such small deer", as Shakespeare has it' (pp. 237 and 238).[11] In this heavily marked and clearly attributed citation, Renfield takes on the role of *King Lear*'s Edgar disguised as Poor Tom, who tells the mad Lear that he has eaten only rats, mice and small deer for the past seven years. Mad Renfield is the 'unaccommodated man' of *King Lear*'s universe, nothing more than a 'poor, bare, fork'd animal' (*King Lear*, 3.4.106–8).

Within the context of Renfield's maniacal pursuit of Dracula as his 'master', the juxtaposition of references to *King Lear* (from Renfield's perspective) with references to *Hamlet* (from Seward's point of view) places *Dracula*'s events within a framework of competing metaphysics. At least for the moment, Dr Seward lives securely in a Christian world that is based on his understanding of *Hamlet* as a providential work. Mistaking Renfield's enigmatic statement that 'the Master is at hand' for religious mania, Seward remarks that 'The real God taketh heed lest a sparrow fall; but the God created from human vanity sees no difference between an eagle and a sparrow' (p. 96).[12] Seward, of course, may cite the New Testament rather than *Hamlet*, but continuing references to *Hamlet* suggest that the doctor clings to a blindly rationalist reading of Renfield's disorder.[13] Renfield, by contrast, inhabits the more pessimistic world of *King Lear*, in which 'as flies to wanton boys are we to th' gods, / They kill us for their sport' (4.1.36–7). In fact, in *Dracula* the gods not only kill men (and women), but 'eat' them. In this way, Renfield's consumption of the flies thus becomes a paradigm for mankind's fate under the regime of Dracula, while his final reduction to a dismembered body serves as a fitting emblem of unaccommodated man's destiny in a world governed not by loyalty and love, but by abjection, cruelty and destruction – in other words, the world of *Dracula* as filtered through *King Lear*.

Redemptive theatricality: Ophelia, Lady Macbeth and Ellen Terry

The intrusion of *King Lear* into *Dracula* not only signals a meta-physical crisis for its denizens as Dracula stands poised to eradicate London's teeming millions, but also permits a shift from the male-centred plots of *Hamlet* and *Macbeth* to a parent–child drama in which women play a more prominent part. Significantly, the 'good daughter' Cordelia is completely absent from *Dracula*. Instead, the novel foregrounds three Shakespearean heroines with a more complex moral history: Desdemona, although only for a moment; Lady Macbeth, although her name is never mentioned; and Ophelia. As a girl on the brink of womanhood, Lucy Westenra fastens on Shakespeare's Desdemona as a model for her own future adventures. While being courted simultaneously by three different men, Lucy comments in her letter to Mina on the marriage proposal that she has just received from the hearty Texan Quincy Morris: 'I sympathize with poor Desdemona when she had such a dangerous stream poured in her ear, even by a black man' (p. 59). Because Lucy light-heartedly wonders why women cannot marry three men at once, many readers take this identification with Desdemona as a sign of impending weakness or sensuality and a predilection toward all that Dracula represents. But Lucy continues to moralize Desdemona's fate in a way that naturalizes her exotic romantic relationship: 'I suppose that we women are such cowards that we think a man will save us from fears, and we marry him' (p. 59). The dangerous stream poured in Desdemona's ear is not only sexual desire, but also a decent Victorian urge towards comfort and safety. Both Lucy and Mina become subject to Dracula's attack precisely when they have married (in Mina's case) or accepted a proposal of marriage (in Lucy's) – that is, when they are most decorously Victorian.[14]

Once the pleasures of courtship and *Othello*'s youthful adventures are closed to them, the women of *Dracula* gravitate toward other Shakespearean paradigms. The most obvious touchstone for the second half of the novel is Lady Macbeth but, as a model of womanhood, she appears always in tandem with Ophelia. As the men try to save Lucy from Dracula's nocturnal visitations, she is identified with Ophelia as beleaguered virgin. Arrayed in a necklace of garlic flowers provided through the superior wisdom of Professor Van Helsing, Lucy settles down for the night and cheerfully records in her journal: 'Well, here I am to-night, hoping for sleep, and lying, like Ophelia in the play, with "virgin crants and maiden strewments". I never liked garlic before, but to-night it is delightful!' (p. 122, citing *Hamlet*, 5.1.231–2). How Lucy comes by her Shakespearean knowledge is never made clear, although she, perhaps even more than any of the educated English characters in this novel, has the Bard explicitly at her fingertips. But for her, as for the other Europeans, knowledge of Shakespeare does not necessarily bring with it knowledge of self and the world. While Lucy's first impulse is to find the flowers charming, if mundane, Lucy's mother dislikes their odour and the stuffiness caused by the closed windows and so removes the garland that protects Lucy against Dracula. In the end, the analogy between Ophelia's and Lucy's flowers underscores the 'doubtful' nature of their deaths – the doubt, in Ophelia's case, referring to the possibility of suicide, and in Lucy's case, to the incompleteness of her passing.

When Lucy returns from the dead to the London scene as the 'bloofer lady' who haunts Hampstead Heath in search of small children and their blood, she seems to have stepped fully into the role of Lady Macbeth, combining her sleepwalking with a new penchant for infanticide. In this transformation, Lucy is identified specifically with Ellen Terry as actress. In a 25 September article on the 'Hampstead Mystery', the fictional *Westminster Gazette* reports that in the wake of a rash of disappearances among young children from that area of London, the children have taken up in their play Lucy Westenra's post-mortem role as the 'bloofer lady':

A correspondent writes us that to see some of the tiny tots pretending to be the 'bloofer lady' is supremely funny. Some of our caricaturists might, he says, take a lesson in the grotesque by comparing the reality and the picture ... Our correspondent naively says that even Ellen Terry could not be so winningly attractive as some of these grubby-faced little children pretend themselves to be.

(p 160)

From this newspaper piece, it is impossible to tell exactly what the 'bloofer lady' looks like and therefore what role by Terry they might be imitating. What the band of men see when they discover Lucy as a young vampire harvesting her first victims, however, is this:

> [F]ar down the avenue of white yews we saw a white figure advance – a dim white figure, which held something dark at its breast. The figure stopped, and at the moment a ray of moonlight fell between the masses of driving clouds and showed in startling prominence a dark-haired woman dressed in the cerements of the grave. We could not see the face, for it was bent down over what we saw to be a fair-haired child ... It was now near enough for us to see clearly, and the moonlight still held. My own heart grew cold as ice, and I could hear the gasp of Arthur, as we recognized the features of Lucy Westenra. Lucy Westenra, but yet how changed. The sweetness was turned to adamantine, heartless cruelty, and the purity to voluptuous wantonness ... Van Helsing raised his lantern and drew the slide; by the concentrated light that fell on Lucy's face we could see that the lips were crimson with fresh blood, and that the stream had trickled over her chin and stained the purity of her lawn death-robe.
>
> (p. 187)

Like the storm scene, this one is tantalizingly but ambiguously populated with Shakespearean vocabulary. Lucy's particular brand of evil – 'adamantine', 'heartless cruelty' that flaunts its 'voluptuous wantonness' – brings together a heady mixture of descriptive and moralizing words from *Macbeth* and *A Midsummer Night's Dream*. What solidifies the identification between this apprentice vampire and a particular Shakespeare role, however, is the gesture of infanticide. Like Lady Macbeth, who would dash out her nursing babe's brains, Lucy, 'with a careless gesture', 'flung to the ground, careless as a devil, the child that up to now she had clutched strenuously to her breast, growling over it as a dog growls over a bone' (p. 188).

The scene does not resonate particularly with the most familiar image of Terry as Lady Macbeth, the portrait by John

Singer Sargent that depicts her in the famous dark, iridescent, beetle-wing robe, holding aloft triumphantly the crown as a token of her own ambition and power. In fact, Lucy's figure here is more reminiscent of a much reproduced photograph of Terry as Ophelia; the image shows her in the mad scene of act 4, dressed in a simple white gown with Grecian folds (actually made from a bedsheet trimmed with rabbit) and clutching a bunch of flowers to her breast (see figure 1). Clement Scott describes the scene on stage: 'A more tenderly plaintive and ideally pathetic rendering of the sweet mad girl cannot be imagined; and the entrance of Ophelia in her clinging white robe, her fair, clustering hair, and a lily branch in her hand, will be an abiding memory.'[15] Lucy's behaviour with the garlic flowers that hung around her neck had been noted earlier in the novel; when asleep, she pushes them away; when awake, she clutches them to her. Post-mortem, the fair-haired child has replaced Ophelia's flowers as well as Lady Macbeth's child. The three figures thus merge into one paradoxical icon. When confronted by the vampire hunters, however, Lucy loses her resemblance to Shakespeare's young heroine: her colour becomes 'livid', her eyes throw out 'sparks of hellfire', her brows are wrinkled like Medusa's snakes and her blood-stained mouth widens into the black square of the mouth-hole in a Grecian or Japanese actor's mask. The delicate pathos with which Lucy, as Terry in the role of Ophelia, advances toward the men dissipates into a bifurcated image of cold theatricality and flamboyant horror. After death, however, Lucy reverts to type as an Ophelia figure who, as Van Helsing assures the vampire hunters and as Laertes insists about his own sister, is now ready to join the 'angels'.

Just as their shared kinship with Hamlet bring Jonathan Harker and Dracula disturbingly close to one another, the Lady Macbeth of Ellen Terry functions as a threatening doppelgänger to her Ophelia, and this kinship is important to the symbolic function of women in *Dracula*. Terry herself saw Lady Macbeth as evil but intensely feminine. She is, as Terry kept reminding herself when she played the part, 'damned charming, charming Macbeth to her plan of murder'.[16] As a contemporary spectator, Austin Brereton agreed that Terry's character was in 'total sympathy' with Irving's:

'Without such an affectionate, determined woman as Miss Terry makes Lady Macbeth, the newly invented Thane of Cawdor, as illustrated by Mr Irving, would never have laid violent hands on Duncan.'[17] After the murder, however, as Brereton notes, Lady Macbeth relinquishes all control; her pathetic lament, 'Nought's had, all's spent, / Where our desire is got without content', is spoken with the same 'beauty and tone of feeling' as was Ophelia's lament for Hamlet's madness.[18]

Thus, while the Lady Macbeth imagined by Sargent is a commanding figure, Lady Macbeth as she appeared in the 1892 Lyceum production was visually and emotionally reminiscent of Ophelia. For her sleepwalking scene in particular, Irving insisted that Terry play the character as a document in madness, with dishevelled, Pre-Raphaelite hair: 'Lady M should certainly have the appearance of having got out of bed, to which she is returning when she goes off. The hair to my mind should be wild and disturbed, and the whole appearance as distraught as possible, and disordered.'[19] Photographs and sketches of Terry in the sleepwalking scene confirm that she wore a white Grecian garment with a hood as she descended the castle stairs (see figure 2). The *Morning Post* saw her in this scene as a phantom:

> No less wonderful was the creature who, with hair blanched with sorrow and eyes steeped in a slumber that was not rest, stood like a spirit at the foot of the stairs, as she came to visit the scenes of past suffering and crimes, and sought in vain to cleanse her hands from the imaginary stain. A creature so spiritual, so ineffable has never perhaps been put on the stage.[20]

Visually, as well as intellectually, innocent Ophelia and demonic Lady Macbeth merge into one figure.

The horrifying prospect of a world in which Ophelia can become Lady Macbeth unfolds in *Dracula* when the count seeks to replace Lucy with Mina as his prime victim. As the men burst through the door of Mina's bedroom, they discover Dracula, Jonathan and Mina in a surreal *ménage à trois*, with Dracula forcing Mina into a reverse transfusion of blood:

With his left hand he held both Mrs Harker's hands, keeping them away with her arms at full tension; his right hand gripped her by the back of the neck, forcing her face down on his bosom. Her white nightdress was smeared with blood, and a thick stream trickled down the man's bare breast, which was shown by his torn-open dress. The attitude of the two had a terrible resemblance to a child forcing a kitten's nose into a saucer of milk to compel it to drink.

(p. 247)

In this scene, as Anne Williams has noted, Dracula plays the terrible mother or bloody Madonna.[21] Dracula's melodramatic threat to 'dash out' Jonathan's brains if Mina resists him (p. 251) indicates as well that he has appropriated the role of Lady Macbeth for his own melodrama. But he also struggles *with* Mina for the role of Ophelia. By a metalepsis or a chain of symbolic displacements, Dracula clutches Mina, as a child, to his breast, just as Lucy, as vampire, had clutched a fair-haired child to her breast and, before that, the garlic flowers that metamorphosed her – as she herself recognized – into the figure of Ophelia. To make the tableau work, however, Dracula must hold Mina's arms awkwardly at full length within one of his own hands. Dr Seward's bathetic comparison between Mina and the kitten with its nose in a saucer of milk registers rhetorically the strain that marks Dracula's attitude, but also inverts the motherly gesture in which Mina herself had comforted Arthur by letting him cry on her shoulder. As in the case of Jonathan, with whom Dracula shared the role of Hamlet, Dracula reflects back to Mina not difference, but a dangerous sameness.

Yoked at once to Lucy, Ophelia and Lady Macbeth by her white clothing and dramatic predicament, Mina instinctively understands that like all three, she is 'Unclean, unclean!' (p. 248) and subsequently seeks refuge in Ophelia's role by offering to commit suicide. As long as she bears the scar from the host seared into her forehead, Mina is not free from the taint of evil; the blood-stained lawn robe linking Mina to Lucy and turning Ophelia into Lady Macbeth – she of the blood-stained hands and sleepless nights – marks out the extent of Mina's spiritual endangerment. But this Shakespearean echo, the last emphatic one in the novel, also points towards the possibility of Mina's redemption. When she receives the stigmata of the host on her forehead, Mina cries out again, 'Unclean! Unclean! Even the Almighty shuns my polluted flesh!' (p. 259). Mina's understanding of Shakespeare here is only partial. At his sister's grave, Laertes insists on Ophelia's purity in relation to the Church that curtails her burial rites:

> Lay her i' th' earth,
> And from her fair and unpolluted flesh
> May violets spring! I tell thee, churlish priest,
> A minist'ring angel shall my sister be
> When thou liest howling.
>
> (*Hamlet*, 5.1.238–42)

Like Laertes, Van Helsing constructs his own radical brand of theology to insist that the female vampire, once subjected to impalement and decapitation, is free from taint. Lucy, he assures the men, is with God; it is safe for Arthur finally to kiss her. Mina, too, escapes from her ordeal unscathed by virtue of Dracula's eradication. While Ophelia has a dangerous kinship with Lady Macbeth, her dramatic trajectory – through love and madness into death and the afterlife – provides *Dracula* with a feminine figure whose 'unpolluted' flesh finally resists vampiric inscription and replication. That redemptive quality, which is perforce contingent and volatile, is located in the figure of Ellen Terry as Shakespearean actress.

What makes the actress equally enchanting and dangerous – at once Ophelia and Lady Macbeth – is her ability to embody the women she portrays. Stoker, as well as the English public, lionized Terry for the naturalness, charm and pathos of her acting. Stoker says that 'Ellen Terry's art is wonderfully true. She has not only the instinct of truth but the ability to reproduce it in the different perspective of the stage.' In so doing, she 'incorporates' the characters she acts:

When Ellen Terry has taken hold of a character it becomes, whilst her thoughts are on it, a part of her own nature. In fact, her own nature

'Is subdued
To what it works in, like the dyer's hand'.[22]

Perceiving both agency and instinct in Terry's art, Stoker avoids relegating her completely to what Gail Marshall has called the 'Galatea Myth', the idea that a great actress is shaped in response to and is dependent on masculine directorial will.[23] Nevertheless, while Stoker's praise for Terry draws on stock Romantic praise for Shakespeare and echoes Irving's assessment that Terry possessed the power of pathos, within the context of *Dracula* Terry's ability to 'incorporate' Shakespeare's female characters and to 'reproduce' them on stage suggests an unsettling analogy between actress and vampire. It is only through remembering Ophelia, as performed by Terry on the Lyceum stage in 1878, that redemptive femininity is re-membered from the bits of Shakespeare in the body of *Dracula*.

Coda: Shakespearean citation as technology and art

In many ways, Stoker's novel is a tribute to Ellen Terry, an apotheosis of her as an exemplar of Shakespearean womanhood. But the actress with whom Stoker worked on a daily basis was no Mina Harker. Both are career woman, but while Mina mocks the New Woman and her pretensions to gender equality, by the mid-1890s Terry was on her way to becoming something of a New Woman. Where Mina is a good Victorian wife with legitimate children, Terry was a loving mother of illegitimate children, and her marriages and romantic liaisons were multiple and varied. Like Stoker himself, whose life revolved around homosocial relations and ideals, *Dracula* shows a certain ambivalence toward its feminine avatar, subordinating the actress's life force to the theatrical and novelistic control of men in a way that is more subtle than the reigning 'Galatea Myth' for actresses, but perhaps more powerful for its subtlety. This control functions through a technology of replication.

As critics have recognized, Stoker's novel plays with the relation between narrative and its material record. Mina Harker knows shorthand and learns to type; Dr Seward records his case studies on the wax cylinders of a phonograph; telegraphs spread the word among the vampire hunters. Typescript, in particular, becomes a powerful weapon against the vampire, not only by arranging disparate pieces of the story in chronological order and providing a blueprint for Dracula's defeat but also by making his story iterable, capable of endless replication and widespread distribution.[24] Although at the end the vampire hunters are left with 'hardly one authentic document', just as 'a mass of typewriting', this mass-produced and mechanized writing is the key to their triumph over Dracula (p. 326). As Jennifer Wicke has demonstrated, the typewriter's machinations are themselves potentially 'vampiric', engaged in a cycle of consumption and replication that is characteristic of culture in the age of mechanical reproduction.[25] At the same time, women's secretarial labours become powerful when put into the hands of chivalric men. A similar paradox governs *Dracula*'s other epistemological touchstone, the Shakespearean drama. For Terry's gift of pathos, like the typewriter's products, is at once natural and spontaneous and artificial and mass produced; she embodies Shakespeare's women, but also 'reproduces' them, night after night, on the Lyceum stage. Terry's performance is therefore 'natural' only within the context and confines of scenic perspective.[26] Her acting is as much a technology as an effect of nature, and that technology is controlled and deployed by men – most notably, Irving as the Lyceum's actor-manager and Stoker himself as novelist.

From where Stoker stands as *Dracula*'s author – at the end of a grand, nineteenth-century tradition of scenic drama and at the advent of an age of mechanical reproduction in the form of photography and then film, technology is not opposed to drama, but complementary with it. Like typescript, stage technology provides the necessary distance that makes embodied emotion comprehensible, and even 'damned charming'. Technology also serves, importantly, as an aide-memoire. In *Dracula*, Mina's type-script reconstructs Jonathan's lost memories, which were erased by a brain fever, and Dr Seward's lost words after Dracula's destruction of his phonograph. Stoker's novel also provides a similar record of past events. As Irving's star was sinking and the

Lyceum's domination of English drama waning, Stoker's evocation of its Shakespearean triumphs was nostalgic, dependent on memory and, indeed, on technological aids to memory.

A photograph of Terry in her very first Shakespearean role illustrates the point. This old-fashioned daguerreotype shows Terry as Mamillius and Charles Kean as Leontes in *The Winter's Tale* (see figure 3). In his *Reminiscences*, Stoker declares it hard to believe that Terry, 'so long a force of womanly charm and radiant beauty', had begun her career as a slim, timid 'child dragging the odd-looking go-cart, which the early daguerreotype recorded as Mamillius in Charles Kean's production of *A Winter's Tale*'.[27] Terry herself remembered this performance as awkward and humiliating. In *The Story of My Life*, she reports that 'it was my duty to drag this little cart about the stage, and on the first night, when Mr Kean as Leontes told me to "go play", I obeyed his instructions with such vigour that I tripped over the handle and came down on my back!'[28] A photograph can never capture the 'truth' of live drama: what we see in the aged daguerreotype is merely the stiff figure of a child staring out solemnly at the camera. But without that technology, in the case of Terry's Mamillius, truth would be lost to memory.

Dracula is another such memory aid. Just as the photograph memorializes Terry and *Dracula* memorializes both her performances and Irving's directorial vision in *Hamlet* and *Macbeth*, the Shakespearean citations in Stoker's novel function as an epistemological machine to refresh and sustain his readers' cultural memory of the Lyceum, its star players and its triumphs. For the canny reader of *Dracula*, the ability of citations to call up characters – Hamlet, Ophelia, the Ghost, Lady Macbeth, Macbeth and even Poor Tom – points the way towards an understanding of vampirism, its discontents and its antidote. The liminal and shifting nature of these citations – their 'haunting' quality – gives Stoker's quotation machine the grander claim to be art. By asking us to re-member Shakespeare through his novel, Stoker thus casts himself as the most recent, if the least august, in a line of dramatic creators. Stoker is not Dracula, an illegitimate propagator of Shakespearean figures. He is not Hamlet, nor was he meant to be, for that role belonged to Irving alone. Rather, Stoker casts himself as Laertes, a man whose love, homage and imagination allow him a privileged vision of Ophelia's apotheosis among the angels and of Ellen Terry as the epitome of English and Shakespearean womanhood.

Notes

[1] Bram Stoker, *Dracula*, ed. Nina Auerbach and David J. Skal, Norton Critical Edition (New York: Norton, 1997), p. 38. Further references to *Dracula* will be to this edition and will be included within the body of the text.

[2] *Hamlet*, 1.5.107. All references to Shakespeare's works are to *The Riverside Shakespeare*, ed. G. Blakemore Evans et al. (2nd edn; Boston: Houghton Mifflin, 1997) and will be incorporated into the body of the text.

[3] Douglas Lanier, *Shakespeare and Modern Popular Culture*, Oxford Shakespeare Topics (Oxford: Oxford University Press, 2002), p. 53.

[4] Alan Hughes, *Henry Irving, Shakespearean* (Cambridge: Cambridge University Press, 1981), p. 30.

[5] Bram Stoker, *Personal Reminiscences of Henry Irving* (2 vols; London: Macmillan, 1906), vol. 2, p. 198.

[6] Ellen Terry, *The Story of My Life: Recollections and Reflections* (New York: McClure Company, 1908), p. 178; Stoker, *Personal Reminiscences*, vol. 2, p. 199.

[7] See the discussion by Hughes, *Henry Irving*, pp. 38–52, especially p. 39.

[8] Marjorie Garber, '*Hamlet*: Giving up the ghost', in Susanne L. Wofford (ed.), *William Shakespeare*, Hamlet, Case Studies in Contemporary Criticism (Boston and New York: Bedford/St Martin's, 1994), p. 310; italics in original.

[9] Dr Seward notes that 'Bats usually wheel and fly about, but this one seemed to go straight on, as if it knew where it was bound for or had some intention of its own' (p. 103).

[10] Charles Lamb, 'On the Tragedies of Shakspear', in Joan Coldwell (ed.), *Charles Lamb on Shakespeare* (London: Colin Smythe, 1978), p. 36.

[11] For stage production, Irving's text of *King Lear* cut heavily from Edgar's role as Poor Tom. This particular reference does not appear in the acting text, as published in 1892 (*King Lear, a Tragedy in Five Acts, by William Shakespeare, as arranged by Henry Irving and presented at the Lyceum Theatre, November 10, 1892* (London: Nassau Steam Press, 1892)).

[12] The relevant citation from *Hamlet* is: 'Not a whit, we defy augury. There is special providence in the fall of a sparrow. If it be [now,] 'tis not to come; if it be not to come, it will be now; if it be not now, yet it will come – the readiness is all' (5.2.219–24).

[13] It can be difficult to disentangle Shakespearean from biblical allusions in Stoker's writing; for his use of biblical parallels, see William Hughes, *Beyond Dracula: Bram Stoker's Fiction and its Cultural Context* (Houndmills, Basingstoke: Macmillan, 2000), pp. 14–53.

14 For a different reading of the Desdemona reference, see Rebecca Pope, 'Writing and biting in *Dracula*', *LIT*, 1 (1990), 199–216, reprinted in Glennis Byron (ed.), *'Dracula': Contemporary Critical Essays*, New Caseboooks (New York: St Martin's, 1999), pp. 75–6.

15 Clement Scott, *The Drama of Yesterday and Today* (2 vols; London: Macmillan and Company, 1899), vol. 2, p. 61.

16 Nina Auerbach, *Ellen Terry, Player in Her Time* (New York: W. W. Norton, 1987), p. 254.

17 Austin Brereton, *The Lyceum and Henry Irving* (London: Lawrence and Bullen, 1893), pp. 270–1.

18 Ibid., p. 272.

19 Roger Manvell, *Ellen Terry* (New York: G. P. Putnam's Sons, 1968), p. 196.

20 Ibid., pp. 200–1.

21 Anne Williams, *Art of Darkness: A Poetics of Gothic* (Chicago: University of Chicago Press, 1995), pp. 128–9.

22 Stoker, *Personal Reminiscences*, vol. 2, pp. 196 and 197.

23 Gail Marshall, *Actresses on the Victorian Stage: Feminine Performance and the Galatea Myth* (Cambridge: Cambridge University Press, 1998). Marshall notes, however, that throughout his *Reminiscences*, Stoker preferred to see Terry as instinctive rather than intellectual (pp. 180–1).

24 For more information on the typewriter at the end of the nineteenth century, see Leonard Wolf, *The Annotated Dracula* (New York: Clarkson N. Potter, 1975), p. 307.

25 Jennifer Wicke, 'Vampiric typewriting: *Dracula* and its media', *ELH: English Literary History*, 59, 2 (summer 1992), pp. 467–93.

26 Stoker, *Reminiscences*, vol. 2, p. 197.

27 Ibid., vol. 2, p. 207.

28 Terry, *The Story of My Life*, p. 18, cited in Auerbach, *Ellen Terry*, p. 40.

10

'Rites of Memory': the Heart of Kenneth Branagh's Hamlet

SUSAN ALLEN FORD

Set in the ominous darkness of nineteenth-century imperial Europe, Kenneth Branagh's 1996 film version of *Hamlet* discovers a world in which statues come to life, walls conceal doors to hidden passages, ghosts walk, the business of the state is conducted in a hall of mirrors, young women suffering from 'madness' are bound in constraints and confined in cells and the very ground bubbles and shifts. *Hamlet*, of course, has long been allied to the Gothic tradition. In 1802, Ann Radcliffe analysed the power of the ghost, with 'all its attendant incidents of time and place … which excite forlorn, melancholy and solemn feelings and dispose us to welcome, with trembling curiosity, the awful being that draws near; and to indulge in that strange mixture of horror, pity and indignation, produced by the tale it reveals'.[1] Horace Walpole cited *Hamlet* as an example he emulated in *The Castle of Otranto* for its mixture of modes; and he clearly owes the novel's revenge plot and catalytic spectres to this play.[2] Indeed, Branagh's version of the ghost, a statue come to life and then reduced to fragments by the end of the film, seems to stride forth from Walpole's pages. There is more, however, than merely a Gothic vocabulary at work here. This *Hamlet* mines the Gothic not only for its trappings and suits but also for its tactics, vision and effects.

What is it about Shakespeare's *Hamlet* that allows it to be read retrospectively in Gothic terms? The Gothic describes a world of mystery and a world of imprisonment. *Hamlet* presents, from its very first scene, a world defined by darkness, mysterious presences and secrets, by labyrinths and imprisoning structures that are physical, social and psychological. This darkness can signify a kind of brutishness that threatens the light of reason and virtue that the play also represents. The Gothic often evokes the past (or, as Jerrold Hogle has it, a counterfeit version of the past) as a safer or less obscured space against which the psychological and political contests of the present may be played out.[3] Not only does Shakespeare set his play in medieval Denmark, but this Denmark is defined in a way that evokes the overriding concerns of that past-in-present: the carceral hold of the past on the living and the tyrannical authority of the father's law. This conflict is played out within the family – or families – defined and dissolved by the play. Indeed, as Anne Williams suggests, the 'Gothic is created when a narrative is organized by the implied latent structure of the patriarchal family – and its related symbolic manifestations'.[4] Even *Hamlet*'s vexed cultural, textual and generic identity suggests its affinity with the Gothic. The play is haunted by its possible sources: the *Historiae Danicae* of Saxo Grammaticus (1514), Belleforest's *Histoires Tragiques* (1570) and, most intriguingly, the undiscovered Ur-*Hamlet* (revived in 1594). Its very text is unstable, foregrounding questions of textual identity. And, finally, the point to which the Gothic journey tends is the revelation of both the mysteries of the past and the secrets of identity. For Hamlet, those past secrets become a means of leading him further into darkness and imprisonment but also, ultimately, to the heart of his own mystery.

Branagh's film treatment of Shakespeare's play, then, actualizes its Gothic potential rather than investing it with something foreign. 'Gothic signifies a writing of excess', argues Fred Botting.[5] Through his authoritative attempts to present, and possess, the totality of *Hamlet*, Branagh creates a kind of sublime excess. He asserts the textual authority of that so-called 'complete text' of the play, the folio text supplemented with passages appearing in Q2. He asserts the visual authority of the 70 mm image, a size used most typically for epics. He asserts interpretive and narrative authority through tracking shots and intercut flash-backs. And, finally, he asserts the personal authority of an actor–director whose marketing campaign portrayed him as the new Olivier and as one who assumed from his Claudius, Sir Derek Jacobi, the most royal designation of 'the Hamlet of the next generation'.[6]

At the same time, those very claims to authority, the creation of that sublime excess, disrupt the fictive experience of *Hamlet*, underscoring the film's transgressions of naturalistic, realistic and even theatrical boundaries. For many, this generic instability reveals a distorting flaw in Branagh's vision of the play. Iska Alter contends that '[t]hese generic slippages indicate a loss of control over the structural patterns that shape the film's energy'.[7] I want to read that generic instability, however, as essential to the film's Gothic identity. As Botting puts it, '[i]t is in the spilling over of boundaries, in its uncertain effects on audiences, that Gothic horrors are most disturbing'. The postmodern Gothic, he suggests, depends on a kind of generic transgression: 'The hybrid mixing of forms and narratives has uncanny effects, effects which make narrative play and ambivalence another figure of horror, another duplicitous object to be expelled from proper orders of consciousness and representation.'[8] The film's very transgression of generic boundaries, then, is integral to Branagh's Gothic vision. Branagh's *Hamlet* uses Gothic conventions to explore not only its own history but also a landscape of political and domestic violence, in which fathers and sons struggle for power and women are ultimately powerless. Paradoxically, it also highlights and deploys the filmic equivalent of Gothic narrative tactics in order to exert narrative and temporal control, attempting to bring history to a halt at the movie's end.

Actions that a man might play

In a short video, 'To be … on camera: a history with *Hamlet*', Kenneth Branagh says: 'This film *Hamlet* is something that's an expression, for what it's worth, of everything I have thought about it all, reacted to it all, and so it is an obsession.'[9] Although since the release of *Henry V* in 1989 Kenneth Branagh's career has increasingly been defined by cinema, he also brought to his movie version of *Hamlet* a rich personal history of engagement with the play on stage. In a 1994 interview with Samuel Crowl, Branagh acknowledged that he had earlier 'felt ... crushingly the weight of the ghosts of other performances'.[10] His own experience of *Hamlet* on the stage, however, contributed much to his movie version of the play, particularly, as his own metaphor might suggest, to his Gothic vision. Not only an evolution of Branagh's understanding of Hamlet but also his interest in the text – elements of setting (both spatial and temporal), thematic emphases (domestic relationships, paternal tyranny, the role of women) and definitions of character and casting – can all be traced to earlier stage productions of *Hamlet*.

Both as an adolescent spectator and a student actor, Branagh was awed by the play's mysterious power. In his introduction to the *Hamlet* screenplay, Branagh recounts watching, at the age of eleven, Richard Chamberlain's performance as Hamlet and the 'unsettling' scene in which the Ghost appears. At fifteen, Derek Jacobi's Hamlet confronted him with what seemed 'a genuine force of nature', the memory of which 'made me glad to be alive'; in consequence, he 'resolved to become an actor'.[11] Branagh's audition for the Royal Academy of Dramatic Arts included a soliloquy from *Hamlet*, and for the school's seventy-fifth anniversary celebration he delivered 'O what a rogue and peasant slave am I', rehearsing the speech before John Gielgud, 'the Hamlet of the century'.[12] By his own account, Branagh was influenced by Tyrone Guthrie's advice

> to do as many of the great roles as you could as early as possible, so there would be more chance of getting them right later on ... I wanted one day to be a great Hamlet ... I wanted to play Hamlet as many times as possible, so that each time I played it I would get better in the role, and would get closer to the truth of the character.[13]

He played Hamlet first in 1980, his final year at RADA.

Branagh's work on the play over the next fifteen years reveals changes in his understanding and presentation of the character Hamlet and sources for a collection of ideas and actors that he could incorporate into his own production. In 1984, Branagh played Laertes in a Royal Shakespeare Company (RSC) production starring Roger Rees and directed by Ron Daniels. In 1988, he starred as Hamlet in a production of his own Renaissance Theatre Company (RTC) that was directed by Derek Jacobi. In 1992, the RTC, in cooperation with BBC Radio, released an audio production of the play, starring Branagh as Hamlet and this time directed by himself and Glyn Dearman. And in 1992–3, he starred in an RSC production directed by Adrian Noble.

The 1984 Royal Shakespeare Company production contributed design and thematic elements, as well as casting ideas, to Branagh's film of *Hamlet*. According to Michael Billington, the production had 'no real sense of the political'; it was the 'most *domestic*' production Christopher Edwards could remember seeing.[14] For other critics, this *Hamlet* was 'a sort of fairy tale for adults', with the set emphasizing the story's archetypal and domestic dimensions: 'less a court than … a family mansion full of staircases and memories' (see figure 4).[15] These features were stylized rather than realistic in design, but the balanced stairways defining the space seem to have resided in Branagh's memory until they were appropriated for his own Elsinore's State Hall. Another import might have been Branagh's interest in and understanding of the Polonius family, which he was able to view 'from within. I was made aware of the double family tragedy.'[16] Indeed, much of the blocking of that production emphasized the contrasts and connections between the two families, particularly between the two sons. Roger Warren remarked on the affection apparent in the Polonius family and on the complexity of Polonius himself, who was 'neither a sinister operator nor an old fool'.[17] The Ghost was a figure of power rather than of affection or pathos, 'played less as a spectre than as a stern, silvery, pale but full-bodied image of potent voice and natural authority'.[18] 'Mark me' and 'Pity me not' (1.5.2, 5) were delivered in a commanding manner meant to induce awe and terror. Fortinbras's dominance in Branagh's film may also be traced to this production; as the lights went down,

Fortinbras occupied the centre of the stage. There are, as well, other links to Branagh's film: in the roles of the Ghost and the First Player, Daniels cast actors (Richard Easton and Bernard Horsfall) 'schooled in an older Shakespearean style'.[19] Branagh's multigenerational casting may stem from his experience with that effect. Further, in his *Hamlet* film Branagh uses two actors from this early production in significant roles: Brian Blessed, Claudius during the play's 1984 Stratford run, reappears as the film's Ghost; and Nicholas Farrell played Horatio in both play and film.

The 1988 Renaissance Theatre Company's production of *Hamlet*, directed by Derek Jacobi, featured Branagh, in his own words, as 'a hectic Hamlet, high on energy but low on subtlety and crucially lacking depth'.[20] Again, certain features of the production foreshadow the Gothic elements of Branagh's later work. Evoking a past world with strong connections to the present, the production used an Edwardian setting to capture a society on the point of military change. The production was 'highly theatrical ... acknowledg[ing] the rich store of theatrical imagery' in Shakespeare's play.[21] In order to emphasize the effect of the play's events on its women, Ophelia and Gertrude were given more time on stage, with lines 'even re-allocated'.[22] Fortinbras was more than usually violent: 'Go bid the soldiers shoot' was the signal to eliminate those remaining in the Danish court.[23] Certain aspects of the play's staging are also significant. In that 1988 production, Jacobi directed that 'To be or not to be' should be delivered not as a soliloquy but, as in his own 1977 *Hamlet* at the Old Vic, directly *to* Ophelia.[24] In Branagh's film, the soliloquy is delivered before a mirrored door, on the other side of which are Claudius and Polonius. In the 1988 Renaissance Theatre Company's production, Hamlet drew a curtain to reveal the concealed Claudius and Polonius; in the film, one of many secret doors swings shut just as Hamlet enters the room in which they have been hiding.

One of the most significant aspects of the 1988 production was the participation of Derek Jacobi, not only the Hamlet of Branagh's adolescence but also the director who had chosen this particular play. The connection between the director with the previous title to the role and the star and head of the company generated what must have been an interesting and fruitful creative tension. Branagh was quite aware of a very specific legacy personified by Derek Jacobi and of his own place in relation to it. In a documentary about the RTC production, Branagh said: 'There seems to be a kind of natural agreement as it were, a tacit understanding that this is both my Hamlet and Derek's *Hamlet*, because it's Derek's *Hamlet* as he wishes to see the play and my Hamlet as I wish to play the character, with a lot of give on both sides.'[25] The complexity of that 'natural agreement' emerges in Branagh's autobiography:

> At first I resisted his suggestions, and I was determined not to be hurried or over-awed ... Derek directed my Hamlet with amazing sensitivity – I had my own instincts, and he shaped them. There wasn't an acting problem in the part that he hadn't already faced and analysed himself, and the alternatives he offered me were fascinating.[26]

The competition in these pronouns for ownership and agency is revealing, and the film's obsession with the tradition of Hamlets, as well as with fathers both biological and spiritual, seems especially apparent.

The 1992 BBC/RTC audio production allowed Branagh to recognize *Hamlet*'s connection between the domestic and the political – a familiar feature of the Gothic – as well as to involve some of those figures with whom he would work on the film project. The audio production was Branagh's 'first taste of the full text, and a splendid opportunity to explore the play's language with a focus and significance that was uniquely offered by the medium, in which the spoken word dominates'.[27] It provided for Branagh, he acknowledged, an enlarged sense of the play: 'The restored lines are not mere padding but enforce the idea that the play is about a national as well as a domestic tragedy.'[28] In this audio version, Jacobi played Claudius as an initially sympathetic figure whose steely edge appears in act 1, scene 2, rather earlier than it does in the film. Richard Briers played Polonius, in Branagh's words, as someone who is 'cunning and has the spy's practised slyness'.[29] Patrick Doyle composed the music for this version, as he did for Branagh's *Hamlet* film (and other Branagh movies).

The 1992–3 *Hamlet* directed by Adrian Noble for the Royal Shakespeare Company seems to have emphasized features of the play – the definition of the text, the concept of the prince, the historical setting, the emphasis on family – that proved particularly useful to Branagh's film-making. Once again, the full text was used. Branagh's conception of the prince had also developed. In the RTC performance he had been, according to Billington, 'all reckless impulsiveness and danger: what he missed was Hamlet's inwardness. But now he [had] the part totally within his sights'. This was, according to John Peter, a 'brooding, self-possessed' Hamlet, dressed with 'obsessive care … Branagh's Hamlet knows that grief is an invasion: one way of defending yourself is to retreat behind the fortifications of dress and impeccable manners'.[30] For Anthony Dawson, however, a dominant aspect of the performance was the 'cultural cachet' the star brought to the role: 'Branagh is not seen as a rebel or a challenge to authority so much as a highly successful entrepreneur – he embodies aspiration for success rather than for liberation.'[31] At the play's end, Hamlet was borne off the stage in a crucified posture, an image used again for the film's climax.

Although this version of *Hamlet* was set in a 'disintegrating Edwardian world', Noble's production 'emphasized the domestic over the political, family over state', again looking forward to Branagh's film.[32] Jack Tinker of the *Daily Mail* also cited the production's domestic focus: 'Seldom have I understood so powerfully the deep family ties at the heart of this play: father and son; sister and brother; son and mother.'[33] Ophelia's closet – with bed, cupboard, washstand and piano – was an important space in the play, the scene for her conversations with Laertes and Polonius (1.3) as well as for the 'Get thee to a nunnery' conversation with Hamlet (3.1); its later disintegration evoked the disintegration of her family, as well as her own loss of self.

Noble's emphasis on domestic drama also shaped the play's supernatural effects. Before act 1, scene 1, the Ghost rose up from beneath a garden at the front of the stage, as Peter Holland described it, 'like a corpse in a poor horror film'.[34] In act 1, scene

5, Hamlet's kneeling posture before the Ghost as he received his instructions is quoted by Branagh in the film (see figure 5). Although in Noble's production the Ghost gave his son the sword with which to avenge his murder, he was also a tender ghost, touching Hamlet at the command 'Taint not thy mind' and, in the closet scene, caressing Gertrude's cheek and holding Hamlet's hand. At the end, Hamlet was borne off towards the Ghost, who received him. For Paul Taylor, however, this final image of father–son connection was powerful but troubling: 'To have this as the climactic stage picture risks obscuring the fact that the play is about the futility of revenge, not its rewards. The image stirs but simplifies.'[35] In Branagh's film, the father–son dynamics would be more multidimensional, more complex.

Many confines, wards and dungeons

By the time Kenneth Branagh arrived at the filming of *Hamlet*, then, not only were his Gothic vision and his facility with a Gothic vocabulary well established through his direction of the movies *Dead Again* (1991), *Mary Shelley's Frankenstein* (1994) and *In the Bleak Midwinter* (1996), but his ideas about the play itself had developed in compatible directions. The movie *Hamlet* is haunted by the past – by Branagh's own cinematic and stage history as well as by the history of other *Hamlet*s. This film translates that haunting into a Gothic world in which past and present are unexpected doors opening into a multifaceted and multivalent universe, labyrinths leading to a still-beating heart. In this *Hamlet*, Branagh marshals Gothic conventions to explore the masculine exercise of power both over the women that men control and over the sons whom they educate to inherit but would prevent from doing so.

The landscape of Branagh's film *Hamlet* emphasizes both the domestic and the political. The nineteenth-century world he depicts probably bears as much resemblance to nineteenth-century Denmark as the world presented on the Globe's stage did to medieval Denmark. As Hogle points out, '*Gothic* has long been a term used to project modern concerns into a deliberately vague, even fictionalized past'.[36] Both Tanja Weiss's contention that 'in the world around there is nothing other than snow and the eerie forest' and H. R. Coursen's complaint that the cold never seems to penetrate a castle without central heating are objections to the lack of realism in this cinematic world.[37] But Hogle's point that the Gothic has always been 'fake and counterfeit' is a useful one.[38] The signs by which Branagh registers the nineteenth century – clothing, sets, Blessed's Fuseli-inspired Ghost, visual echoes of Pre-Raphaelite paintings – remind us of certain features of the Victorian world, only to draw us back to our own millennial, postmodern one. As Williams suggests, 'Gothic conventions represent the culture's "then" and "there" (as opposed to its "here" and "now"); i.e., Gothic systematically represents "otherness", which is, of course, always a relative term.'[39] It is also a term that brings us back, via reflection, to the self. So what is that other? Branagh's film *Hamlet* captures a moment of change between an old order and a new: between the world of Claudius and Gertrude, in which diplomacy is carried out in a confectionary court with the 'daily brazen cast of cannon' hidden beneath, and the world of Fortinbras's army, moving across snowy plains and bursting through Elsinore's mirrored walls; between a world defined by the eighteenth-century fantasy of statues come to life and the twentieth-century politic of statues toppled and smashed. In Coursen's formulation, '[t]he nineteenth century surrenders to the twentieth, and anything of value lies back there as the new century swings in on a steel hinge'.[40]

In underscoring this political aspect of the film, Branagh himself attempted to enforce a distinction between *Hamlet*'s archetypal Gothic castle (as seen in a film like Olivier's, all dark corridors and fog) and the image provided by Blenheim Palace: 'For me (and perhaps it's due to my age and being at the end of the twentieth century), Blenheim, rather than being a Gothic castle, [is a place in which] you feel that the fates of nations can be decided.'[41] Blenheim, Winston Churchill's birthplace and Queen Anne's reward to the duke of Marlborough for his military victories, is immediately identifiable as an icon of political and military power. Branagh defines it in specifically political terms:

It's the kind of building that makes you wonder why there's never been a proper revolution in England. That sense of power was very important to convey and to show that it's not just the life of one man and one family that will change but the life of an entire nation.[42]

However, Branagh's Elsinore, despite its rational, geometric design both inside and out, is revealed as a truly Gothic space, with mirrored walls, secret doors, hidden passages, a chapel, even a padded cell off the State Hall. As Philippa Sheppard says, 'it is exactly [Elsinore's] normalcy, this glaring brightness' that makes it the perfect Gothic backdrop: 'The macabre is only magnified by being contrasted to the quotidian.'[43] The Gothic castle, as Williams suggests, can represent male culture and power *as well as* the feminine other:

> [A] castle is a *man*-made thing, a cultural artefact linked with the name of a particular family. This structure has a private and a public aspect; its walls, towers, ramparts suggest external identity, the 'corridors of power', consciousness; whereas its dungeons, attics, secret rooms and dark hidden passages connote the culturally female, the sexual, the maternal, the unconscious. It is a public identity enfolding (and organizing) the private, the law enclosing, controlling, dark 'female' otherness … The structure embodies the principles of cultural order.[44]

Indeed, this organization also helps define the mystery of Elsinore. The hidden doors engender an atmosphere of secrecy and paranoia. In Branagh's film, it is the male characters who control the secret doors through which viewers, most of the time, cannot follow. This enlarged access underscores the limits not merely for Ophelia but also for the viewers. The conventions of film seem to highlight that sense of limitation. In the theatre, the stage is infinitely transformable, and characters exit into the mysterious backstage of the 'reality' behind the play's mystery. The true magic, the magic of theatrical transformation, takes place before our eyes. In the cinema, however, with its pledge of realism, we feel that we *can* travel with any character, as this camera, with its continuous movement and long tracking shots, encourages us to believe. When we are prevented from following, however, we feel our division from the mystery. Truth lies in an undiscovered country to which we cannot travel. Film, paradoxically *because* of its realistic claims, seems to have more ability than the theatre to evoke a sense of Gothic imprisonment.

Another aspect of the politics of Branagh's Gothic *Hamlet* is its commentary on gender. The later part of the nineteenth century betokens a world of increasing freedoms for women. Gertrude's role as 'imperial jointress to this warlike state'[45] is developed through her signing of state documents following the return of Voltemand and Cornelius from Norway. Ophelia is dressed in quasi-military garb for the wedding and, in the early scenes, walks through the palace and its grounds with seeming liberty. But, of course, any power for Gertrude or Ophelia is illusory. The real decisions are made by groups of men: Claudius in consultation with Polonius, or Rosencrantz and Guildenstern, or later, with Laertes; Polonius with Reynaldo. Gertrude is increasingly powerless, her presence a ceremonial representation of feeling, and Ophelia's agency is taken over by the men in her life and then completely curtailed. Williams's formulation of the gender politics of the Gothic is helpful here:

> Like all dreams – even nightmares – Gothic narratives enabled their audiences to confront and explore, and simultaneously to deny, a theme that marks the birth of the Romantic (and modern) sensibility: that 'the Law of the Father' is a tyrannical *paterfamilias* and that we dwell in his ruins.[46]

Bound in filial obligation

Though Branagh's film is conscientious about developing *Hamlet's* political dimensions through its setting, its family plot is also emphasized through the nineteenth-century landscape and the film's version of the Gothic castle. As Williams argues, 'family structure ... generates the plots that occur within Gothic, for it imposes a certain balance of power, both personal and political ... Literally and metaphorically, Gothic plots are family plots; Gothic romance is family romance.'[47] Although initial views of the

Polonius family suggest strong bonds of affection, closer scrutiny reveals that the family replicates the incestuous power dynamics evident elsewhere in Elsinore. As Laertes and Ophelia 'walk with their arms around each other', for example, the screenplay specifies that 'they are very, some might say unnaturally, close' and that he gives her a 'big kiss on the lips'.[48] Julie Sanders points out that Branagh's 'text constructs Hamlet and Laertes as duelling lovers as well as grieving sons'.[49] Further, Laertes' protective fear for his sister's sexuality – that she will her 'chaste treasure open' (*Hamlet*, 1.3.31) – identifies him with the father's law. Indeed, as Branagh's screenplay indicates, he 'become[s] pompous. A little too much of his father's son.'[50]

The relationship between Polonius, as father, and both son and daughter suggests the more corrupt, violent and incestuous aspects of paternal law. Although Douglas Lanier describes the scene in which Polonius delivers his advice to Laertes as 'a touching, intimate, entirely unironic expression of a father's love for his son' that the chapel setting 'gently sacralize[s]', the chapel's Gothic definition as a space of repressed and codified desire suggests subterranean elements of the father's relationship with his children.[51] Once Laertes leaves, Polonius closes the gates upon Ophelia and, in a tone 'quiet but menacing', questions her about her relationship to Hamlet – a conversation that explodes into muted violence as he pushes her against the confessional.[52] Later, as Polonius sets Reynaldo – defined in the screenplay as a 'pimp' for Polonius – to spy on his son, his affectionate fathering is revealed as a façade. The two men 'reek of corruption', and the young prostitute with whom Polonius has just finished is grabbed and then 'brutally pushe[d] away' by Reynaldo. When Ophelia enters Polonius' room to describe Hamlet's mad behaviour, after Polonius questions whether she has given Hamlet hard words, she rushes in tears to the bed recently vacated by the prostitute and 'curls up on it'.[53] The connection between Polonius's use of the young prostitute and his use of his daughter is underscored in Branagh's version, as Polonius forces Ophelia to read Hamlet's letter to the king and queen.

Branagh's *Hamlet* underscores Ophelia's role as an increasingly powerless and victimized Gothic heroine. She is used as bait by

the king and Polonius, who cower behind a mirrored door while
Hamlet squashes her face against it. Ophelia is subject to Hamlet's
violence as he grabs her 'with great force', drags her around the
State Hall, 'shoves her hard against the mirrored door behind
which her father stands' and, after opening that door, flings her to
the floor of the antechamber. At 'To a nunnery, go', Ophelia 'stays
where he pushed her, wrecked in every sense'.[54] Hamlet also
publicly taunts her at the play, making Ophelia – and her sexuality
– part of the spectacle. Following the murder of Polonius, soldiers
searching for Hamlet invade Ophelia's room and search her bed –
in an allusion to Edmund Burke's image of a victimized Marie
Antoinette, a sentimental image of beauty in distress at the hands
of masculine and brutish (revolutionary) power. At Ophelia's
consequent madness, the detachment of court and of movie audience in relationship to her victimization is underscored. From
above, they (and we) view Ophelia in her padded cell. Before she
is released from her straightjacket, 'she pushes her squashed face
along the floor, unable to get up'.[55] (In the Noble version, while
assuming his antic disposition, Branagh's Hamlet had worn an
unfastened straightjacket as a jester's cape or stage property. Here,
Ophelia's complete imprisonment and powerlessness are underscored by the contrast.) Horatio (and we) also watch through a
spyhole as she is hosed down, a harsh and punishing therapy.
Finally, in her coffin Ophelia appears as a Pre-Raphaelite image,
dreamy voluptuousness transformed into a dead saintliness over
which Hamlet and Laertes can struggle.

In Branagh's film, Hamlet himself is also, of course, embedded
in a family plot, most particularly a struggle against the father.
Hogle points out that

> the features of Anglo-European-American Gothic have helped to
> prefigure and shape Freud's notion of Oedipal conflict in the
> middle-class family. In some way the Gothic is usually about some
> 'son' both wanting to kill and striving to be the 'father' and thus
> feeling fearful and guilty about what he most desires.[56]

Indeed, Crowl points out that Branagh 'see[s] the play as dominated by fathers and brothers rather than mothers and lovers',

while Starks calls it 'the most Oedipal of all *Hamlets* on screen'.[57] Certainly, there are multiple father-figures visualized in Branagh's version: the Ghost/Old Hamlet (Brian Blessed), Old Norway (John Mills), Claudius (Derek Jacobi), Polonius (Richard Briers), the Player King (Charlton Heston) and Priam (John Gielgud). These father-figures function in multiple spheres: besides appearing as fathers within the plot of the movie, they define the lineage of stage and cinema, of Hamlets and of *Hamlets* that Branagh wants both to join and to replace.

Hamlet's Gothic relationship with his father is darkly mirrored in Branagh's relationship with his own predecessors, a tension underscored in the film. In a kind of tribute to the history of stage and cinema, Branagh stocks his film with actors from earlier generations, other Hamlets and the casts of other productions. With the exception of Jacobi, these older actors appear in marginal, usually powerless roles. Branagh uses John Gielgud, Noel Sloboda argues, to displace the competing figure of Laurence Olivier,[58] but Gielgud is also the mentor before whom the student Kenneth Branagh had rehearsed his soliloquy. Gielgud, significantly, plays here a frail and mute king killed off in the course of a speech. The displacement of Olivier is particularly overt. In March 1993, during the Adrian Noble production, Branagh had described Olivier's film as '[a] great piece of cinema, in my opinion undoubtedly Olivier's best Shakespearean film'.[59] As Buhler suggests, Branagh then had used *In the Bleak Midwinter* – a film about a group of misfit actors preparing a holiday production of *Hamlet* as a benefit to save themselves and a church threatened with destruction by a local developer – to explore Olivier's seminal *Hamlet*. Just before shooting on *Hamlet* began, however, Branagh cleared a space for himself by arguing that Olivier 'was perhaps not an absolute natural for the role':

> In *Hamlet*, Olivier tries to ape it, and it's not his natural suit, and so what one gets is a beautiful sounding voice that is in a sort of vacuum ... Which is inhuman in a way. You have a tone of melancholy. A beautiful tone of melancholy. But you don't get the character.[60]

This kind of Oedipal tension is replicated throughout Branagh's *Hamlet* (in another version of Gothic excess), through narrative technique as well as through the staging of relationships between the characters. It may even extend to Branagh's relationship with Shakespeare himself: Peter Donaldson suggests that while Olivier's attitude toward Shakespeare is '*incorporative* rather than competitive, ... for Branagh the making of a film enacts a struggle or competition for power'.[61] The flashcuts that explain Shakespeare's text – footage documenting the sexual relationship between Hamlet and Ophelia, scenes of the prelapsarian happy family, images of Claudius in the garden after the poisoning – control interpretation rather than allow for interpretive ambivalence or ambiguity. As Alter points out, the camera 'insistently literalizes meaning'. The images we are shown of Old Hamlet's murder, for example, 'cut the heart out of the play's mystery'.[62] And, while the film begins with an image that recognizes the play's monumental status, the name *HAMLET* carved into a stone plinth, the author *William Shakespeare* appears in the more ephemeral lettering of the opening credits, a function of the director's discretion.

However, Hamlet's relationship with his two closest father-figures, Claudius and Old Hamlet, most clearly explicates the Oedipal tensions that Branagh's Gothic film enacts. Hamlet's, and perhaps Branagh's, most threatening paternal figure is Derek Jacobi's Claudius, who, as Crowl contends, 'repeatedly gives Hamlet reflection, not difference'.[63] Their Scandinavian blondness and sober military dress heighten the resemblance; Branagh's use of long tracking shots for both characters creates another form of doubling.[64] There are also psychological linkages: Hamlet's flashcut visualization of his mother's corset being unlaced comes from Claudius's perspective; the image of Claudius's murder of his brother, with blood spurting out of the ears, is replicated in Hamlet's murderous fantasies of stabbing Claudius through the confessional, where blood spurts from the same orifice. Perhaps that identity accounts for the gusto with which Claudius is eliminated. Jacobi's on-screen death seems the very image of excess: he is pinioned by a poisoned sword that is thrown, 'javelin like', from across the hall,[65] then struck and trapped by a flying chandelier so that poisoned wine can be forced down his throat. Jacobi's death, in fact, had been played out previously, and just as excessively, in Branagh's thriller, *Dead Again*. Thus, Courtney Lehmann argues that 'Branagh was able to get his revenge by playing Hamlet to Jacobi's Claudius, as well as by directing the film himself, consolidating his creative energies in an effort to replace the memory of his theatrical father in the popular imagination'.[66]

Both the film's Gothic excess and its Oedipal structure are manifested in the Ghost of Old Hamlet. The forest meeting between Hamlet and the Ghost has been a target for particular criticism for its obvious fakery, as well as for the distance maintained between the two figures, who never appear together in the frame. While Weiss defines its strategies as 'intentionally sensational' and 'bound to their cinematic tradition', Coursen argues that 'the film suffers from special effects that make the Ghost a ludicrous intruder from a Grade B horror film'.[67] Branagh acknowledged dissatisfaction with the effects, suggesting that 'money and budget and quite frankly lack of imagination on my part' were obstacles.[68] Kliman suggests, however, that Branagh's 'undermining' of the Ghost might point to 'a psychological struggle within Branagh between himself and [Brian] Blessed, one of his father figures, who has played a key role in Branagh's films and his career'.[69]

However, there is more than lack of funds or vision or even mixed motivations at work here. The excess of this representation of the Ghost gets at the complexity of Hamlet's relationship to it: simultaneous opposition and identity, allegiance and resistance. Brian Blessed's Ghost – particularly in his statuary incarnation – is identified with a past world, particularly through the muscled armour and pointed helmet seemingly inspired by Henry Fuseli's 1789 painting, *Hamlet and the Ghost*, for Boydell's Shakespeare Gallery. Old Hamlet is defined visually in terms of emotion and of a vital, though aged, physicality and, by association, with the statue as well as the history of the conflict with Norway, in terms of military force. Crowl gets at the complexity of this Oedipal drama: 'Branagh's film makes visually clear the ways in which Hamlet has mistakenly idealized his father, for Blessed's old Hamlet bears a much greater resemblance to Hamlet's description of Claudius than that of the dead king.'[70] Branagh captures the identity even through difference of father and son, suggesting also perhaps the futility of any attempts at rebellion.

Breaking down the pales and forts of reason

At the same time as Hamlet and Branagh are confronting the father's authority, they must also face the monstrous Other. From the beginning, the movie sets up Fortinbras as a dark foil for Hamlet. Indeed, the camera introduces Fortinbras to illustrate Horatio's explanation to Marcellus and Barnardo for the 'sweaty haste' of the preparations for war (1.1.77). This explanation, the screenplay indicates, acts as an alternative to our focus on the Ghost: Horatio is 'grateful to be diverted from his ghostly fears'. The camera then flashes to a council chamber: 'We see but cannot hear the dark, wild young man, as he leans yelling across a table' at 'frightened advisers ... a group of surly mercenaries'. It is a some-what disorienting scene: 'The Camera rushes with the crazed FORTINBRAS from his campaign table to a board where we see him rip off and tear up a map of Denmark. This ferocious young man wants revenge.'[71] The dark, wild young man, whose language we cannot hear, appears as a kind of negative precursor to the blond, still young man, whose language defines him. Thus, the cinematic representation of Hamlet's replacement by Fortinbras is also a meta-cinematic representation announcing the replacement of Shakespeare's play by Branagh's film. Not only is Branagh's scene not in Shakespeare's text, but it is a moment defined (except for the voice-over) by its silence and its visual busyness. Later, the report of Cornelius and Voltemand to Claudius is illus-trated with the scene of Fortinbras's rebuke by, submission to and reward from Old Norway – in ways that mirror Hamlet's connec-tion to his own father. Fortinbras, like Hamlet, is set in opposition to the fathers' word.

In Branagh's revision, Hamlet's dark foil develops into a looming presence. In addition to invading and conquering Denmark's centre of power, Fortinbras invades and threatens the emotional and thematic centre of *Hamlet*. The film's conclusion, in fact, highlights the triumph of Fortinbras. As Robert Willson points out, the camera's visualization of Fortinbras in the early stages of the film and the climactic cross-cutting between Hamlet's duel with Laertes and Fortinbras's assault on the palace leads to '[t]he inevitable conclusion … that the true hero is about to seize the throne, not to expire near it'.[72] Crowl remarks that 'Fortinbras is the monster that Branagh's Hamlet and *Hamlet* creates, and the film might be amusingly retitled *Dr Hamlet and Mr Fortinbras*'.[73]

The opposition between Fortinbras and Hamlet illustrates the contest between the corporal violent self and the intellectual reflective self, wildness and civility, passion and reason. For most of the play, Hamlet struggles between these extremes. When he returns from the aborted trip to England, however, he is changed – a change we feel in the passage of time, in the differences in his clothing, in the reflective nature of his conversation with the gravedigger and in the philosophy with which he answers Horatio's fears for his life. But, while Shakespeare's play seeks to validate Hamlet's new-found calm, in which 'the readiness is all' (4.2.218), the film cannot 'let be'. This Hamlet becomes a reflection of Fortinbras. Hence, the excessive physicality of the duel, with its Errol Flynn leaps and shattering glass. The establishment of Fortinbras's rule, for which Hamlet's corpse is marshalled as a piece of funereal stage- and statecraft, is defined as a triumph of the new order by which Hamlet himself has been co-opted. The old order so vigorously destroyed is represented not by the corpse of the canny Claudius but by the destruction of the fair and warlike statue of Old Hamlet, who had come from the grave to tell us something was rotten. Branagh's film never shows – or even attempts to show – the distinction between the world of Old Hamlet and the world of Claudius. Such difference is never defined except as Hamlet's thinking makes it so. The shattered pieces of the statue piled up by Fortinbras's soldiers represent, rather, the triumph of military force, the replacement of one force by another.

Branagh's Gothic spectacle, then, continuously creates and dissolves the myth and mystery of *Hamlet*. This tragedy has no cathartic sense of a world restored or renewed. In the final moments of this 'full text' *Hamlet*, the pieces of the statue fall in front of the plinth so that finally, in slow motion, the head obscures the legend, as the screenplay tells us, 'gradually oblit-erat[ing] the name HAMLET. For ever. As we … fade to black.'[74] The final image – termed 'heavy-handed' by Sloboda[75] – is the eradication of a monument, a textual destruction, the erasure of the narratives that have made up this history. The Gothic figure of horror is the image of the end of narrative, simultaneously conclusive and inconclusive, as Branagh fades to black his history of twentieth-century *Hamlet*.

But *forever*? For at least one artist, ambitious for adaptation himself, Branagh's closure is an opening. In 2000, at the beginning of the new century and the new millennium, in the afterword to his novel *Gertrude and Claudius*, John Updike acknowledges Kenneth Branagh's 'four-hour film', to which he 'owes a revivi-fied image of the play and of certain off-stage characters such as Yorick and King Hamlet'.[76] Updike's emphasis on time, his image of bringing the dead back to life, and the vision of characters who exist only in memory, all suggest the imaginative power of Branagh's adaptation while underscoring something of its Gothic character. But they also testify that fading to black, rather than closing off corridors, only temporarily obscures labyrinths for new Gothic journeys. Just as Branagh's film simultaneously paid tribute to and pre-empted his artistic and theatrical predecessors, so Updike's novel both acknowledges a debt to Branagh and makes him an approving audience (no doubt weighing delight and dole) for the next revolution. Updike's narrative prequel reshapes our understanding of Shakespeare's text and so of Branagh's, pre-empting both according to the novelistic rites and rituals of memory.

Notes

[1] 'On the supernatural in poetry', *New Monthly Magazine*, 16 (1826), 145–52, reprinted in E. J. Clery and Robert Miles (eds), *Gothic Documents: A Sourcebook, 1700–1800* (Manchester: Manchester University Press, 2000), p. 166.

2   Horace Walpole, *The Castle of Otranto*, in Peter Fairclough (ed.), *Three Gothic Novels* (New York: Penguin, 1968), pp. 44–5.

3   Jerrold E. Hogle, 'Introduction: the Gothic in Western culture', in Jerrold E. Hogle (ed.), *Cambridge Companion to Gothic Fiction* (Cambridge: Cambridge University Press, 2002), pp. 1–20.

4   Anne Williams, *Art of Darkness: A Poetics of Gothic* (Chicago: University of Chicago Press, 1995), p. 249.

5   Fred Botting, *Gothic* (New York: Routledge, 1996), p. 1.

6   Russell Jackson, 'Film diary', in Kenneth Branagh, *Hamlet, by William Shakespeare* (New York: Norton, 1996), p. 206.

7   Iska Alter, '"To see or not to see": interpolations, extended scenes and musical accompaniment in Kenneth Branagh's *Hamlet*', in Hardin L. Asand (ed.), *Stage Directions in* Hamlet: *New Essays and New Directions* (Madison, NJ: Fairleigh Dickinson University Press, 2003), p. 166.

8   Botting, *Gothic*, pp. 167–8 and 169.

9   David Castell (dir.), *To be . . . on Camera: A History with Hamlet*, on *Hamlet*, dir. Kenneth Branagh, video cassette, Time Warner, 1996.

10 Samuel Crowl, 'Hamlet "most royal": an interview with Kenneth Branagh', *Shakespeare Bulletin*, 12, 4 (fall 1994), 6.

11 Kenneth Branagh, 'Introduction' to *Hamlet, by William Shakespeare* (New York: Norton, 1996), pp. xi–xii.

12 Branagh, *Beginning* (New York, Norton, 1990), pp. 66–7.

13 Ibid., p. 69.

14 Michel Billington, review of *Hamlet*, dir. Ron Daniels, Royal Shakespeare Company, *Guardian*, 7 September 1984, italics added; Christopher Edwards, review of *Hamlet*, dir. Ron Daniels, Royal Shakespeare Company, *Spectator*, 8 September 1984, italics added.

15 Don Chapman, review of *Hamlet*, dir. Ron Daniels, Royal Shakespeare Company, *Oxford Mail*, 6 September 1984; Edwards, review of *Hamlet*.

16 Branagh, 'Introduction' to *Hamlet, by William Shakespeare*, p. xiii.

17 Roger Warren, 'Shakespeare at Stratford-upon-Avon', review of *Hamlet*, dir. Ron Daniels, Royal Shakespeare Company, *Shakespeare Quarterly*, 36 (1985), 80.

18 Gareth Lloyd Evans, review of *Hamlet*, dir. Ron Daniels, Royal Shakespeare Company, *Stratford-upon-Avon Herald*, 14 September 1984.

19 Warren, review, 80.

20 Branagh, 'Introduction' to *Hamlet*, p. xiii.

21 Branagh, *Beginning*, p. 209.

22 Ibid., p. 210.

23 Sarah Hatchuel, *A Companion to the Shakespearean Films of Kenneth Branagh* (Niagara Falls: Blizzard, 2000), p. 70; John W. Mahon, 'A Derek Jacobi fest', *Shakespeare Newsletter*, 47, 1 (spring 1997), 1 and 6–8.

24 Anthony B. Dawson, *Hamlet*, Shakespeare in Performance (Manchester: Manchester University Press, 1995), p. 219; Mahon, 'Derek Jacobi Fest', 8; Mark Olshaker, *Discovering Hamlet*, video cassette, PBS, 1990.

25 Olshaker, *Discovering Hamlet*.

26 Branagh, *Beginning*, p. 210.

27 Branagh, 'Introduction' to *Hamlet, by William Shakespeare*, pp. xiii–xiv.

28 Hatchuel, *Companion*, p. 70.

29 Ibid., p. 71.

30 Michael Billington, review of *Hamlet*, dir. Adrian Noble, Royal Shakespeare Company, *Guardian*, 21 December 1992; John Peter, review of *Hamlet*, dir. Adrian Noble, Royal Shakespeare Company, *Sunday Times*, 27 December 1992.

31 Dawson, *Hamlet*, p. 238.

32 Billington, review of *Hamlet*, dir. Adrian Noble; Crowl, 'Hamlet "most royal"', 5.

33 Jack Tinker, review of *Hamlet*, dir. Adrian Noble, Royal Shakespeare Company, *Daily Mail*, 23 December 1992.

34 Peter Holland, *English Shakespeares: Shakespeare on the English Stage in the 1990s* (Cambridge: Cambridge University Press, 1997), p. 147.

35 Paul Taylor, review of *Hamlet*, dir. Adrian Noble, Royal Shakespeare Company, *Independent*, 12 December 1992.

36 Hogle, 'Introduction', p. 16; italics in original.

37 Tanja Weiss, *Shakespeare on the Screen: Kenneth Branagh's Adaptations of Henry V, Much Ado about Nothing, and* Hamlet (2nd revised edn; Frankfurt: Lang, 2000), p. 147; H. R. Coursen, *Shakespeare in Space: Recent Shakespeare Productions on Screen* (New York: Peter Lang, 2002), p. 233.

38 Hogle, 'Introduction', p. 15.

39 Williams, *Art of Darkness*, p. 18.

40 Coursen, *Shakespeare in Space*, p. 236.

41 Ramona Wray and Mark Thornton Burnett, 'From the horse's mouth: Branagh on the Bard', in Mark Thornton Burnett and Ramona Wray (eds), *Shakespeare, Film, Fin de Siècle* (New York: St Martin's, 2000), p. 170.

42 Ibid.

43 Phillipa Sheppard, 'The castle of Elsinore: Gothic aspects of Kenneth Branagh's *Hamlet*', *Shakespeare Bulletin*, 19, 3 (summer 2001), 36.

44 Williams, *Art of Darkness*, p. 44; italics in original.

45 *Hamlet*, in *The Riverside Shakespeare*, ed. G. Blakemore Evans et al. (2nd edn; Boston: Houghton Mifflin, 1997), 1.2.9. Further references will appear in the body of the text.

46 Williams, *Art of Darkness*, p. 24.

47 Ibid., pp. 22–3.

48 Branagh, *Hamlet, by William Shakespeare*, pp. 23 and 25.

49 Julie Sanders, 'The end of history and the last man: Kenneth Branagh's *Hamlet*', in Mark Thornton Burnett and Ramona Wray (eds), *Shakespeare, Film, Fin de Siècle* (New York: St Martin's Press, 2000), p. 158.

50 Branagh, *Hamlet, by William Shakespeare*, p. 25.

51 Douglas Lanier, '"Art thou base, common and popular?" The cultural politics of Kenneth Branagh's *Hamlet*', in Courtney Lehmann and Lisa S. Starks

(eds), *Spectacular Shakespeare: Critical Theory and Popular Cinema* (Madison, NJ: Fairleigh Dickinson University Press, 2002), p. 160.

52 Branagh, *Hamlet, by William Shakespeare*, p. 27.

53 Ibid., pp. 43, 44, 44 and 47.

54 Ibid., pp. 80–1.

55 Ibid., p. 125.

56 Hogle, 'Introduction', p. 5.

57 Samuel Crowl, *Shakespeare at the Cineplex: The Kenneth Branagh Era* (Athens: University of Ohio Press, 2003) p. 149; Lisa S. Starks, 'The displaced body of desire: sexuality in Kenneth Branagh's *Hamlet*', in Christy Desmet and Robert Sawyer (eds), *Shakespeare and Appropriation* (London: Routledge, 2000), p. 178.

58 Noel Sloboda, 'Visions and revisions of Laurence Olivier in the *Hamlet* films of Franco Zeffirelli and Kenneth Branagh', *Studies in the Humanities*, 27 (2000), 152–4.

59 Graham Bostock, 'Excalibur aloft', *West Midlands What's On*, March 1993.

60 Paul Meier, 'Kenneth Branagh with utter clarity: an interview', *The Drama Review: The Journal of Performance Studies*, 41, 2 (1997), 86 and 87.

61 Peter S. Donaldson, 'Taking on Shakespeare: Kenneth Branagh's *Henry V*', *Shakespeare Quarterly*, 42 (1991), 61–2; italics in original.

62 Alter, '"To see or not to see"', pp. 162 and 165.

63 Crowl, *Shakespeare at the Cineplex*, p. 153.

64 Ibid., p. 152.

65 Branagh, *Hamlet, by William Shakespeare*, p. 169.

66 Courtney Lehmann, *Shakespeare Remains: Theatre to Film, Early Modern to Postmodern* (Ithaca: Cornell University Press, 2002), pp. 182–3.

67 Weiss, *Shakespeare on the Screen*, p. 155; Coursen, *Shakespeare in Space*, p. 32.

68 Crowl, 'Communicating Shakespeare: an interview with Kenneth Branagh', *Shakespeare Bulletin*, 20, 3 (summer 2002), 27.

69 Bernice W. Kliman, 'The unkindest cuts: flashcut excess in Kenneth Branagh's *Hamlet*', in Deborah Cartmell and Michael Scott (eds), *Talking Shakespeare: Shakespeare into the Millennium* (London, Palgrave, 2001), p. 154.

70 Crowl, *Shakespeare at the Cineplex*, p. 150.

71 Branagh, *Hamlet, by William Shakespeare*, pp. 7 and 8.

72 Robert F. Willson, Jr, 'Kenneth Branagh's *Hamlet*, or the revenge of Fortinbras', *Shakespeare Newsletter*, 47, 1 (spring 1997), 7.

73 Crowl, *Shakespeare at the Cineplex*, p. 150.

74 Branagh, *Hamlet, by William Shakespeare*, p. 173.

75 Sloboda, 'Visions and revisions', 150.

76 John Updike, *Gertrude and Claudius* (New York: Knopf, 2000), p. 211.

Afterword: Shakespearean Gothic

FREDERICK BURWICK

> *What injury (short of the theatres) did not Boydell's 'Shakespeare Gallery'*
> *do me with Shakespeare! To have Opie's Shakespeare, Northcote's*
> *Shakespeare, light-headed Fuseli's Shakespeare, heavy-headed Romney's*
> *Shakespeare, wooden-headed West's Shakespeare (though he did the best in*
> *'Lear'), deaf-headed Reynolds's Shakespeare, instead of my, and every-*
> *body's Shakespeare. To be tied down to an authentic face of Juliet! To have*
> *Imogen's portrait!*
>
> Charles Lamb, letter to Samuel Rogers (December 1833)

The rise of Gothic drama followed quickly upon the spreading popularity of the Gothic novel, and both phenomena coincided with the era of Shakespearean Bardolatry. Paradoxically, the ascendancy of Shakespeare's reputation in the latter half of the eighteenth century was marked by three stunning failures: first, the Shakespeare Jubilee of September 1769, organized by the actor and Drury Lane manager, David Garrick, ended dismally when heavy rains dampened the celebrations at Stratford-upon-Avon; secondly, John Boydell's Shakespeare Gallery opened with great fanfare in May 1789 but closed in bankruptcy fifteen years later; and thirdly, Shakespeare papers were discovered by William Henry Ireland and published by his father, Samuel Ireland, as the *Miscellaneous Papers and Legal Instruments under the Hand and Seal of William Shakespeare; including the Tragedy of King Lear and a small fragment of Hamlet* (1795; dated 1796) but were quickly exposed as forgeries by the eminent Shakespearean scholar, Edmond Malone.[1] All three of these events, as Jonathan Bate points out, were motivated by entrepreneurial interests in Shakespeare as a lucrative commercial commodity.[2]

Shakespeare as a money-making, box-office attraction was not an inconvenient companion to Shakespeare as literary model par excellence.[3] Shakespearean themes were easily absorbed into the Gothic mode. Horace Walpole's *The Castle of Otranto* (1764) established a model for the narrative of mystery and terror – dark forebodings, guilty secrets, imminent madness, haunting spirits – sequestered amidst the dank decay of a Gothic castle.[4] The setting, plot and characters of the Gothic novel were soon adapted for the stage. *The Count of Narbonne* (Covent Garden, November 1781), by Robert Jephson, was the first dramatization of Walpole's novel. As Jessica Walker observes, the Gothic elements were readily available in Shakespeare plays.[5] Although the presence of these elements by no means argues that Shakespeare was a Gothic play-wright, it is nevertheless true that the performance of his plays became emphatically Gothicized during the period in which Gothic drama enjoyed popularity on the British stage. The essays in this volume abundantly demonstrate how Shakespeare was adapted to the emergent fascination with Gothic horror. The influence, however, was two-way: just as Shakespeare influenced the Gothic drama, the Gothic drama influenced the performance of Shakespeare's plays.

One of the first examinations of Shakespeare's use of the supernatural was by the German playwright and critic, Ludwig Tieck. Deriving his argument from Aristotle's advocacy of 'prob-able impossibilities' as preferable to 'improbable possibilities',[6] Tieck considers the strategies that enable Shakespeare to lend a seeming probability to the impossible. Tieck's term '*das Wunderbare*' (the marvellous) comprises the ghosts and witches of *Macbeth*, as well as the magic and fairy-tale enchantment in *A Midsummer Night's Dream* and *The Tempest*. Credibility is gained by initiating the audience gradually rather than confronting them all too abruptly with phenomena beyond the natural order. As a revealing example of Shakespeare's preparation for the supernatural moment, Tieck cites the opening of *Hamlet*. Not until act 1, scene 4 does Hamlet see the Ghost, and not until scene 5 does the Ghost speak to Hamlet. To prepare for this encounter, Shakespeare opens the play, in act 1, scene 1, with the report of Francisco and Bernardo, who had seen the Ghost on the previous night. They are joined by Horatio and Marcellus, who witness the Ghost's return. In scene 2, Horatio and Marcellus inform Hamlet of the apparition. By the time that Hamlet himself sees and speaks to the Ghost, the audience is prepared by the testimony of the four witnesses and their own experience of the silent figure stalking the stage. For Tieck, Shakespeare's skill goes far beyond the mere mastery of creating stage illusion: he uses the psychology of deliberate delay to heighten anticipation and, with it, a readiness to accept the supernatural. The supernatural does not intrude upon the natural world; rather, the natural world is seen to depend upon the supernatural.[7]

As strongly as he praised Shakespeare's genius in introducing the marvellous on stage, Tieck felt that the artists of Boydell's Shakespeare Gallery frequently missed the mark, not by halting the dynamics of dramatic action but by depicting scenes ill suited for painting. In representing a scene from a play, Tieck reasoned, the artist should not rely on stage performance but endeavour to recreate the characters and action through the visual imagination. To copy from the performance, Tieck explained, was to copy a copy rather than to engage directly with the vitality of the original. In terms of this criterion, one might expect Tieck to be tolerant of the depiction of an off-stage event. Yet he faults William Hodges for taking the subject of 'Melancholy Jacques' 'not from the scene itself but from a description of one of the speaking persons'. He raised the same objection to James Northcote's depiction of the murdered princes in *Richard III*, a scene that occurs not on stage but only in the description of Tyrel. And Fuseli's exaggerations make him, Tieck declared, 'the worst of Michelangelo's imitators'.[8]

In England, however, Boydell's Shakespeare Gallery met with enthusiastic public response. That it ultimately failed in bankruptcy was due to the generous commissions Boydell paid to his artists and to his overly optimistic expectations that the large crowds who attended during the gallery's opening years would continue to come regularly when new paintings were no longer being added to the collection. Some of the paintings, such as Fuseli's, were indeed, as Tieck said that he wanted, inspired by imaginative responses to Shakespeare's text. Others were representations of actual performances. Some were 'copies of copies' in an additional sense, for several of the artists, among them William Hodges and Julius Caesar Ibbetson, found lucrative commissions in painting stage scenery and backdrops for theatre performance and might thus paint the actors performing before their own backdrop scenery.[9]

The representation on stage of the supernatural involves the paradox of rendering the invisible visible, the impalpable palpable, and the Artistotelian 'probable impossibilities' not only probable but also physically present. Yet they must, at the same time, appear only tenuously present. In *Romanticism and the Forms of Ruin*, Thomas McFarland posits a contrast between two artistic modes: the mimetic represents 'what is there', and the meontic represents 'what is not there'.[10] The staging of the supernatural creates the illusion of the meontic passing into the mimetic, of the 'not there' appearing as 'there'. When oxygen-fed lamps were introduced at the end of the eighteenth century, remarkable new stage effects were introduced that made it possible to project phantom images onto the stage. To be sure, no stagecraft of the period could reproduce Fuseli's visions of the supernatural, but even if they had little to do with what was actually staged, their popular appeal indicated that Fuseli had caught the imaginative temper of the contemporary theatre audience, especially their predilection for the Gothic.

Although 'upstaged' by Hamlet's struggle to escape Horatio's restraining grasp, the Ghost of Hamlet's father nevertheless commands the stage in Fuseli's eerie depiction of the scene. Standing before the moonlight and glaring through the sea mists, the Ghost is not, as one might expect, silhouetted. Rather, the moonlight seems to reach around him or even to penetrate through him. Indeed, the light of the moon seems to gleam through his ghostly eyes and to flame from his outspread beard. Horatio and Marcellus are frightened and attempt to hold Hamlet back. Hamlet, however, pushes against Horatio and seems to be pulled magnetically by the Ghost's commanding gesture with his sword. At the Ghost's feet, also heightened by the glaring moon, Fuseli has painted a surging sea lapping at the stone platform before the palace of Elsinore (see figure 6).[11]

Although Fuseli uses the platform to create a stage-like setting, the scene itself may owe little to any particular performance of *Hamlet*. What it does owe to the stage, however, is Fuseli's reliance on the pose of Robert Bensley as his Ghost. Bensley's features are recognizable from other portraits in the National Portrait Gallery.[12] John Genest, who ranked the Ghost in *Hamlet* among Bensley's best parts, granted that, although his voice was not generally pleasing, his sepulchral tones were nevertheless well suited to the haunting Ghost in *Hamlet*, and his delivery seemed to rise from the dead.[13] At the very time that Fuseli was preparing his painting for Boydell, Bensley appeared twice as the Ghost: at Haymarket (18 August 1795) and again at Drury Lane (29 April 1796).[14]

The ghosts of Gothic drama are not always frightening. A ghost haunts the site of murder to wreak vengeance on the perpetrator or to reveal the villain's crime. A ghost may also appear as a protective spirit, to prevent evil from befalling a son or daughter. In Samuel Taylor Coleridge's poem, the ghost of Christabel's mother appears, only to be banished by Geraldine: 'Off, wandering mother! Peak and pine! / I have power to bid thee flee' (ll. 205–6).[15] In M. G. Lewis's *The Castle Spectre*, the ghost of Evelina intervenes to protect her daughter Angela from the murderous Osmond.[16] When John Philip Kemble played Hamlet, he followed Fuseli's telling dramatic gesture: Hamlet is attracted to, not frightened by, the Ghost of his father. When he broke free from Horatio's restraining hold, he turned his sword away from the Ghost, not towards it; and when the Ghost sank into the earth, Hamlet slowly dropped to his knees for the close of the scene.[17]

In depicting the encounter of Macbeth and Banquo with the three witches in *Macbeth*, Fuseli again utilized the muscular posturing of the supernatural scene from *Hamlet*. Horatio's restraining grasp – the right leg bent, the left leg stretched back to

balance the weight of the forward-thrusting body – is duplicated
in the pose of Banquo. The muscular display of heroic gesture is
masculine bravado responding to the supernatural powers of the
'weird sisters'. The three witches hail Macbeth with the prophecy
that he shall be king and Banquo with the news that he shall be
both 'lesser' and 'greater'. The stage direction simply states,
'Witches vanish'. Banquo asks, 'Whither?' and Macbeth replies,
'Into the air; and what seemed corporal / Melted as breath into
the wind' (1.3.78, 79–80).[18] While such an exit could not be
performed in quite those terms upon the stage, Fuseli
commanded in painting more extensive powers of illusion. Just as
the moonlight shines through his Ghost, the mists carry his
witches aloft. He depicts them in the very moment of vanishing,
caught up in the wind and ascending on billowing clouds (see
figure 7).[19]

Robert Thew, who also engraved Fuseli's scene from *Hamlet*,
obviously had a much more difficult time engraving Sir Joshua
Reynolds's scene with Macbeth in Hecate's cave. Fuseli's vision of
the Shakespearean Gothic was, as Tieck not unjustly observed,
exaggeratedly Michelangelesque in its heroic posturing. Although
Fuseli, in his scenes from *A Midsummer Night's Dream*, could
crowd his canvas with an eroticized fecundity of fantastic creatures,[20] his scenes with ghosts and witches allowed no clutter to
distract from the stark emotional impact of supernatural terror.
Reynolds's approach was just the opposite: skulls, toads and all the
artefacts of horror emerge from dark recesses and are scattered
underfoot. It may well be wondered why Reynolds, renowned for
his elegant portraits of English aristocracy, should have turned to
this sort of grotesquerie. Among the first of the artists whom
Boydell approached in November 1786, Reynolds himself chose
this scene as his subject. By 1789, his failing eyesight forced him
to give up painting, but still he struggled to complete his contribution to a tradition that included Salvator Rosa's four *Scenes with
Witches* (1645–9)[21] and the younger Jacques de Gheyn's *Witches'
Kitchen* (1604).[22] Inspired by de Gheyn, Reynolds, too, hints at
rituals of infanticide. The ugly witches, positioned on either side
of the enthroned Hecate, are modelled after the Sybils on the
ceiling of Michelangelo's Sistine Chapel, and their ugliness

contrasts with the three beautiful sirens, 'the best of our delights', who arise with the vapours from the bubbling cauldron (*Macbeth*, 4.1.144).

In spite of his appropriations from other artists, Reynolds was attentive to the Shakespearean text. Each of the apparitions conjured by the witches has been worked into this picture: armed head; bloody child; child crowned, with a tree in his hand; shadowy kings, one bearing a mirror; and the ghost of Banquo (4.1.83–127). Even granting that stage designers may well have borrowed from the same sources that influenced Reynolds, it is unlikely that such ghastly disarray was recreated in the theatre. Hecate raises one finger as she admonishes Macbeth, who stands aghast before her, draped with a Scottish tartan and posed dramatically, with raised dagger and out-thrust arms.[23] Unlike the ugly hags to her left and right, the figure of Hecate is sternly handsome and muscular (see figure 8). Reynolds's model for Hecate was the twenty-two-year-old actor, John Darley, who had just performed the role of Hecate in the production of *Macbeth* at Covent Garden on 16 November 1787. Darley was described as manly, with a well-proportioned person and a rich and resonant voice;[24] Reynolds apparently was impressed by the muscular masculinity of the sorceress from the underworld. When Reynolds died in London on 23 February 1792, the painting, now hanging at Petworth, was still unfinished. Boydell, however, was reluctant to lose from his folio edition of the prints a work for which he had paid a high sum. Among the first commissioned, it was one of the last to be engraved. Thew filled in the missing details, and the engraving was published in December 1802.

John Philip Kemble played Macbeth annually throughout his career at Drury Lane in the 1790s and after he moved to Covent Garden in 1793. His own adaptations of the text – published in 1794, 1798, 1803 and 1814 – followed David Garrick's revisions of William Davenant's version. For the first scene with the witches (1.3), Kemble dimmed the lights, opened with 'thunder and lightning' and provided musical accompaniment to the witches' songs. For the second scene in Hecate's cave (4.1), Kemble used stage traps for the 'Apparitions of the Kings', each sudden appearance and vanishing accompanied by 'thunder and lightning'. As in Reynold's painting, a bubbling cauldron sent up vapours into the semi-darkened space.[25]

Also hanging at Petworth, the 'Death of Cardinal Beaufort' was Reynolds's only other painting for Boydell's Shakespeare Gallery. The scene is from *2 Henry VI* (3.3) where the cardinal hallucinates, clutches the bed in terror and bemoans his part in the death of Humphrey, duke of Gloucester (see figure 9). Henry Fuseli had already drawn this same scene in 1772.[26] As in his painting of Macbeth and Hecate, Reynolds was attentive to Shakespeare's text. Haunted by his own guilt, the cardinal sees the murdered Humphrey before him:

> O, torture me no more – I will confess.
> Alive again? Then show me where he is.
> I'll give a thousand pound to look upon him.
> He hath no eyes! The dust hath blinded them.
>
> (*2 Henry VI*, 3.3.11–14)

Witnessing the cardinal's torment, the king utters the futile command to 'beat away the busy meddling fiend / That lays strong siege unto this wretch's soul' (ll. 21–2). Warwick exclaims, 'See how the pangs of death do make him grin' (l. 24). Reynolds took the king's metaphor literally. Opposite the king, who stands at the bedside with raised hand, Reynolds painted the 'meddling fiend', glowering from the draperies above the cardinal's head. In Reynold's painting, the cardinal's horrific grimace, his hand clutching the bedding, was a clear revelation of the dying man's haunted conscience. As accustomed as the gallery visitors were to scenes of Shakespearean Gothic, which recurred in many other paintings on display, the public and critics alike objected to this all too blatant representation of the cardinal's guilt. In response to criticism from Walpole and others, Boydell instructed Caroline Watson, who executed the stunning stipple engraving, to remove the 'meddling fiend'. The first version of the engraving was published in June 1790. The second, published in August 1792, shows only a shadowy swirl where once the demon had appeared. The demon also vanished from Reynolds's painting.

The villains of Gothic drama owed much to the malignancy of Shakespeare's Richard III and Iago. The cruel and evil females of Gothic drama also followed those in Shakespeare: Lady Macbeth, who goads her husband into murder; Tamora, who has her sons rape and mutilate Lavinia, the daughter of Titus Andronicus; and Margaret of Anjou,

> She-wolf of France, but worse than wolves of France,
> Whose tongue more poisons than adder's tooth –
> ...
> Women are soft, mild, pitiful, and flexible;
> Thou stern, obdurate, flinty, rough, remorseless.
>   (*3 Henry VI*, 1.4, 111–12 and 142–3)[27]

Married at fifteen to the weak-minded and ineffectual Henry VI, Margaret of Anjou is portrayed as adulterous, ambitious and domineering. She appears in all three *Henry VI* plays, as well as in *Richard III*. In spite of their promotion of such a powerful villainess, the three parts of *Henry VI* were among the least performed of Shakespeare's history plays during the eighteenth century. Parts 1 and 2, as adapted by John Crowne, were performed at Dorset Garden in 1681; part 1 was staged at Covent Garden on 13 March 1738; and the altered version of *Henry VI* by Theophilus Cibber played at Drury Lane on 5 July 1723.

Even if the *Henry VI* plays were not familiar on stage, both Reynolds and Opie were confident that the reading public was thoroughly familiar with *Henry VI*. Opie's rendition of Eleanor's visit to Mother Jourdain, like Reynolds's depiction of Macbeth in the cave of Hecate, adheres to the established tradition of witches in art. Both artists visualized *Henry VI* not as a play revealing the factions that gave rise to the Wars of the Roses[28] but, rather, as a play revealing a Gothic curse that haunts the houses of Lancaster and York. Both chose to represent the dramatic action in terms of the play's demonic moments. In thus emphasizing the Gothic elements of Shakespeare's play, Reynolds gave centrality to a brief scene of just thirty lines. The scene in which Eleanor, duchess of Gloucester, seeks the witch's prophecy is more substantial, being forty-three lines long, and more pertinent to the plot.

Shakespeare sets the event in Gloucester's garden and indicates thunder and lightning when the spirit Asmath appears and departs. Opie has chosen to envelop the scene in darkness. In Shakespeare's text, Bolingbroke commands Mother Jourdain, 'Be you prostrate and grovel on the earth' (*2 Henry VI*, 1.4.10). The stage directions indicate the ritual to be performed: 'Here do the ceremonies belonging, and make the circle.' Opie has given that ritual its full ghastly detail. Mother Jourdain has drawn the circle with an infant's blood. She still clutches the bloody knife, and the dead baby lies at her feet among the scattered bones of other human remains. She passes her wand over the steaming cauldron, and the demon spirit arises. Bolingbroke asks the demon to reveal the fate of King Henry. Opie has the demon point his finger at Bolingbroke when delivering the fatal answer: 'The Duke yet lives that Henry shall depose; / But him outlive, and die a violent death' (ll. 29–30) (see figure 10).[29]

The significant literary antecedent of this scene of conjuration is Saul's visit to the Witch of Endor (1 Samuel 28:7–25). As was Samuel's, Eleanor's interview with the witch is a violation of the law. The difference is that Margaret of Anjou has tricked Eleanor into seeking this interview so that Eleanor can be arrested and imprisoned. Trick though it may be, the prophecies of the demon Asmath are nevertheless true. In the struggle for power between the houses of York and Lancaster, Richard Plantagenet, duke of York aspires to the throne. Because Gloucester is next in line to the throne, the Lancastrians plot to get rid of him by enlisting the help of Margaret. She already dominates the weak king, but she sees Gloucester as a hindrance. Thus, she plots to use Eleanor, duchess of Gloucester, to bring about her husband's downfall. When Eleanor is arrested for sorcery, the shame forces Gloucester to resign his role as Lord Protector. The conspirators – Margaret, Suffolk, the duke of York and Beaufort (bishop of Winchester, later cardinal) – are not content with his resignation; instead, they want to be rid completely of Gloucester and so arrange for his imprisonment on an accusation of treason.

The conjuring scene therefore is crucial to the plot of *2 Henry VI*. As with the revelations of the witches in *Macbeth*, the demonic prophecies are true. Shakespeare makes the most of these prophecies by having them told twice. When Asmath answers Bolingbroke's questions, Southwell records in a book the fateful predictions: the duke shall depose Henry but 'die a violent death' (*2 Henry VI*, 1.4.30); Suffolk 'by water shall … die, and take his end' (l. 32); and Somerset is advised to 'shun castles' and seek safety 'upon the sandy plains' (ll. 34, 35). The interview with the demon is no sooner concluded than York and Buckingham arrive with their guard to arrest 'these traitors and their trash' (l. 36). From Suffolk's book, York then reads 'the devil's writ' (l. 55). Asmath's predictions are thus heard a second time but dismissed by York as vague and obscure: 'These oracles are hardily attained / And hardly understood' (ll. 58–9).

For an age of Gothic melodrama, Edmund Kean's performance as Richard III more fully realized the expectation of lurid villainy from 'that bottled spider … this bunch-backed toad' (*Richard III*, 1.3.240, 244). Kemble, however, chose to play the role with cold aloofness and cunning reserve. When Kemble was invited to the artist's studio to pose for the scene in which Richard 'meets the Princes' (3.1), Northcote complained that he showed too little passion. This restraint was crucial to Kemble's interpretation of Richard's dispassionate and calculating ruthlessness.[30] Kemble, of course, performed Colly Cibber's, not Shakespeare's *Richard III*, which he adapted in his own versions of the play, published in 1810, 1811 and 1814. Other than trimming a few speeches and adding small bits of the Shakespearean original, Kemble did little to change Cibber's text. When he came to the ghostly encounters in Richard's tent (5.5), Kemble modelled the set after William Hogarth's famous painting of David Garrick as Richard III.[31] But he also strove to enhance the supernatural stage effects. In *Macbeth*, he kept the witches upstage, but in *Richard III* he wanted to startle the audience by having the ghosts pop up through downstage traps front right, left and centre. The lights are dimmed, and groans are heard as the ghosts of Richard's victims – King Henry, Lady Anne, the young princes – arise to condemn him. With a clap of thunder, the ghosts vanish.[32]

Kemble did not perform in *Julius Caesar* until late in his career, and when he did, on 29 February 1812, he spent an unusual amount of effort on preparation, preparing one prompt book in

1811, and because of continuing adjustments, a second prompt book for the opening in 1812.[33] Remarkably, *Julius Caesar* had not been performed on the London stage in over thirty years.[34] Thus, when Richard Westall painted *Brutus and the Ghost of Caesar* (4.3), he was relying not on any performance but on his own interpretation of the text. As Westall would have it, there is no fear, nor even any sign of intimidation, in Brutus's response to the Ghost. To make Brutus appear all the more stoically aloof, Westall has given the Ghost a most threatening, glowering expression. To the Ghost's prophecy of death, Brutus answers with cold disdain, 'Why, I will see thee at Philippi then' (*Julius Caesar*, 4.2.337).[35] Kemble's interpretation is very different. He played the scene of Brutus in his tent much as he played Richard III in his tent, with Brutus registering the same fear but without the downstage traps. At the Ghost's entrance, Kemble's stage directions call for the lights to be gradually dimmed. As the Ghost stalks from stage left with measured step, Brutus challenges it to declare its identity:

> I think it is the weakness of mine eyes
> That shapes this monstrous apparition.
> It comes upon me. Art thou any thing?
> Art thou some god, some angel, or some devil,
> That mak'st my blood cold, and my hair to stare?
> Speak to me, what thou art.

(ll. 327–32)

The Ghost answers, 'Thy evil spirit, Brutus' (l. 333). Brutus asks whether they will meet again. Crossing to stage right, the Ghost turns to reply, 'Ay, at Philippi' (l. 336). Only after the Ghost has vanished does Brutus regain his composure: 'Now I have taken heart, thou vanishest. / Ill spirit, I would hold more talk with thee' (ll. 337–8).[36]

While it is true that supernatural elements abound in Shakespeare and that in the later eighteenth century authors of Gothic literature adapted these elements to their purpose, it would require an anachronistic and backward reading of literary history to identify Shakespeare as a playwright of Gothic drama. Nevertheless, precisely such an anachronistic and backward reading took place in the staging of Shakespeare's plays during this same period. The popular fascination with Gothic horror led to performances of Shakespeare that emphasized the Gothic potentiality of scenes with ghosts and witches. No wonder that Charles Lamb protested: 'What injury (short of the theatres) did not Boydell's "Shakespeare Gallery" do me with Shakespeare!'[37] Ostensibly, Lamb's objection was to restricting the infinite array of possibilities, of imposing upon the imagination specific and concrete images. Any performance, any painting of Shakespeare limited the illimitable. In his essay, 'The tragedies of Shakspeare, considered with reference to their fitness for stage representation' (1811), Lamb had already concluded that Shakespeare was less fit for the physical stage than other playwrights because he had much more to offer in the theatre of the mind. This curious argument makes a bit more sense when Lamb gives examples of the sort of specificity to which he objects most strongly. The supernatural can be 'realized' mentally in reading, but on stage it must be 'materialized'; spirits and fairies cannot be represented, they cannot even be painted – they can only be objects of belief.

The worst consequence of performance is its levelling effect. Shakespeare's play is placed on the same stage with the play of a far less capable playwright; both can make us weep or make us laugh, and both are judged by the power of their emotional impact, so that their differences in psychological complexity and aesthetic merit are forgotten. The audience therefore can be moved as much by Sarah Siddons in the role of Mrs Beverly in *The Gamester* as by her performance as Lady Macbeth. Lamb cites the response to George Barnwell in George Lillo's *The London Merchant*: 'Barnwell is a wretched murderer; there is a certain fitness between his neck and the rope; he is the legitimate heir to the gallows; nobody who thinks at all can think of any alleviating circumstances in his case to make him a fit object of mercy.' Shakespeare's villains – Macbeth, Richard, Iago – may be reduced to the same criminal level in performance, but not so while we read and meditate on their actions: 'We think not so much of the crimes which they commit, but of the ambition, the aspiring spirit, the intellectual activity, which prompts them to overleap those moral fences.'[38]

Lamb, no less than other late eighteenth- and early nineteenth-century adapters of Shakespeare, could transform the Bard to suit the conventions of Gothic romance. On the one hand, he argued that an encounter with a ghost was intimately personal – as an encounter with a memory, or guilt, or fear. It was a matter of one's own conscience, not of public display.[39] On the other hand, he certainly saw the mental and moral value of encouraging readers to participate in a character's torment. The supernatural scenes are fully indulged in the Lambs' *Tales from Shakespear*. In dividing the telling of these tales with his sister, Lamb was responsible for the tragedies. His retelling of *Macbeth* presents Lady Macbeth as the play's center of evil· she is a 'hardened being' and 'one of Shakespeare's worst characters', a 'bad, ambitious woman'. Her madness and suicide are not simply the consequence of remorse and guilt but rather of pride exposed to 'public hate'.[40] In relating Macbeth's encounter with the witches on the heath and Hecate in her cave, Lamb masters the prose of Gothic tales for children.[41] Whatever had been Lamb's objections to the 'materializing' of the imagination through the Shakespeare Gallery and stage performance, the first edition of *The Tales of Shakespear* (1807) was illustrated with the Lambs' own gallery of twenty plates by William Mulready, which included, among other Gothic moments, 'The Witches' Cauldron'.[42]

Shakespeare's plays provided source material for the Gothic literature of the eighteenth and nineteenth centuries. Not only were scenes from his plays, indeed entire plots, adapted to the new Gothic literature, but the plays themselves were also reshaped to satisfy public expectations for Gothic horror on stage. As documented in the Boydell Shakespeare Gallery and as evident in Kemble's prompt books, the supernatural moments in such plays as *Hamlet*, *Macbeth* and *Richard III* were fully exploited for their Gothic impact. Even Charles Lamb, critic of the unwarranted 'materialization' of the subjective experience, was caught up in the compelling sweep of the Gothic mode.

Notes

1   In this volume, see ch. 3, Jeffrey Kahan, 'The curse of Shakespeare'.

2   Jonathan Bate, *Shakespearean Constitutions: Politics, Theatre, Criticism, 1730–1830* (Oxford: Clarendon Press, 1989), p. 45; see also Richard D. Altick, *The Shows of London* (Cambridge, MA: Belknap Press, 1978), pp. 106–9.

3   Frederick Burwick, 'Shakespeare and the Romantics', in Duncan Wu (ed.), *The Blackwell Companion to Romanticism* (London: Blackwell, 1997), pp. 512–19.

4   In this volume, see ch. 1, Anne Williams, 'Reading Walpole reading Shakespeare'.

5   In this volume, see ch. 8, Jessica Walker, '"We are not safe": history, fear and the Gothic in *Richard III*'.

6   'Probable impossibilities', chapter 25 of Aristotle, *Poetics*, in *The Basic Works of Aristotle*, ed. Richard McKeon (New York: Random House, 1941), pp. 1485–6.

7   Ludwig Tieck, 'Über Shakespeare's Behandlung des Wunderbaren' (1793), in *Schriften*, ed. Jans Peter Balmes, Manfred Frank, Achim Hölter et al. (12 vols; Frankfurt/aM: Deutsche Klassiker Verlag, 1991), vol. 1, pp. 685–722. See, as well, Frederick Burwick, *Illusion and the Drama: Critical Theory of the Enlightenment and Romantic Era* (University Park: Pennsylvania State University Press, 1991), pp. 61–74.

8   Tieck, 'Über die Kupferstiche nach der Shakespearschen Galerie in London', in *Schriften*, vol. 1, pp. 653–80: 'Statt dieser Gegenstände aber hat *Hodges* die erste Szene des zweiten Akts gewählt, – und nicht die Szene selbst, sondern eine Schilderung im Munde einer der sprechenden Personen', vol. 1, pp. 665–6; italics in original.

9   *Boydell Shakespeare Gallery*, ed. Walter Pape and Frederick Burwick (Bottrop: Peter Pomp, 1996), pp. 190–1.

10   Thomas McFarland, *Romanticism and the Forms of Ruin* (Princeton: Princeton University Press, 1981), pp. 384–418.

11   *Boydell Shakespeare Gallery*, p. 285.

12   National Portrait Gallery, NPG D12183, 'Robert Bensley' (1738–1817), soft-ground etching by William Daniell, after the painting by George Dance (20 April 1795); published 2 April 1814. See also NPG D15501, 'Robert Bensley', line engraving by Philipp Audinet, after the painting by Samuel de Wilde; published by John Bell, 23 February 1793; NPG D9544, 'A scene in *The Fair Circassian*' (Drury Lane, 27 November 1781), Robert Bensley as Omar, Elizabeth Farren as Almeida; etching by James Sayers (1781). An earlier rendering of this scene was painted in 1768–9 by Benjamin Wilson, with Hamlet (William Powell), Horatio (Thomas Hull), Marcellus and the Ghost (Robert Bensley). The human figures are small, and the vast landscape is dominated by dark clouds and the sea.

13   John Genest, *Some Account of the English Stage from the Restoration in 1660 to 1830* (10 vols; Bath: H. E. Carrington, 1832), vol. 7, pp. 252–3: 'He

frequently delivered dialogue with such propriety of emphasis and nicety of discrimination, that plainly evinced a sound and comprehensive judgement … he showed a mind labouring, as it were, against natural defects.'

14 Ibid., vol. 7, pp. 224 and 240.
15 Samuel Taylor Coleridge, 'Christabel', in *Poetical Works: Part 1, Poems (Reading Text)*, vol. 16 of *The Collected Works of Samuel Taylor Coleridge*, ed. J. C. C. Mays (Princeton: Princeton University Press, 2001), pp. 477–504, p. 489.
16 M. G. Lewis, *The Castle Spectre*, in Jeffrey Cox (ed.), *Seven Gothic Dramas: 1789–1825* (Athens: Ohio University Press, 1992), pp. 150–224, p. 219.
17 James Boaden, *Memoirs of the Life of John Philip Kemble* (2 vols; London: Longman, Hurst, Rees, Orme, Brown and Green, 1825), vol. 1, pp. 88–133.
18. All references to Shakespeare's plays are to *The Norton Shakespeare*, ed. Stephen Greenblatt et al. (New York: Norton, 1997). Further references will be incorporated into the body of the text.
19 *Boydell Shakespeare Gallery*, p. 230.
20 Ibid., pp. 222–4; Boydell, 1:20 and 1:21.
21 A series of four paintings (Morning, Day, Evening, Night), Cleveland Museum of Art, Cat. 1977.37.1, 2, 3 and 4.
22 Claudia Swan, *Art, Science and Witchcraft in Early Modern Holland: Jacques de Gheyn II (1565–1629)* (Cambridge: Cambridge University Press, 2005), especially 'Part 2: Unnatural sights, witchcraft and phantasia', pp. 123–94; *Witches' Kitchen* (1604), p. 125.
23 *Macbeth* was first performed with Scottish costumes at Covent Garden, 23 October 1773; Genest, *Some Account of the English Stage*, vol. 5, pp. 414–15.
24 Genest, *Some Account of the English Stage*, vol. 6, p. 488. Darley subsequently emigrated to America and began performing in Philadelphia in 1794.
25 Charles H. Shattuck (ed.), *John Philip Kemble Promptbooks* (11 vols; Charlottesville: Published for the Folger Shakespeare Library by the University Press of Virginia, 1974), vol. 5: *Macbeth*, scenes 4, 8–10, 29–30 and 44–8.
26 Henry Fuseli, 'The Death of Cardinal Beaufort' (1772); pen and wash, Walker Art Gallery, Liverpool.
27 Before being stabbed by Queen Margaret and Clifford, the duke of York condemns her with these words.
28 Although the commissioned artists – Opie, Reynolds and Northcote – painted other scenes, Josiah Boydell represented the Wars of the Roses with the allegorical scene in which Plantagenet and Somerset pluck the white and red roses. See Boydell, 2:14, 'The Temple Garden' (*1 Henry VI*, 1.6); Josiah Boydell, engraved by John Ogborne (1 January 1795).
29 *Boydell Shakespeare Gallery*, p. 259.
30 Ibid.; Boydell, 2:22 (*Macbeth*, 3.1); James Northcote, 'Meets the Princes' (*Richard III*, 3.1); engraved by Robert Thew (1 March 1791).
31 William Hogarth, 'David Garrick as Richard III' (1745), Walker Art Gallery, Accession Number WAG634.
32 Shattuck, *Kemble Promptbooks*, vol. 7: *Richard III*, 1.3.65–7.

33   Ibid., vol. 4: *Julius Caesar*, 1.2.

34   Genest, *Some Account of the English Stage*, vol. 6, p. 131; performed at Drury Lane, 24 January 1780.

35   *Boydell Shakespeare Gallery*; Boydell, 2:30, Richard Westall, 'Brutus and the Ghost of Caesar' (*Julius Caesar*, 4.3); engraved by Edward Scriven (1 December 1802).

36   Shattuck, *Kemble Promptbooks*, vol. 4: *Julius Caesar* (1811), p. 64; *Julius Caesar* (1812), p. 61.

37   Charles Lamb to Samuel Rogers (December 1833), in *The Letters of Charles Lamb, to which are added those of his sister Mary Lamb*, ed. E. V. Lucas (3 vols; London: Methuen, 1933), vol. 3, p. 394.

38   Charles Lamb, 'On the tragedies of Shakspeare considered with reference to their fitness for stage representation', in Joan Coldwell (ed.), *Charles Lamb on Shakespeare* (Gerrards Cross: Colyn Smythe, 1978), pp. 24–41, here 33 and 35–6; see also Burwick, *Illusion and the Drama*, pp. 74–81.

39   Charles Lamb, 'G. F. Cooke in "Richard the Third"', *Morning Post* (8 January 1802), cited in *Charles Lamb on Shakespeare*, ed. Coldwell, pp. 18–21.

40   Lamb, *Tales from Shakespear*, pp. 96, 98–9 and 103.

41   Ibid., pp. 95 and 101–2.

42   Charles Lamb [and Mary Lamb], *Tales from Shakespear* (2 vols; London: Printed for Thomas Hodgkins, at the Juvenile Library, 1807). The illustrations are by William Mulready; the engraving of the twenty plates has been attributed, without justification, to William Blake.

Bibliography

❧

A'Beckett, Gilbert Abbott, *Timour, the Cream of All Tartars* (London: W. S. Johnson, 1845).

Adelman, Janet, 'Male bonding in Shakespeare's comedies', in Peter Erickson and Coppélia Kahn (eds), *Shakespeare's Rough Magic: Renaissance Essays in Honour of C. L. Barber* (Newark: University of Delaware Press, 1985), pp. 73–103.

Adolphus, J.[ohn] L.[eycester], *Letters to Richard Heber, Esq., Containing Critical Remarks on the Series of Novels Beginning with 'Waverley', and an Attempt to Ascertain Their Author* (London: Rodwell and Martin, 1821).

Alexander, Catherine M. S., 'Shakespeare and the eighteenth century: criticism and research', *Shakespeare Survey*, 51 (1998), 1–15.

Alter, Iska, '"To see or not to see": interpolations, extended scenes and musical accompaniment in Kenneth Branagh's *Hamlet*', in Hardin L. Assand (ed.), *Stage Directions in* Hamlet: *New Essays and New Directions* (Madison, NJ: Fairleigh Dickinson University Press, 2003), pp. 161–9.

Altick, Richard D., *The Shows of London* (Cambridge, MA: Belknap Press, 1978).

'Ann Radcliffe', *Annual Biography and Obituary*, 8 (1824).

Aristotle, *Poetics*, in *The Basic Works of Aristotle*, ed. Richard McKeon (New York: Random House, 1941), pp. 1455–87.

Armstrong, Philip, *Shakespeare in Psychoanalysis* (London and New York: Routledge, 2001).

Atwood, Margaret, *Cat's Eye* (New York: Doubleday, 1989).

Auerbach, Nina, *Ellen Terry, Player in Her Time* (New York: W. W. Norton, 1987).

Austen, Jane, *Northanger Abbey*, ed. Claire Grogan (Peterborough, Ont: Broadview Literary Texts, 1996).

Baines, Paul, *The House of Forgery in Eighteenth-Century Britain* (Aldershot: Ashgate, 1999).

Baker, Susan, 'Shakespearean authority in the classic detective story', *Shakespeare Quarterly*, 46, 4 (1995), 428–48.

Bakhtin, Mikhail, *Rabelais and His World*, trans. Helen Iswolsky (Bloomington: Indiana University Press, 1968).

Barbauld, Anna Laetitia, 'Mrs Radcliffe', biographical preface to *The Romance of the Forest*, vol. 43 of *The British Novelists* (London: Rivington, 1810), pp. i–viii.

Barbour, Judith, '"The meaning of the tree": the tale of Mirra in Mary Shelley's *Mathilda*', in Syndy M. Conger, Frederick S. Frank and Gregory O'Dea (eds), *Iconoclastic Departures: Mary Shelley after Frankenstein* (Madison, NJ: Fairleigh Dickinson University Press, 1997), pp. 98–114.

Bate, Jonathan, *Shakespeare and the English Romantic Imagination* (Oxford: Clarendon Press, 1986).

——, *Shakespearian Constitutions: Politics, Theatre, Criticism, 1730–1830* (Oxford: Clarendon Press, 1989).

—— (ed.), *The Romantics on Shakespeare* (London and New York: Penguin, 1992).

Bedford, Kristina, '"This castle hath a pleasant seat": Shakespearean allusion in *The Castle of Otranto*', *English Studies in Canada*, 14, 4 (December 1988), 415–35.

Besnault, Marie-Hélène, and Michel Bitot, 'Historical legacy and fiction: the poetical reinvention of King Richard III', in Michael Hattaway (ed.), *The Cambridge Companion to Shakespeare's History Plays* (Cambridge: Cambridge University Press, 2002), pp. 106–25.

Betsky, Aaron, *Queer Space: Architecture and Same-Sex Desire* (New York: William Morrow, 1997).

Billington, Michael, review of *Hamlet*, dir. Ron Daniels, Royal Shakespeare Company, *Guardian*, 7 September 1984.

——, review of *Hamlet*, dir. Adrian Noble, Royal Shakespeare Company, *Guardian*, 21 December 1992.

Blakemore, Steven, 'Matthew Lewis's black mass: sexual, religious inversion in *The Monk*', *Studies in the Novel*, 30, 4 (1998), 521–39.

Bleiler, E. F., 'Horace Walpole and *The Castle of Otranto*', in *Three Gothic Novels*, E. F. Bleiler (ed.) (New York: Dover, 1966), pp. viii–ix.

Bloom, Harold, *The Anxiety of Influence* (1973; reprint, New Haven: Yale University Press, 1997).

—— (ed.), *William Shakespeare's* King Lear (New York and Philadelphia: Chelsea House, 1987).

Boaden, James, *Memoirs of the Life of John Philip Kemble, esq., Including a History of the Stage, from the Time of Garrick to the Present Period* (2 vols; London: Longman, Hurst, Rees, Orme, Brown and Green, 1825).

Booth, Stephen, King Lear, Macbeth, *Indefinition and Tragedy* (New Haven: Yale University Press, 1983).

Bostock, Graham, 'Excalibur aloft', *West Midlands What's On*, March 1993.

Botting, Fred, *Gothic* (New York: Routledge, 1996).

——, 'Monstrosity', in Marie Mulvey-Roberts (ed.), *The Handbook of Gothic Literature* (New York: New York University Press, 1998), p. 163.

Boutin, Aimee, 'Shakespeare, women and French Romanticism', *Modern Language Quarterly*, 65, 4 (December 2004), 505–29.

Boydell Shakespeare Gallery, Walter Pape and Frederick Burwick (eds) (Bottrop: Peter Pomp, 1996).

[Boyle, Henry], *The Universal Chronologist, and Historical Register, From the Creation to the Close of the Year 1825* (London: Sherwood, Gilbert and Piper, 1826).

Bradley, Simon, 'The Englishness of Gothic: theories and interpretations from William Gilpin to J. H. Parker', *Architectural History*, 45 (2002), 325–46.

Branagh, Kenneth, *Beginning* (New York: Norton, 1990).

——, *Hamlet, by William Shakespeare* (New York: Norton, 1996).

—— (dir.), *In the Bleak Midwinter*, US title *A Midwinter's Tale* (1996; video cassette, Columbia Tristar, 1996).

—— (dir.), *Mary Shelley's Frankenstein* (1994; DVD, Columbia TriStar, 1998).

—— (dir.), *Dead Again* (1991; DVD, Paramount, 2000).

—— (dir.), *Hamlet* (1996; video cassette, Time Warner, 2000).

—— and Glyn Dearman, dirs, *Hamlet* (1992; audio cassette, Random, 1992).

Branam, George C., 'The genesis of David Garrick's *Romeo and Juliet*', *Shakespeare Quarterly*, 35, 2 (1984), 170–9.

Brereton, Austin, *The Lyceum and Henry Irving* (London: Lawrence and Bullen, 1893).

Brightwell, Cecilia Lucy, *Memorials of the Life of Amelia Opie, Selected and Arranged from Her Letters* (London: Longman, Brown, 1854).

Brooke, John, 'Horace Walpole and the politics of the early years of the reign of George III', in Warren Hunting Smith (ed.), *Horace Walpole: Writer, Politician and Connoisseur: Essays on the 250th Anniversary of Walpole's Birth* (New Haven: Yale University Press, 1967), pp. 3–23.

Brown, Marshall, *The Gothic Text* (Stanford: Stanford University Press, 2005).

Brownell, Morris R., *The Prime Minister of Taste: A Portrait of Horace Walpole* (New Haven and London: Yale University Press, 2001).

Bruhm, Steven, *Gothic Bodies: The Politics of Pain in Romance Fiction* (Philadelphia: University of Pennsylvania Press, 1994).

Bucke, Charles, *On the Beauties, Harmonies and Sublimities of Nature* (new edn; 3 vols; London: T. Tegg and Sons, 1837).

Budra, Paul, *A Mirror for Magistrates and the De Casibus Tradition* (Toronto: University of Toronto Press, 2000).

Buhler, Stephen M., *Shakespeare in the Cinema: Ocular Proof* (Albany: State University of New York Press, 2002).

Burke, Edmund, *A Philosophical Enquiry into the Origin of Our Ideas of the Sublime and Beautiful* (London: R. and J. Dodsley, 1757).

Burnett, Mark Thornton, *Constructing 'Monsters' in Shakespearean Drama and Early Modern Culture* (New York: Palgrave Macmillan, 2002).

Burney, E. L., 'Shakespeare in *Otranto*', *Manchester Review*, 12 (winter 1972), 61–4.

Burnim, Kalman A., *David Garrick, Director* (Carbondale: Southern Illinois University Press, 1973).

Burwick, Frederick, *Illusion and the Drama: Critical Theory of the Enlightenment and Romantic Era* (University Park: Pennsylvania State University Press, 1991).

——, 'Shakespeare and the Romantics', in Duncan Wu (ed.), *A Companion to Romanticism* (London: Blackwell, 1998), pp. 512–19.

Butler, Marilyn, *Jane Austen and the War of Ideas* (1975; reprint, Oxford: Oxford University Press, 1987).

Byrne, Paula, *Jane Austen and the Theatre* (London: Hambledon and London, 2002).

Cakebread, Caroline, 'Shakespeare in transit', in Christy Desmet and Robert Sawyer (eds), *Harold Bloom's Shakespeare* (New York: Palgrave, 2002), pp. 199–211.

Callaghan, Dympna C., 'The ideology of romantic love: the case of *Romeo and Juliet*', in Dympna Callaghan, Lorraine Helms and Jyotsna Singh, *The Weyward Sisters: Shakespeare and Feminist Politics* (Oxford/ Cambridge: Blackwell, 1994), pp. 59–101.

Castell, David, dir., *To be … on Camera: A History with Hamlet*, on *Hamlet*, dir. Kenneth Branagh, video cassette, Time Warner, 1996.

Chapman, Don, Review of *Hamlet*, dir. Ron Daniels, Royal Shakespeare Company, *Oxford Mail*, 6 September 1984.

Chatterjee, Ranita, '*Mathilda*: Mary Shelley, William Godwin and the ideologies of incest', in Syndy M. Conger, Frederick S. Frank and Gregory O'Dea (eds), *Iconoclastic Departures: Mary Shelley after Frankenstein* (Madison, NJ: Fairleigh Dickinson University Press, 1997), pp. 130–49.

Clemit, Pamela, '*Frankenstein, Matilda* and the legacies of Godwin and Wollstonecraft', in Esther Schor (ed.), *The Cambridge Companion to Mary Shelley* (Cambridge: Cambridge University Press, 2003), pp. 26–44.

Clery, E. J., *The Rise of Supernatural Fiction, 1762–1800* (New York: Cambridge University Press, 1995).

——, 'Introduction' to Horace Walpole, *The Castle of Otranto: A Gothic Story*, ed. W. S. Lewis (Oxford: Oxford University Press, 1996), pp. vii–xxxiii.

——, 'Horace Walpole's *The Mysterious Mother* and the impossibility of female desire', in Fred Botting (ed.), *The Gothic* (Cambridge: Brewer, 2001), pp. 23–46.

——, 'The genesis of "Gothic" fiction', in Jerrold E. Hogle (ed.), *The Cambridge Companion to Gothic Fiction* (Cambridge: Cambridge University Press, 2002), pp. 21–39.

Coleridge, Samuel Taylor, *Remains*, in Jonathan Bate (ed.), *The Romantics on Shakespeare* (London and New York: Penguin, 1992), pp. 385–94.

——, *Poetical Works: Part 1, Poems (Reading Text)*, vol. 16 of *The Collected Works of Samuel Taylor Coleridge*, ed. J. C. C. Mays (Princeton: Princeton University Press, 2001).

Colie, Rosalie, *Shakespeare's Living Art* (Princeton: Princeton University Press, 1974).

Collick, John, *Shakespeare, Cinema and Society* (Manchester: Manchester University Press, 1989).

Commons, Jeffrey, *100 Years of Italian Opera* (London: Opera Rara, 1982).

Congreve, William, *Incognita: Or, Love and Duty Reconciled: A Novel* (London: Printed for Peter Buck, 1692).

Copeland, Nancy, 'The sentimentality of Garrick's *Romeo and Juliet*', *Restoration and Eighteenth-Century Theatre Research*, 4, 2 (1989), 1–13.

Coursen, H. R., *Shakespeare in Space: Recent Shakespeare Productions on Screen* (New York: Peter Lang, 2002).

Cowden-Clarke, Mary, *The Girlhood of Shakespeare's Heroines* (3 vols; London: W. H. Smith and Son, 1850–2).

Crowl, Samuel, 'Hamlet "most royal": an interview with Kenneth Branagh', *Shakespeare Bulletin*, 12, 4 (fall 1994), 5–8.

——, 'Communicating Shakespeare: an interview with Kenneth Branagh', *Shakespeare Bulletin*, 20, 3 (summer 2002), 24–8.

——, *Shakespeare at the Cineplex: The Kenneth Branagh Era* (Athens: University of Ohio Press, 2003).

Danchin, Pierre (ed.), *The Prologues and Epilogues of the Restoration, 1660–1700* (Nancy: Presses Universitaires de Nancy, 1978).

Daniels, Ron (dir.), *Hamlet*, by William Shakespeare, Stratford-upon-Avon, Royal Shakespeare Theatre, August 1984, Archival video, Shakespeare Centre Library.

Dawson, Anthony B., *Hamlet*, Shakespeare in Performance (Manchester: Manchester University Press, 1995).

Dawson, Carl, *Thomas Love Peacock* (London: Routledge and Kegan Paul, 1968).

de Chénier, Marie-Joseph, *Tableau historique de l'état et des progrès de la littérature française, depuis 1789* (Paris, 1816).

de Grazia, Margreta, *Shakespeare Verbatim: The Reproduction of Authenticity and the 1790 Apparatus* (Oxford: Clarendon Press, 1991)

DeLamotte, Eugenia, *Perils of the Night: A Feminist Study of Nineteenth-Century Gothic* (Oxford: Oxford University Press, 1990).

Demme, Jonathan (dir.), *The Silence of the Lambs*. Perf. Jodie Foster, Anthony Hopkins. Orion Pictures Corporation, 1991.

Desens, Marliss C., *The Bed-Trick in English Renaissance Drama: Explorations in Gender, Sexuality and Power* (Newark: University of Delaware Press, 1994).

Desmet, Christy and Robert Sawyer (eds), *Shakespeare and Appropriation* (London: Routledge, 2000).

—— and —— (eds), *Harold Bloom's Shakespeare* (New York: Palgrave, 2002).

Dibdin, Charles, *A Complete History of the English Stage* (London: Printed for the author, 1800).

Dobson, Michael, *The Making of the National Poet: Shakespeare, Adaptation and Authorship, 1660–1769* (Oxford: Clarendon, 1992).

Dodd, William, *The Beauties of Shakespeare, Regularly Selected from Each Play* (London: T. Waller, 1752).

Donaldson, Peter S., 'Taking on Shakespeare: Kenneth Branagh's *Henry V*', *Shakespeare Quarterly*, 42 (1991), 60–71.

Drake, Nathan, *Literary Hours: or Sketches Critical, Narrative and Poetical* (3rd edn; 3 vols; London: T. Cadell and W. Davies, 1804).

Dryden, John, *Troilus and Cressida*, in vol. 13 of *The Works of John Dryden*, ed. Alan Roper and Vinton A. Dearing (20 vols; Berkeley: University of California Press, 1956–84), pp. 219–355.

——, 'Prologue' to the April 1679 performance of *Troilus and Cressida, or Truth Found Too Late*, in Pierre Danchin (ed.), *The Prologues and Epilogues of the Restoration, 1660–1700* (Nancy: Presses Universitaires de Nancy, 1978).

Dubrow, Heather, '"The infant of your care": guardianship in Shakespeare's *Richard III* and early modern England', in Kari Boyd McBride (ed.), *Domestic Arrangements in Early Modern England* (Pittsburgh: Duquesne University Press, 2002), pp. 147–68.

Dugas, Don-John, *Marketing the Bard: Shakespeare in Performance and Print, 1660–1740* (Columbia and London: University of Missouri Press, 2006).

Dunlop, John, *The History of Fiction* (3 vols; London: Longman, Hurst, Rees, Orme, Brown and Green, 1814).

Dusinberre, Juliet, *Shakespeare and the Nature of Women* (3rd edn; Basingstoke, Hampshire, New York: Palgrave Macmillan, 2003).

Edwards, Christopher, review of *Hamlet*, dir. Ron Daniels, Royal Shakespeare Company, *Spectator*, 8 September 1984.

Ellis, Kate, *The Contested Castle: Gothic Novels and the Subversion of Domestic Ideology* (Urbana: University of Illinois Press, 1989).

Ellison, Julie, *Cato's Tears and the Making of Anglo-American Emotion* (Chicago: University of Chicago Press, 1999).

Enquiry into the Origin of the Authorship of Some of the Earlier Waverley Novels (Bolton: J. Hudsmith, 1856).

Evans, Gareth Lloyd, review of *Hamlet*, dir. Ron Daniels, Royal Shakespeare Company, *Stratford-upon-Avon Herald*, 14 September 1984.

[Excelmans, Baron Karlo], *Life of Napoleon* (4 vols; London: John Cumberland, 1828).

Feinsten, Elaine and the Women's Theatre Group, *Lear's Daughters*, in Daniel Fischlin and Mark Fortier (eds), *Adaptations of Shakespeare* (London: Routledge, 2000), pp. 215–32.

Fenner, Theodore, *Opera in London: Views of the Press, 1785–1830* (Carbondale: Southern Illinois University Press, 1994).

[Fenton, Richard], *Tour in Quest of Genealogy, Through Several Parts of Wales, Somersetshire and Wiltshire* (London: Sherwood, Neely and Jones, 1811).

[Fielding, Thomas], *Proverbs of All Nations: Illustrated with Notes and Comments* (London: Longman, Hurst, Rees, Orme, Brown and Green, 1824).

Fincher, Max, *Queering Romanticism in the Romantic Age: the Penetrating Eye* (New York and London: Palgrave, 2007).

Fitzgerald, Lauren, 'The sexuality of authorship in *The Monk*', in Michael O'Rourke and David Collings (eds), *Queer Romanticism, Romanticism on the Net*, 36–37 (November 2004–February 2005), *http://www.erudit.org/revue/ron/2004/v/n36–37/011138ar.html* (accessed 16 February 2007).

Foakes, R. A., 'Tragedy at the children's theatres after 1600: a challenge to the adult stage', in David Galloway (ed.), *The Elizabethan Theatre, II* (Toronto: Archon Books, 1970), pp. 37–59.

——, *Hamlet Versus Lear: Cultural Politics and Shakespeare's Art* (Cambridge: Cambridge University Press, 1993).

Fordyce, James, *Sermons to Young Women* (London: Printed for A. Millar and T. Cadell, 1766).

Fowles, John, *The Collector* (New York: Little, Brown and Company, 1963).

Freud, Sigmund, 'The theme of the three caskets', in *The Standard*

Edition of the Complete Psychological Works, ed. James Strachey et al. (24 vols; London: Hogarth Press, 1953–74), vol. 12, pp. 290–301.

——, 'On family romances', in Peter Gay (ed.), *The Freud Reader* (New York: Norton, 1989), pp. 297–300.

Gajowski, Evelyn, *The Art of Loving: Female Subjectivity and Male Discursive Traditions in Shakespeare's Tragedies* (Newark: University of Delaware Press, 1992).

Gamer, Michael, *Romanticism and the Gothic: Genre, Reception and Canon Formation* (Cambridge: Cambridge University Press, 2000).

Garber, Marjorie, '*Hamlet*: giving up the ghost', in Susanne L. Wofford (ed.), *William Shakespeare*, Hamlet, Case Studies in Contemporary Criticism (Boston and New York: Bedford/St Martin's, 1994), pp. 297–331.

——, *Shakespeare After All* (New York: Anchor Books, 2004).

Garrett, Margaret Davenport, 'Writing and re-writing incest in Mary Shelley's *Mathilda*', *Keats-Shelley Journal*, 45 (1996), 44–60.

Garrett, Peter K., *Gothic Reflections: Narrative Force in Nineteenth-Century Fiction* (Ithaca: Cornell University Press, 2003).

Gay, Penny, *Jane Austen and the Theatre* (Cambridge: Cambridge University Press, 2002).

Genest, John, *Some Account of the English Stage from the Restoration in 1660 to 1830* (10 vols; Bath: H. E. Carrington, 1832).

Genlis, Stéphanie Félicité Ducrest de St-Aubin, Countess of, *Adelaide and Theodore; or Letters on Education* (3 vols; London: T. Cadell, 1783).

Gerard, Alexander, *An Essay on Genius* (London: Printed for W. Strahan, T. Cadell and W. Creech at Edinburgh, 1774).

Gilbert, Sandra and Susan Gubar, *The Madwoman in the Attic: The Woman Writer and the Nineteenth-Century Literary Imagination* (New Haven and London: Yale University Press, 1978).

Gildon, Charles, *Remarks on the Plays of Shakespear* (London: Printed for E. Curll and E. Sanger, 1710).

Gilfillan, George, 'Female authors. no. 1 – Mrs Hemans', *Tait's Edinburgh Magazine*, n.s., 14 (1847), 350–63.

Goddard, Harold C., 'King Lear', in Harold Bloom (ed.), *William Shakespeare's* King Lear (New York and Philadelphia: Chelsea House, 1987), pp. 9–43.

Goldberg, Jonathan, '*Romeo and Juliet's* open R's', in Jonathan Goldberg (ed.), *Queering the Renaissance* (Durham: Duke University Press, 1994), pp. 218–35.

Griffith, Elizabeth, *The Morality of Shakespeare's Drama Illustrated* (London: T. Cadell, 1775).

Grimes, Kyle, 'Verbal jujitsu: William Hone and the tactics of satirical conflict', in Steven E. Jones (ed.), *The Satiric Eye: Forms of Satire in the Romantic Period* (New York: Palgrave Macmillan, 2003), pp. 173–84.

Groom, Nick, *The Forger's Shadow: How Forgery Changed the Course of Literature* (London: Picador, 2002).

Guthrie, William, *A Reply to the Counter-Address & etc.* (London: W. Nicoll, 1764).

Haggerty, George E., 'Literature and homosexuality in the late eighteenth century: Walpole, Beckford and Lewis', *Studies in the Novel*, 18, 4 (1986), 341–52.

———, *Men in Love: Masculinity and Sexuality in the Eighteenth Century* (New York and London: Columbia University Press, 1999).

———, *Queer Gothic* (Urbana and Chicago: University of Illinois Press, 2006).

———, 'Queering Horace Walpole', *Studies in English Literature*, 46, 3 (summer 2006), 543–62.

Halliday, F. E., *The Cult of Shakespeare* (London: Gerald Duckworth & Co., Ltd., 1957).

Halsband, Robert, 'Walpole versus Lady Mary', in Warren Smith (ed.), *Horace Walpole: Writer, Politician and Connoisseur: Essays on the 250th Anniversary of Walpole's Birth* (New Haven: Yale University Press, 1967), pp. 215–26.

Haraszti, Zoltan, *The Shakespeare Forgeries of William-Henry Ireland: The Story of a Famous Literary Fraud* (Boston: Trustees of the Public Library, 1934).

Harbeson, W. B., 'The Elizabethan influence on the tragedy of the late eighteenth and the early nineteenth centuries', Ph.D. dissertation, University of Pennsylvania, 1921.

Harfst, Betsy Perteit, *Horace Walpole and the Unconscious: An Experiment in Freudian Analysis* (New York: Arno Press, 1980).

Harpold, Terence, '"Did you get Mathilda from Papa?": seduction fantasy and the circulation of Mary Shelley's *Mathilda*', *Studies in Romanticism*, 28, 1 (1989), 49–67.

Hatchuel, Sarah, *A Companion to the Shakespearean Films of Kenneth Branagh* (Niagara Falls: Blizzard, 2000).

Hattaway, Michael, 'The Shakespearean history play', in Michael Hattaway (ed.), *The Cambridge Companion to Shakespeare's History Plays* (Cambridge: Cambridge University Press, 2002), pp. 3–24.

Hawkes, Terrence (ed.), *Coleridge's Writings on Shakespeare: A Selection of the Essays, Notes and Lectures of Samuel Taylor Coleridge on the Poems and Plays of Shakespeare* (New York: Capricorn Books, 1959).

Haywood, Ian, *The Making of History: A Study of the Literary Forgeries of James Macpherson and Thomas Chatterton in Relation to Eighteenth-Century Ideas of History and Fiction* (Rutherford, NJ: Fairleigh Dickinson University Press, 1986).

Hazlitt, William, *Characters of Shakespear's Plays* (2nd edn; London: Taylor and Hessey, 1818).

——, 'Mr Kean's Hamlet', *Morning Chronicle*, 14 March 1814, in William Archer and Robert Lowe (eds), *Hazlitt on Theatre* (New York: Hill and Wang, 1957), pp. 9–14.

——, 'On Shakespeare and Milton', in Jonathan Bate (ed.), *The Romantics on Shakespeare* (London: Penguin, 1992), pp. 180–8.

Himes, Audra Dibert, '"Knew shame, and knew desire": Ambivalence as structure in Mary Shelley's *Mathilda*', in Syndy M. Conger, Frederick S. Frank and Gregory O'Dea (eds), *Iconoclastic Departures: Mary Shelley after Frankenstein* (Madison, NJ: Fairleigh Dickinson University Press, 1997), pp. 115–29.

Hoeveler, Diane Long, *Gothic Feminism: The Professionalization of Gender from Charlotte Smith to the Brontës* (University Park: Pennsylvania State University Press, 1998).

—— and Sarah Davies Cordova, 'Gothic opera as romantic discourse in Britain and France: a cross-cultural dialogue', in Larry H. Peer and Diane Long Hoeveler (eds), *Romanticism: Comparative Discourses* (Aldershot: Ashgate, 2006), pp. 11–34.

Hogle, Jerrold E., 'The ghost of the counterfeit in the genesis of the Gothic', in Allan Lloyd Smith and William Hughes (eds), *Gothick Origins and Innovations* (Amsterdam and Atlanta: Rodopi, 1994), pp. 23–33.

—— (ed.), *The Cambridge Companion to Gothic Fiction* (Cambridge: Cambridge University Press, 2002).

Holland, Peter, *English Shakespeares: Shakespeare on the English Stage in the 1990s* (Cambridge: Cambridge University Press, 1997).

Hughes, Alan, *Henry Irving, Shakespearean* (Cambridge: Cambridge University Press, 1981).

Hughes, William, *Beyond Dracula: Bram Stoker's Fiction and its Cultural Context* (Houndsmills, Basingstoke, Hampshire: Macmillan, 2000).

Hunter, J. Paul, 'The world as stage and closet', in Shirley Strum Kenny (ed.), *British Theatre and Other Arts, 1660–1800* (Washington, DC and London: Folger Shakespeare Library and Associated University Presses, 1983), pp. 271–87.

Hurd, Richard, *Letters on Chivalry and Romance* (London: A. Millar, W. Thurlbourn and J. Woodyer, 1762).

Ingleby, C. M., *The Shakespeare Fabrications* (London: J. R. Smith, 1859).

Ingram, John Henry, *The True Chatterton: A New Study from Original Documents* (London: T. Fisher Unwin, 1910).

Ireland, Samuel, *Miscellaneous Papers and Legal Instruments under the Hand and Seal of William Shakespeare; including the Tragedy of King Lear and a small fragment of Hamlet* (London: Mr Egerton, 1796).

Ireland, William Henry, *An Authentic Account of the Shaksperian Manuscripts, &c.* (London: J. Debrett, 1796).

——, Correspondences and press clippings, 1777–1835, British Library MS 30346, 30347, 30349; Bodleian MS, Montagu d 5, fo.

——, *The Abbess* (4 vols; London: Earle and Hemet, 1799).

——, *Vortigern, An Historical Tragedy, in Five Acts; Represented at the Theatre Royal, Drury Lane, Saturday, April 2, 1796* (London: J. Barker, 1799).

——, *Rimualdo: or the Castle of Badajos. A Romance. By W. H. Ireland, author of 'The Abbess', &c. In Four Volumes* (4 vols; London: A. Strahan for T. N. Longman and O. Rees, 1800).

——, *A Woman of Feeling* (4 vols; London: D. N. Shury, 1804).

——, *The Confessions of William-Henry Ireland* (New York: Burt Franklin, 1805).

——, *Gondez, the Monk: A Romance* (4 vols; London: W. Earle and J. W. Hucklebridge, 1805).

——, *The Catholic, An Historical Romance* (3 vols; London: W. Earle, 1807).

[——], *The Death-Bed Confessions of the Late Countess of Guernsey* (London: J. Fairburn, [1821]).

——, *Vortigern; An Historical Play; With An Original Preface. Represented at the Theatre Royal, Drury Lane, on Saturday, April 2, 1796, as a Supposed Newly-Discovered Drama of Shakspeare* (London: J. Thomas, 1832).

——, 'Monody on Shakespeare', Folger Shakespeare Library, MS D.a. 54., ca. 1833.

——, *The Abbess*, (4 vols; 1799), facsimile with Introduction by Benjamin Franklin Fisher, IV, ed. (New York: Arno, 1974).

——, and G. P. R. James, *Rizzio; or, Scenes in Europe During the Sixteenth Century* (3 vols; London: T. C. Newby, 1849).

Irving, Henry, *King Lear, a Tragedy in Five Acts, by William Shakespeare, as arranged by Henry Irving and presented at the Lyceum Theatre, November 10, 1892* (London: Nassau Steam Press, 1892).

Jackson, Russell, 'Film diary', in Kenneth Branagh, *Hamlet, by William Shakespeare* (New York: Norton, 1996), pp. 175–208.

Jacobi, Derek, dir., *Hamlet*, Birmingham, Birmingham Repertory, May 1988; London, Phoenix Theatre, September 1988.

Jameson, Anna, *Shakespeare's Heroines: Characteristics of Women, Moral, Political and Historical* (new edn; 2 vols; London: George Bell, 1889).

Jephson, Robert, *The Count of Narbonne*, in Temple James Maynard (ed.), *The Plays of Robert Jephson* (New York: Garland, 1980).

Johnson, Samuel, *Miscellaneous Observations on the Tragedy of Macbeth* (London: E. Cave, 1745).

——, *Johnson on Shakespeare*, in vols 7 and 8 of *The Yale Edition of the Works of Samuel Johnson*, ed. Arthur Sherbo (New Haven: Yale University Press, 1968).

Jones, Ann, *Ideas and Innovations: Best Sellers of Jane Austen's Age* (New York: AMS, 1986).

Jones, Darryl, *Critical Issues: Jane Austen* (Houndmills: Palgrave Macmillan, 2004).

Jones, Steven E., 'Introduction: forms of satire in the Romantic period', in Steven E. Jones (ed.), *The Satiric Eye: Forms of Satire in the Romantic Period* (New York: Palgrave Macmillan, 2003), pp. 1–9.

Jones, Wendy, 'Stories of desire in *The Monk*', *ELH: English Literary History*, 57 (1990), 129–50.

Kahan, Jeffrey, *Reforging Shakespeare* (Bethlehem, PA: Lehigh University Press, 1998).

Kahn, Coppélia, 'Coming of age in Verona', *Modern Language Studies*, 8, 1 (1978), 5–22.

Keats, John, *The Letters of John Keats, 1814–1821*, ed. Edward Rollins Hyder (2 vols; Cambridge, MA: Harvard University Press, 1958).

——, *The Poems of John Keats*, ed. Jack Stillinger (Cambridge: Harvard University Press, 1978).

Kemble, Mary Thérèse, *Smiles and Tears, or, The Widow's Stratagem* (London: John Miller, 1816).

Ketton-Cremer, Robert Wyndham, *Horace Walpole: A Biography* (3rd edn; Ithaca: Cornell University Press, 1966).

Kidnie, Margaret Jane, 'Where is *Hamlet*? Text, performance and adaptation', in Barbara Hodgdon and W. B. Worthen (eds), *A Companion to Shakespeare and Performance* (Malden, MA: Blackwell, 2005), pp. 101–20.

Kiernan, Robert F., *Frivolity Unbound: Six Masters of the Camp Novel: Thomas Love Peacock, Max Beerbohm, Ronald Firbank, E. F. Benson, P. G. Wodehouse, Ivy Compton-Burnett* (New York: Continuum, 1990).

Kilgour, Maggie, *The Rise of the Gothic Novel* (London and New York: Routledge, 1995).

Kimball, David, *Italian Opera* (Cambridge: Cambridge University Press, 1991).

Kliman, Bernice W., 'The unkindest cuts: flashcut excess in Kenneth Branagh's *Hamlet*', in Deborah Cartmell and Michael Scott (eds), *Talking Shakespeare: Shakespeare into the Millennium* (London, Palgrave, 2001), pp. 151–67.

Know-Shaw, Peter, *Jane Austen and the Enlightenment* (Cambridge: Cambridge University Press, 2004).

Kramnick, Jonathan Brody, *Making the English Canon: Print Capitalism and the Cultural Past, 1700–1770* (Cambridge: Cambridge University Press, 1998).

Kristeva, Julia, *Powers of Horror: An Essay on Abjection*, trans. Leon S. Roudiez (New York: Columbia University Press, 1982).

Lamb, Charles, 'G. F. Cooke in "Richard the Third"', *Morning Post*, 8 January 1802.

——, *The Letters of Charles Lamb, to which are added those of his sister Mary Lamb*, ed. E.V. Lucas (3 vols; London: Methuen, 1933).

——, 'On the tragedies of Shakspear, considered with reference to their fitness for stage representation', in Joan Coldwell (ed.), *Charles Lamb on Shakespeare* (Gerrards Cross: Colyn Smythe, 1978), pp. 24–42.

—— [and Lamb, Mary], *Tales from Shakespear. Designed for the use of young persons. Embellished with copper-plates* (2 vols; London: Printed for Thomas Hodgkins, at the Juvenile Library, 1807).

Lang, S., 'The principles of Gothic revival in England', *The Journal of the Society of Architectural Historians*, 25, 4 (December 1966), 240–67.

Lanier, Douglas, *Shakespeare and Modern Popular Culture*, Oxford Shakespeare Topics (Oxford: Oxford University Press, 2002).

——, '"Art thou base, common and popular?" The cultural politics of Kenneth Branagh's *Hamlet*', in Courtney Lehmann and Lisa S. Starks (eds), *Spectacular Shakespeare: Critical Theory and Popular Cinema* (Madison, NJ: Fairleigh Dickinson University Press, 2002), pp. 149–71.

Le Brun, Charles, *Méthode pour apprendre à dessiner les passions* (Amsterdam: Chez François van-der Plaats, 1702).

Lee, Harriet, *The Mysterious Marriage, Or the Heirship of Roselva. A Play, in Three Acts* (London: Printed for G. G. and J. Robinson, 1798).

Lehmann, Courtney, *Shakespeare Remains: Theatre to Film, Early Modern to Postmodern* (Ithaca: Cornell University Press, 2002).

Lennox, Charlotte, *Shakespear Illustrated* (3 vols; London: A. Millar, 1753).

Levine, Nina S., *Women's Matters: Politics, Gender and Nation in Shakespeare's Early History Plays* (Newark: University of Delaware Press, 1998).

Lévi-Strauss, Claude, *The Savage Mind* (Chicago: University of Chicago Press, 1966).

Lévy, Maurice, *Le Roman 'Gothique' anglais, 1764–1824* (Toulouse: Association des Publications de la Faculté des Lettres et Sciences Humaines, 1968).

Lewis, M. G., *Timour the Tartar: A Grand Romantic Melo-drama in Two Acts* (London: Lowndes & Hobbs, 1811).

——, *The Monk*, ed. Dennis Wheatley (London: Sphere Books Ltd., 1974).

——, *The Castle Spectre*, in Jeffrey Cox (ed.), *Seven Gothic Dramas, 1789–1825* (Athens: Ohio University Press, 1992), pp. 150–224.

——, *The Monk: A Romance*, ed. Howard Anderson (Oxford: Oxford University Press, 1998).

Lewis, Wilmarth Sheldon, *Horace Walpole*, A. W. Mellon Lectures in the Fine Arts (London: Rupert Hart Davis, 1961).

——, *Rescuing Horace Walpole* (New Haven and London: Yale University Press, 1978).

——— (ed.), 'Notes by Horace Walpole on several characters of Shakespeare', *Miscellaneous Antiquities* (Windham, CT: Hawthorne House, 1940).

'Literary forgeries', *The Monthly Mirror* (May 1803), 294–5.

Longueil, Alfred E., 'The word "Gothic" in eighteenth-century criticism', *Modern Language Notes*, 38, 8 (December 1923), 453–60.

Lull, Janis, 'Plantagenets, Lancastrians, Yorkists and Tudors: *1–3 Henry VI, Richard III, Edward III*', in Michael Hattaway (ed.), *The Cambridge Companion to Shakespeare's History Plays* (Cambridge: Cambridge University Press, 2002), pp. 89–105.

Lynch, Deidre Shaun, *The Economy of Character: Novels, Market Culture and the Business of Inner Meaning* (Chicago: University of Chicago Press, 1998).

McFarland, Thomas, *Romanticism and the Forms of Ruin* (Princeton: Princeton University Press, 1981).

Macgregor, Margaret E., *Amelia Opie, Wordling and Friend* (Northampton, MA: Smith College Studies in Modern Languages, 1933).

McLean, Clara D., 'Lewis's *The Monk* and the matter of reading', in Linda Lang-Peralta (ed.), *Women, Revolution and the Novels of the 1790s* (East Lansing: Michigan State University Press, 1999), pp. 111–31.

Madoff, Mark, 'The useful myth of Gothic ancestry', *Studies in Eighteenth-Century Culture*, 8 (1979), 337–50.

Mahon, John W., 'A Derek Jacobi fest', *Shakespeare Newsletter*, 47, 1 (spring 1997), 1, 6–8.

Malone, Edmond, *Inquiry into the Authenticity of Certain Miscellaneous Papers* (London: W. Baldwin, 1796).

Manvell, Roger, *Ellen Terry* (New York: G. P. Putnam's Sons, 1968).

Marcus, Leah, 'Shakespearean editing and why it matters', *Literature Compass*, 2 (2005), 1–5.

Marienstras, Richard, 'Of a monstrous body', in Jean-Marie Maguin and Michèle Willems (eds), *French Essays on Shakespeare and His Contemporaries: 'What Would France with Us?'* (London: Associated University Presses, 1995), pp. 153–74.

Marsden, Jean I., *The Re-Imagined Text: Shakespeare, Adaptation and Eighteenth-Century Literary Theory* (Lexington: University Press of Kentucky, 1995).

———, 'Daddy's girls: Shakespearean daughters and eighteenth-century ideology', *Shakespeare Survey*, 51 (1998), 17–26.

Marshall, Gail, *Actresses on the Victorian Stage: Feminine Performance and the Galatea Myth* (Cambridge: Cambridge University Press, 1998).

Marshall, Peter, *William Godwin* (New Haven and London: Yale University Press, 1984).

Mathias, Thomas James, *The Pursuits of Literature, or What You Will* (London: J. Owen, 1794).

Meier, Paul, 'Kenneth Branagh with utter clarity: an interview', *The Drama Review: The Journal of Performance Studies*, 41, 2 (1997), 82–9.

Mellor, Anne K., *Mary Shelley: Her Life, Her Fiction, Her Monsters* (New York: Routledge, 1988).

Merrill, Lisa, *When Romeo Was a Woman: Charlotte Cushman and Her Circle of Female Spectators* (Ann Arbor: University of Michigan Press, 1999).

Meyerstein, E. H. W., *Thomas Chatterton* (London: Ingpen and Grant, 1930).

Mighall, Robert, *A Geography of Victorian Gothic Fiction* (Oxford: Oxford University Press, 1998).

Miles, Robert, *Gothic Writing, 1750–1820: A Genealogy* (London: Routledge, 1993).

——, 'The 1790s: the effulgence of Gothic', in Jerrold E. Hogle (ed.), *The Cambridge Companion to the Gothic* (Cambridge: Cambridge University Press, 2002), pp. 41–62.

——, 'Forging a Romantic identity: Herbert Croft's *Love and Madness* and W. H. Ireland's Shakespeare Ms', *Eighteenth-Century Fiction*, 17, 4 (July 2005), 599–627.

Mills, Howard, *Peacock: His Circle and His Age* (Cambridge: Cambridge University Press, 1969).

Moers, Ellen, *Literary Women* (Garden City, NY: Doubleday, 1976).

Moncrieff, William Thomas, *The Lear of Private Life! or, Father and Daughter: A Domestic Melo-drama in Three Acts* (London: T. Richardson, c.1828).

Montagu, Elizabeth, *An Essay on the Writings and Genius of Shakspeare* (London: Printed for J. Dodsley, J. Walter, T. Cadell and J. Wilkie, 1769).

Moody, Jane, 'Romantic Shakespeare', in Stanley Wells and Sarah Stanton (eds), *The Cambridge Companion to Shakespeare on Stage* (Cambridge: Cambridge University Press, 2002), pp. 37–57.

Morgan, Elizabeth, 'Mary and modesty', *Christianity and Literature*, 54, 2 (2005), 209–33.

Mowl, Timothy, *Horace Walpole: The Great Outsider* (London: John Murray, 1996).

Mullenix, Elizabeth Reitz, *Wearing the Breeches: Gender on the Antebellum Stage* (New York: St Martin's Press, 2000).

Murphy, Arthur, 'Free remarks on the tragedy of *Romeo and Juliet*', in Brian Vickers (ed.), *Shakespeare: The Critical Heritage* (6 vols; London and Boston: Routledge and K. Paul, 1974–1990), vol. 3, pp. 374–9.

Napier, Elizabeth R., *The Failure of Gothic: Problems of Disjunction in an Eighteenth-Century Literary Form* (Oxford: Clarendon, 1987).

Neely, Carol Thomas, *Broken Nuptials in Shakespeare's Plays* (New Haven and London: Yale University Press, 1985).

Newlyn, Lucy, *Reading, Writing and Romanticism: The Anxiety of Reception* (Oxford: Oxford University Press, 2000).

Newman, Gerald, *The Rise of English Nationalism: A Cultural History, 1740–1830* (London: Weidenfield and Nicholson, 1987).

Nitchie, Elizabeth, 'Mary Shelley's *Mathilda*: an unpublished story and its biographical significance', *Studies in Philology*, 40 (1943), 447–62.

Noble, Adrian (dir.), *Hamlet*, London, Barbican, December 1992; Stratford-upon-Avon, Royal Shakespeare Theatre, March 1993, archival videos, Shakespeare Centre Library.

Norton, Rictor, *Mistress of Udolpho: The Life of Ann Radcliffe* (London and New York: Leicester University Press, 1999).

Novy, Marianne, *Love's Argument: Gender Relations in Shakespeare* (Chapel Hill and London: University of North Carolina Press, 1984).

Obituary for Horace Walpole, *The Gentleman's Magazine* (March 1797), 257–60.

Olshaker, Mark, *Discovering Hamlet*, video cassette, PBS, 1990.

Opie, Amelia, *The Father and Daughter, with Dangers of Coquetry*, ed. Shelley King and John B. Pierce (Peterborough, Ont.: Broadview Press, 2003).

Orgel, Stephen, 'The authentic Shakespeare', in *The Authentic Shakespeare and Other Problems of the Early Modern Stage* (New York: Routledge, 2002), pp. 231–56.

Otway, Thomas, *The History and Fall of Caius Marius: A Tragedy (1680)* (London: Cornmarket Press, 1969).

Paër, Ferdinando, *Agnese di Fitz-Henry* (Paris: Janet et Cotelle, 1812).

[Panam, Pauline Adélaide Alexandre], *Memoirs of a Young Greek Lady* (London: J. Fairburn, 1823).

Peacock, Thomas Love, *Headlong Hall* (Philadelphia: M. Carey, 1816).

——, 'The four ages of poetry', in H. F. B. Brett-Smith (ed.), *Peacock's 'Four Ages of Poetry', Shelley's 'Defense of Poetry', Browning's 'Essay on Shelley'* (Oxford: Basil Blackwell, 1947), pp. 3–19.

——, *Nightmare Abbey* (London: Hamish Hamilton, 1947).

Pearlman, E., 'The invention of Richard of Gloucester', *Shakespeare Quarterly*, 43, 4 (winter 1992), 410–29.

Pearson, Jacqueline, *Women's Reading in Britain, 1750–1835: A Dangerous Recreation* (Cambridge: Cambridge University Press, 1999).

Perry, Ruth, *Novel Relations: The Transformation of Kinship in English Literature and Culture, 1748–1818* (Cambridge: Cambridge University Press, 2004).

Peter, John, review of *Hamlet*, dir. Adrian Noble, Royal Shakespeare Company, *Sunday Times*, 27 December 1992.

Pinch, Adela, *Strange Fits of Passion: Epistemologies of Emotion, Hume to Austen* (Stanford: Stanford University Press, 1996).

Pincombe, Michael, 'Horace Walpole's *Hamlet*', in Marta Gibinska and Jerzy Limon (eds), *Hamlet East-West* (Gdansk: Theatrum Gedanebse Foundation, 1998), pp. 125–33.

Plumb, J. H., *Sir Robert Walpole* (2 vols; London: Cresset Press, 1956–60).

Poovey, Mary, *The Proper Lady and the Woman Writer: Ideology as Style in the Works of Mary Wollstonecraft, Mary Shelley and Jane Austen* (Chicago: University of Chicago Press, 1984).

Pope, Rebecca, 'Writing and biting in *Dracula*', *LIT*, 1 (1990), 199–216, reprinted in Glennis Byron (ed.), *'Dracula': Contemporary Critical Essays*, New Caseboooks (New York: St Martin's, 1999), pp. 68–92.

Price, F. W., 'Ann Radcliffe, Mrs Siddons and the character of Hamlet', *Notes and Queries*, n.s., 23, 4 (April 1976), 164–7.

Punter, David, *The Literature of Terror: A History of Gothic Fictions from 1765 to the Present Day* (2nd edn; New York: Longman, 1996).

Rackin, Phyllis, *Stages of History: Shakespeare's English Chronicles* (Ithaca: Cornell University Press, 1990).

Radcliffe, Ann, *The Castles of Athlin and Dunbayne: A Highland Story* (London: T. Hookham, 1789).

——, *A Sicilian Romance* (2 vols; London: T. Hookham, 1790).

——, *The Mysteries of Udolpho, A Romance* (4 vols; London: G. G. and J. Robinson, 1794).

——, *The Romance of the Forest* (4th edn; 3 vols; London: T. Hookham and J. Carpenter, 1794).

——, *A Journey Made in the Summer of 1794, through Holland and the Western Frontier of Germany, with a Return Down the Rhine* (London: G. G. and J. Robinson, 1795).

——, *The Italian, or The Confessional of the Black Penitents* (3 vols; London: T. Cadell and W. Davies, 1797).

——, *Gaston de Blondeville* (4 vols; London: Henry Colburn, 1826).

——.'On the supernatural in poetry', *New Monthly Magazine*, 16 (1826), 145–52, reprinted in E. J. Clery and Robert Miles (eds), *Gothic Documents: A Sourcebook, 1700–1800* (Manchester: Manchester University Press, 2000), pp. 163–72.

Railo, Eino, *The Haunted Castle: A Study of the Elements of English Romanticism* (New York. E. P. Dutton and Sons, 1927).

Rajan, Tilottama, 'Mary Shelley's *Mathilda*: melancholy and the political economy of Romanticism', *Studies in the Novel*, 26, 2 (summer 1994), 43–68.

Ready, Robert, 'Dominion of Demeter: Mary Shelley's *Mathilda*', *Keats-Shelley Journal*, 52 (2003), 94–110.

Reed, Edward, *From Soul to Mind: The Emergence of Psychology from Erasmus Darwin to William James* (New Haven: Yale University Press, 1997).

Review of the Catalogue of the Shakespeare Gallery, *Analytical Review,* 3 (May 1789), 111–12.

Review of *The Mysteries of Udolpho, Critical Review,* 11 (August 1794), 361–72.

Richards, Graham, *Mental Machinery: The Origins and Consequences of Psychological Ideas, Part I: 1600–1850* (Baltimore: Johns Hopkins University Press, 1992).

Richardson, Alan, *British Romanticism and the Science of the Mind* (Cambridge: Cambridge University Press, 2001).

Richardson, William, *Philosophical Analysis and Illustration of Some of Shakespeare's Remarkable Characters* (London: J. Murray, 1774).

Rival Wives: Or, the Greeting of Clarissa to Skirra in the Elysian Shades (London: Printed for W. Lloyd, 1738).

Rival Wives Answer'd: or, Skirra to Clarissa (London: Printed for W. Lloyd, 1738).

Robinson, Mary, *Memoirs of the Late Mrs Robinson, Written by Herself* (London: Printed by Wilkes and Taylor for R. Phillips, 1801).

Ross, Trevor, 'The emergence of "literature": making and reading the English canon in the eighteenth century', *ELH: English Literary History,* 63, 2 (1996), 397–422.

Rowland, Susan, 'Margery Allingham's Gothic: Genre as cultural criticism', *Clues: A Journal of Detection,* 23, 1 (fall 2004), 27–39.

Russell, Charles Edward, *Thomas Chatterton, the Marvelous Boy: The Story of a Strange Life, 1752–1770* (New York: Moffat, Yard and Co., 1908).

Sabor, Peter (ed.), *Horace Walpole: The Critical Heritage* (London and New York: Routledge and Kegan Paul, 1987).

Sanders, Julie, 'The end of history and the last man: Kenneth Branagh's *Hamlet*', in Mark Thornton Burnett and Ramona Wray (eds), *Shakespeare, Film, Fin de Siècle* (New York: St Martin's Press, 2000), pp. 147–64.

[Savary, Anne-Jean-Marie-René], *Memoirs of the Duke of Rovigo, M. Savary* (2 vols; London: Henry Colburn, 1828).

Schmid, Thomas H., *Humor and Transgression in Peacock, Shelley and Byron: A Cold Carnival* (Lewiston, NY: Edwin Mellen, 1992).

Scott, Clement, *The Drama of Yesterday and Today* (2 vols; London: Macmillan and Company, 1899).

Scott, Sir Walter, 'Prefatory memoir to Mrs Ann Radcliffe', *The Novels of Mrs Ann Radcliffe,* vol. 10 of Ballantyne's Novelist's Library (Edinburgh: James Ballantyne, 1824).

Sedley, Sir Charles, *Antony and Cleopatra* (London: Jacob Tonson, 1677).

[Sedley Charles], *The Barouche Driver and His Wife* (2nd edn; 2 vols; London: J. F. Hughes, 1807).

——, *The Infidel Mother* (2nd edn; 3 vols; London: J. F. Hughes, 1807).

——, *The Mask of Fashion* (2 vols; London: J. F. Hughes, 1807).

——, *Asmodeus; Or, The devil in London* (3 vols; London: J. F. Hughes, 1808).

——, *The Faro Table, Or, the gambling mothers: A fashionable fable* (2 vols; London: J. F. Hughes, 1808).

——, *A Winter in Dublin: A descriptive tale* (3 vols; London: J. F. Hughes, 1808).

Seymour, Miranda, *Mary Shelley* (New York: Grove, 2000).

Shakespeare, William, *The Norton Shakespeare*, ed. Stephen Greenblatt et al. (New York: Norton, 1997).

, *The Riverside Shakespeare*, ed. G. Blakemore Evans et al. (2nd edn; Boston: Houghton Mifflin, 1997).

——, *The Arden Edition of the Works of William Shakespeare*, ed. Brian Gibbons (1980; reprint, London: Methuen, 2003).

——, *Hamlet*, ed. Ann Thompson and Neil Taylor, 3rd Arden edn (London: Thomson Learning, 2006).

Shattuck, Charles H. (ed.), *John Philip Kemble Promptbooks* (11 vols; Charlottesville: Published for the Folger Shakespeare Library by the University Press of Virginia, 1974).

Shawe-Taylor, Desmond, 'Performance portraits', *Shakespeare Survey*, 51 (1998), 107–23.

Shelley Mary, *Matilda*, ed. Elizabeth Nitchie (Chapel Hill: University of North Carolina Press, 1959).

——, *Matilda*, in Nora Crook and Pamela Clemit (gen. eds) and Betty Bennett (consulting ed.), *The Novels and Selected Works of Mary Shelley* (8 vols; London, Pickering and Chatto, 1992), vol. 2, pp. 5–67.

——, *The Journals of Mary Shelley: 1814–1844*, ed. Paula Feldman and Diana Scott-Kilvert (Baltimore and London: Johns Hopkins University Press, 1995).

Sheppard, John, *Letters, Descriptive of a Tour through some parts of France, Italy, Switzerland and Germany, in 1816* (2 vols; Edinburgh: Printed for Oliphant, Waugh & Innes, 1817).

Sheppard, Phillipa, 'The castle of Elsinore: Gothic aspects of Kenneth Branagh's *Hamlet*', *Shakespeare Bulletin*, 19, 3 (summer 2001), 36–9.

Sloboda, Noel, 'Visions and revisions of Laurence Olivier in the *Hamlet* films of Franco Zeffirelli and Kenneth Branagh', *Studies in Humanities*, 27 (2000), 140–57.

Smiley, Jane, *A Thousand Acres* (New York: Knopf, 1991).

——, 'Shakespeare in Iceland', in Marianne Novy (ed.), *Transforming Shakespeare: Contemporary Women's Re-Visions in Literature and Performance* (New York: St Martin's, 1998), pp. 159–79.

Smith, Adam, *The Theory of Moral Sentiments* (London: printed for A. Millar, A. Kincaid and J. Bell, 1759).

Smith, Warren Hunting, *Architecture in English Fiction* (New Haven: Yale University Press, 1934).

—— (ed.), *Horace Walpole: Writer, Politician and Connoisseur* (New Haven and London: Yale University Press, 1967).

Starks, Lisa S., 'The displaced body of desire: sexuality in Kenneth Branagh's *Hamlet*', in Christy Desmet and Robert Sawyer (eds), *Shakespeare and Appropriation* (London: Routledge, 2000), pp. 160–78.

Staves, Susan, 'British seduced maidens', *Eighteenth-Century Studies*, 14, 2 (1980), 109–34.

Stein, Jess M., 'Horace Walpole and Shakespeare', *Studies in Philology*, 31 (1934), 51–68.

Stoker, Bram, *Personal Reminiscences of Henry Irving* (2 vols; London: Macmillan, 1906).

——, *Dracula*, ed. Nina Auerbach and David J. Skal, Norton Critical Edition (New York: Norton, 1997).

Stone, George Winchester, Jr, '*Romeo and Juliet*: the source of its modern stage career', *Shakespeare Quarterly*, 15, 2 (spring 1964), 191–206.

Summers, Montague (ed.), *Shakespeare Adaptations* (New York: Benjamin Blom, 1922).

Swan, Claudia, *Art, Science and Witchcraft in Early Modern Holland: Jacques de Gheyn II (1565–1629)* (Cambridge: Cambridge University Press, 2005).

Talfourd, Thomas Noon, 'Memoir of the life and writings of Mrs Radcliffe', prefixed to Ann Radcliffe, *Gaston de Blondeville* (4 vols; London: Henry Colburn, 1826).

Tandon, Bharat, *Jane Austen and the Morality of Conversation* (London: Anthem Press, 2003).

Tarr, Sister Mary Muriel, *Catholicism in Gothic Fiction* (Washington, DC: Catholic University of America Press, 1946).

Tate, Nahum, *The History of King Lear*, in Montague Summers (ed.), *Shakespeare Adaptations* (New York: Benjamin Blom, 1922), pp. 177–254.

Taylor, Gary, *Reinventing Shakespeare: A Cultural History, from the Restoration to the Present* (Oxford: Clarendon, 1993).

Taylor, Paul, review of *Hamlet*, dir. Adrian Noble, Royal Shakespeare Company, *Independent*, 12 December 1992.

Terry, Ellen, *The Story of My Life: Recollections and Reflections* (New York: McClure Company, 1908).

Tieck, Ludwig, *Schriften*, ed. Jans Peter Balmes, Manfred Frank, Achim Hölter et al. (12 vols; Frankfurt/aM: Deutsche Klassiker Verlag, 1991).

Times, Friday, 29 April 1796, issue 3572, p. 3, col. D.

Tinker, Jack, review of *Hamlet*, dir. Adrian Noble, Royal Shakespeare Company, *Daily Mail*, 23 December 1992.

Traub, Valerie, 'Jewels, statues and corpses: containment of female erotic power in Shakespeare's plays', *Shakespeare Studies*, 20 (1987), 215–38.

Tuite, Clara, 'Cloistered closets: Enlightenment pornography, the confessional state, homosexual persecution and *The Monk*', in Frederick Frank (ed.), *Matthew Lewis's* The Monk, *Romanticism on the Net*, 8 (November 1997), *http://www.erudit.org/revue/ron/1997/v/n8/index.html* (accessed 16 February 2007).

Ty, Eleanor, *Empowering the Feminine: The Narratives of Mary Robinson, Jane West and Amelia Opie* (Toronto: University of Toronto Press, 1998).

Updike, John, *Gertrude and Claudius* (New York: Knopf, 2000).

Upton, John, *Critical Observations on Shakespeare* (London: printed for G. Hawkins, 1746).

Varma, Devendra P., *The Gothic Flame* (London: Arthur Barker, 1957).

Wahrman, Dror, *The Making of the Modern Self: Identity and Culture in Eighteenth-Century England* (New Haven and London: Yale University Press, 2004).

Waldie, Jane, *Sketches Descriptive of Italy in the Years 1816 and 1817* (4 vols; London: J. Murray, 1820).

Walpole, Horace, *The Castle of Otranto: A Gothic Story* (3rd edn; London: William Bathoe, 1766).

——, *Historic Doubts on the Life and Reign of King Richard III* (Dublin: G. Faulkner, A. Leathley and W. and W. Smith, 1768).

——, *A Description of the Villa of Mr Horace Walpole* (1784; reprint, London: The Gregg Press Limited, 1964).

——, *The Castle of Otranto*, in Peter Fairclough (ed.), *Three Gothic Novels* (New York: Penguin, 1968).

——, *The Yale Edition of Horace Walpole's Correspondence*, ed. W. S. Lewis et al. (48 vols; New Haven: Yale University Press, 1937–83).

——, *Historic Doubts on the Life and Reign of Richard III*, ed. P. W. Hammond (Gloucester: Alan Sutton, 1987).

——, *The Castle of Otranto: A Gothic Story*, ed. W. S Lewis (Oxford: Oxford University Press, 1996).

——, The Castle of Otranto *and* The Mysterious Mother, ed. Frederick S. Frank (New York: Broadview Literary Texts, 2002).

——, *The Castle of Otranto*, ed. Michael Gamer (New York: Penguin, 2001).

Warren, Roger, 'Shakespeare at Stratford-upon-Avon', review of *Hamlet*, dir. Ron Daniels, Royal Shakespeare Company, *Shakespeare Quarterly*, 36 (1985), 80.

Warton, Joseph, *An Essay on the Writings and Genius of Pope* (2 vols; London: M. Cooper, 1756–82).

Watson, Donald G., *Shakespeare's Early History Plays: Politics at Play on the Elizabethan Stage* (Athens: University of Georgia Press, 1990).

Watson, Robert N. and Dickey, Stephen, 'Wherefore art thou Tereu? Juliet and the legacy of rape', *Renaissance Quarterly*, 58 (2005), 127–56.

Watt, James, *Contesting the Gothic: Fiction, Genre and Cultural Conflict, 1764–1832* (Cambridge: Cambridge University Press, 1999) .

——, 'Gothic', in Thomas Keymer and Jon Mee (eds), *The Cambridge Companion to English Literature, 1740–1830* (Cambridge: Cambridge University Press, 2004), 119–35.

Weiss, Tanja, *Shakespeare on the Screen: Kenneth Branagh's Adaptations of* Henry V, Much Ado about Nothing, *and* Hamlet (2nd revised edn; Frankfurt: Lang, 2000).

Whately, Thomas, *Remarks on some of the Characters of Shakespeare* (London: Printed for T. Payne, 1785).

Whittier, Gayle, 'The sonnet's body and the body sonnetized', *Shakespeare Quarterly*, 40, 1 (spring 1989), 27–41.

Wicke, Jennifer, 'Vampiric typewriting: *Dracula* and its media', *ELH: English Literary History*, 59, 2 (summer 1992), 467–93.

Wieten, A. A. S., *Mrs Radcliffe: Her Relation Towards Romanticism; with An Appendix on the Novels Falsely Ascribed to Her* (Amsterdam: H. J. Paris, 1926).

Williams, Anne, *Art of Darkness: A Poetics of Gothic* (Chicago: University of Chicago Press, 1995).

Willson, Robert F., Jr, 'Kenneth Branagh's *Hamlet*, or the revenge of Fortinbras', *Shakespeare Newsletter*, 47, 1 (spring 1997), 7.

Wilson, Daniel, *Chatterton: A Biographical Study* (London: Macmillan, 1869).

Wilson, Kathleen, *The Island Race: Englishness, Empire and Gender in the Eighteenth Century* (London: Routledge, 2003).

Wilson, Richard, *Shakespeare in French Theory: King of Shadows* (London and New York: Routledge, 2007).

Wiltshire, John, *Recreating Jane Austen* (Cambridge: Cambridge University Press, 2001).

Wolf, Leonard (ed.), *The Annotated Dracula* (New York: Clarkson N. Potter, 1975).

Wolfson, Susan, 'Shakespeare and the Romantic girl reader', *Nineteenth-Century Contexts*, 21, 2 (1999), 191–234.

Works of Shakespeare, with Dr Johnson's Prefaces (London, 1771).

Wray, Ramona and Mark Thornton Burnett, 'From the horse's mouth: Branagh on the bard', in Mark Thornton Burnett and Ramona Wray (eds), *Shakespeare, Film, Fin de Siècle* (New York: St Martin's, 2000), pp. 165–78.

Wright, Julia M., 'Peacock's early parody of Thomas Moore in *Nightmare Abbey*', *English Language Notes*, 30 (1993), 31–8.

Wright, Katherine L., *Shakespeare's* Romeo and Juliet *in Performance: Traditions and Departures* (Lewiston, NY: Edwin Mellen, 1997).

Young, Alan R., *Hamlet and the Visual Arts, 1709–1900* (Newark: University of Delaware Press, 2002).

Žižek, Slavoj, 'I hear you with my eyes; or, the invisible master', in Renata Seleci and Slavoj Žižek (eds), *Gaze and Voice as Love Objects* (Durham: Duke University Press, 1996), pp. 90–126.

Index

Index